Criminological Theory

ASPEN COLLEGE SERIES

Criminological Theory

GEORGE E. HIGGINS, PH.D.

Professor
Department of Criminal Justice
University of Louisville

CATHERINE D. MARCUM, PH.D.

Assistant Professor of Justice Studies
Appalachian State University

Published by Wolters Kluwer in New York.

Wolters Kluwer serves customers worldwide with CCH, Aspen Publishers, and Kluwer Law International products. (www.wolterskluwerlb.com)

To contact Customer Service, e-mail customer.service@wolterskluwer.com,
call 1-800-234-1660, fax 1-800-901-9075, or mail correspondence to:

Wolters Kluwer
Attn: Order Department
PO Box 990
Frederick, MD 21705

Printed in the United States of America.

1 2 3 4 5 6 7 8 9 0

ISBN 978-1-4548-4807-3

Library of Congress Cataloging-in-Publication Data

Higgins, George E.
    Criminological theory / George E . Higgins, PH.D., Professor, Department of Criminal Justice, University of Louisville, Catherine D. Marcum, PH.D., Assistant Professor of Justice Studies, Appalachian State University.
        pages cm.—(Aspen College series)
    Includes bibliographical references and index.
    ISBN 978-1-4548-4807-3 (alk. paper)
    1. Criminology. I. Marcum, Catherine Davis, 1980- II. Title.
    HV6025.H54 2016
    364.01—dc23

                                                                                        2015034471

About Wolters Kluwer Law & Business

Wolters Kluwer Law & Business is a leading global provider of intelligent information and digital solutions for legal and business professionals in key specialty areas, and respected educational resources for professors and law students. Wolters Kluwer Law & Business connects legal and business professionals as well as those in the education market with timely, specialized authoritative content and information-enabled solutions to support success through productivity, accuracy and mobility.

Serving customers worldwide, Wolters Kluwer Law & Business products include those under the Aspen Publishers, CCH, Kluwer Law International, Loislaw, ftwilliam.com and MediRegs family of products.

CCH products have been a trusted resource since 1913, and are highly regarded resources for legal, securities, antitrust and trade regulation, government contracting, banking, pension, payroll, employment and labor, and healthcare reimbursement and compliance professionals.

Aspen Publishers products provide essential information to attorneys, business professionals and law students. Written by preeminent authorities, the product line offers analytical and practical information in a range of specialty practice areas from securities law and intellectual property to mergers and acquisitions and pension/benefits. Aspen's trusted legal education resources provide professors and students with high-quality, up-to-date and effective resources for successful instruction and study in all areas of the law.

Kluwer Law International products provide the global business community with reliable international legal information in English. Legal practitioners, corporate counsel and business executives around the world rely on Kluwer Law journals, looseleafs, books, and electronic products for comprehensive information in many areas of international legal practice.

Loislaw is a comprehensive online legal research product providing legal content to law firm practitioners of various specializations. Loislaw provides attorneys with the ability to quickly and efficiently find the necessary legal information they need, when and where they need it, by facilitating access to primary law as well as state-specific law, records, forms and treatises.

ftwilliam.com offers employee benefits professionals the highest quality plan documents (retirement, welfare and non-qualified) and government forms (5500/PBGC, 1099 and IRS) software at highly competitive prices.

MediRegs products provide integrated health care compliance content and software solutions for professionals in healthcare, higher education and life sciences, including professionals in accounting, law and consulting.

Wolters Kluwer Law & Business, a division of Wolters Kluwer, is headquartered in New York. Wolters Kluwer is a market-leading global information services company focused on professionals.

This book is dedicated to our families
for their support and tolerance through this process.

SUMMARY OF CONTENTS

Table of Contents xi
Preface xix
About the Authors xxi

Chapter 1   Introduction to Criminological Theory 1

Chapter 2   Classical School Theories 7

Chapter 3   Biological and Psychological Theories 27

Chapter 4   Social Disorganization Theory 49

Chapter 5   Strain Theories 63

Chapter 6   Social Learning Theory 81

Chapter 7   Control Theories 97

Chapter 8   Labeling Theories 115

Chapter 9   Conflict and Critical Theories 129

Chapter 10 Feminist Theory 143

Chapter 11 Integrative Theory 159

Glossary 169
Index 183

TABLE OF CONTENTS

Preface   *xix*
About the Authors   *xxi*

CHAPTER 1

Introduction to Criminological Theory 1

Chapter Outline   *1*
Key Words and Concepts   *1*
Introduction   2
Sources of Crime Data   4
   Uniform Crime Report and National Incident Based Reporting System   4
   National Crime Victimization Survey   5
   Self-Report Surveys   5
Outline of the Book   5
References   6

CHAPTER 2

Classical School Theories 7

Chapter Outline   *7*
Key Words and Concepts   *7*
Introduction   8
Early Classical School   9
Modern Deterrence Theory   12
    Case Study 2.1: Speedy Trials as a Method of Deterrence   13
   Empirical Tests of Deterrence   14
Neoclassical School   16
   Rational Choice Theory   16

Routine Activities Theory 17

Policy Implications of Classical School Theories **19**

Case Study 2.2: Countering Classical School *20*
Case Study 2.3: Target Hardening in Cyberspace *22*

Summary 22
Discussion Questions 23
References 23

C H A P T E R   3

Biological and Psychological Theories 27

Chapter Outline 27
Key Words and Concepts 27

Introduction **28**

Biological Theory of Crime Assumptions **29**

Biology to Understand the Criminal **30**
Lombroso 30
Ferri 32
Garofalo 32
Dugdale 33
Hooten 33
Sheldon 34
Biosocial Criminology 35

Case Study 3.1: The Kray Twins *36*

Policy Implications of the Biological School **39**

Psychology and Crime **39**

Assumptions of Psychological Theories of Crime **40**

Progression Through Psychological Theory **41**
Freud 41
Personality Theories 43
Cognitive Theory 44

Policy Implications **44**

Summary 45
Discussion Questions 45
References 46

CHAPTER 4

Social Disorganization Theory 49

Chapter Outline	49
Key Words and Concepts	49
Introduction	50
Origins of Social Disorganization	50
The Criminological Element	52
Revisions of Social Disorganization Theory	54
Empirical Research	55
Policy Implications	57
Case Study 4.1: Too Tough to Fix Broken Windows?	58
Case Study 4.2: Mobilization of Youth	59
Summary	60
Discussion Questions	60
References	61

CHAPTER 5

Strain Theories 63

Chapter Outline	63
Key Words and Concepts	63
Introduction	64
Progression of Strain Theory	65
Merton	65
Case Study 5.1: Bernie Madoff	67
Cohen	67
Miller	68
Cloward and Ohlin	70
Agnew	71
Messner and Rosenfeld	73
Empirical Research	74
Policy Implications	76
Case Study 5.2: STARR	77
Summary	77
Discussion Questions	78
References	79

C H A P T E R   6

Social Learning Theory 81

Chapter Outline   *81*
Key Words and Concepts   *81*

Introduction   **82**

History of Social Learning Theory   **82**

Progression of Social Learning Theory   **84**
    Pavlov   84
    Skinner   84
    Bandura   85
    Wilson and Herrnstein   85

Contemporary Social Learning Theory   **86**
    Sutherland   87
    Burgess and Akers   90
    Akers   91

      Case Study 6.1: Tech Boyz Heist   **94**

Policy Implications   **94**
Summary   *95*
Discussion Questions   *95*
References   *95*

C H A P T E R   7

Control Theories 97

Chapter Outline   *97*
Key Words and Concepts   *97*

Introduction   **98**

Assumptions of Control Theories   **98**

Progression of Control Theories   **99**
    Reiss's Theory of Personal and Social Control   99
    Nye   100
    Reckless   101
    Sykes and Matza   102
    Hirschi   103

Contemporary Control Theories   **104**
    Gottfredson and Hirschi   104

Case Study 7.1: Land Surveyor Fined $3,000 for Verbally
Abusing ICA Officer **109**

Tittle 110

Policy Implications **112**
Summary *112*
Discussion Questions *113*
References *113*

CHAPTER 8

Labeling Theories 115

Chapter Outline *115*
Key Words and Concepts *115*
Introduction **116**
Progression of Labeling Theory **117**
    Tannenbaum 117
    Becker 117
      Case Study 8.1: Impact of Labeling on Juveniles **118**
    Lemert 119
    Braithwaite 120
      Case Study 8.2: Disintegrative Shaming? **121**
Empirical Research **121**
Policy Implications **122**
Summary *125*
Discussion Questions *126*
References *126*

CHAPTER 9

Conflict and Critical Theories 129

Chapter Outline *129*
Key Words and Concepts *129*
Introduction **130**
Conflict Criminology **130**
Development of Conflict Theories **131**

Pluralist Conflict	132
Vold	133
Turk	133
Quinney	134
Blalock	135
Case Study 9.1: Racial Profiling	*135*
Radical Conflict Perspective	136
Critical Criminology	137
Notable Critical Criminologists	**137**
Young	137
Ferrell	138
Pepinsky and Quinney	139
Policy Implications	**139**
Summary	*140*
Discussion Questions	*141*
References	*141*

C H A P T E R   1 0

Feminist Theory 143

Chapter Outline	*143*
Key Words and Concepts	*143*
Introduction	**144**
Chivalry Hypothesis	145
Progression of Feminist Theory	**146**
Adler	146
Simon	147
Hagan	147
Messerschmidt	148
Case Study 10.1: Piper Kerman	*149*
Daly and Chesney-Lind	149
Empirical Research	**150**
Policy Implications	**153**
Case Study 10.2: Outward Bound	*153*
Summary	*154*
Discussion Questions	*155*
References	*155*

CHAPTER 11

Integrative Theory 159

Chapter Outline	*159*
Key Words and Concepts	*159*
Introduction	**160**
Theoretical Competition	**160**
Theoretical Integration	**161**
Elliot and Colleagues	162
Shaming	163
Krohn's Network Analysis	163
Life Course Perspective	164
Case Study 11.1: Turning My Life Around	**165**
Summary	*166*
Discussion Questions	*167*
References	*167*
Glossary	*169*
Index	*183*

PREFACE

Understanding crime and delinquency is of great importance in criminal justice and criminology. The most important tool for understanding crime and delinquency is criminological theory. Criminological theory provides a rational method of examining crime and delinquency using logical links between defined concepts.

The goal of this book is to provide students (undergraduate and graduate), faculty, and scholars exposure to criminological theories. This book provides these groups with a readable presentation of the criminological theories. The readability allows for an easier understanding of the concepts, their connections, and how the literature has found problems with these theories.

This book is written in a manner that focuses on critical thought. The table of contents provides evidence that thinking about crime and delinquency requires a deeper understanding than one theory may be able to provide. Consuming the chapters in this book will help students, faculty, and scholars to better critically analyze crime and delinquency using criminological theories.

This book is not possible without a myriad of assistance. We thank our numerous colleagues, which are too numerous to list, for their support and guidance from reading multiple chapters. Further, we thank the anonymous reviewers of previous drafts of our manuscripts for making the book better. Lastly, we thank David Herzig, Betsy Kenny, and the staff of Wolters Kluwer for their assistance in the publication process.

ABOUT THE AUTHORS

George E. Higgins is a professor in the Department of Criminal Justice at the University of Louisville. He received his Ph.D. in criminology from Indiana University of Pennsylvania in 2001. He is the current editor of the *Journal of Criminal Justice Education*. His most recent publications appear or are forthcoming in *Journal of Criminal Justice, Criminal Justice and Behavior, Justice Quarterly, Deviant Behavior,* and *Youth and Society.*

Catherine D. Marcum is an associate professor in the Department of Government and Justice Studies at Appalachian State University. She received her Ph.D. in criminology from Indiana University of Pennsylvania in 2008. She is currently the associate editor for *Corrections: Policy, Practice, and Research.* Her research interests include criminological theory testing, cybercrime, and correctional issues.

Introduction to Criminological Theory

CHAPTER OUTLINE

Introduction

Sources of Crime Data
Uniform Crime Report and National Incident Based Reporting System
National Crime Victimization Survey
Self-Report Surveys

Outline of the Book

References

Key Words and Concepts

Crime	Micro-level Theory	Scope
Criminological Theory	National Crime	Self-Report Survey
Empirical Falsification	Victimization Survey	Tautology
Empirical Validity	National Incident Based	Testability
General Theory	Reporting System	Theory
Integrated Theory	Parsimonious	Uniform Crime Report
Likelihood	Policy Implications	Usefulness
Logically Consistent	Probabilistic Concept of	
Macro-level Theory	Causality	

Introduction

What is **crime**? Depending upon the audience, we can define crime in several different ways. Legalistically, crime is a violation of criminal laws of the state and government. In the political realm, laws serve those who are politically powerful, and crime is going against the interest of those in power. Sociologists assert that crime is an antisocial act that is an offense against human relationships. Lastly, psychology defines crime as problem behavior that makes living in society difficult for its norm-abiding inhabitants (Schmalleger, 2014). In this book, we will investigate crime in all four ways and determine potential predictors of behaviors through the examination of **criminological theory**.

A **theory** is a set of propositions that describe relationships between variables, often in a causal manner. A **general theory** attempts to explain crime, or at least the majority of it, in an overarching explanation, while **integrated theory** takes concepts from various sources and merges it together to provide a better explanation of crime. The specific purpose of criminological theory is to help us understand why individuals commit crime. Whether the explanation of criminality is simple or complex, abstract or concrete, each criminological theory contributes to our understanding of deviant human behavior. If we derive support that a theory is valid in its assertion of why crime occurs, we use its explanation to create policies to prevent and reduce crime. Police patrol plans and community policing policies were created as a result of criminological theory, as well as sentencing guidelines. Further, punishments and treatments administered by our corrections system are a result of theoretical testing and results.

The majority of criminological theories can be divided into one of two categories: **macro-level** or **micro-level theories**. A macro-level theory attempts to explain the behaviors of groups or societies in a broader spectrum. For example, social disorganization theory (as discussed in Chapter 4) is a macro-level theory. Micro-level theory, on the other hand, focuses on the behavior of individuals. Theories such as routine activities theory or social learning theory are examples of micro-level theories. Akers (1968; 1985) distinguishes between these two types of theories by stating that macro-level theories examine how structural factors affect group criminality, while micro-level theories attempt to explain individual behavior by considering social process factors.

With the introduction of the positivist school in the 19th century, criminological theory became scientific rather than just abstract musings of causes of crime. In other words, theorists began testing their observations and asserted the necessity of repeated support to validate a theory. It is important to note that findings from empirical studies may be factual but never "prove" a causal relationship 100 percent.

Instead, criminological theories demonstrate how variables can increase or decrease the **likelihood** that an event (crime) will occur. For example, rather than stating that psychological theories prove that abnormal mental processes cause criminality, it would be rephrased to say that abnormal mental processes increase the likelihood of an individual committing a crime.

Akers and Sellers (2013) have presented criteria to evaluate a theory. The most important is **empirical validity**, as it demonstrates if a theory can be validated or refuted with gathered evidence. When considering if a theory is good, it is important to determine if a theory can be supported by evidence and if the support is weak or strong. Further, the concept of causality is important with empirical validity. As discussed previously, a good theory does not have to demonstrate that an independent variable (X) always causes a dependent variable (Y). Rather, an empirically valid theory demonstrates the **probabilistic concept of causality**, showing that the presence of X indicates that Y is more likely to occur.

However, there are several other criteria that should also be assessed. First, a good theory must be **logically consistent,** possess **scope,** and be **parsimonious** (Akers & Sellers, 2013). Theories must make sense throughout their entirety and present logical concepts. Scope is the range of criminality that can be explained by the concepts of a theory. A theory that only explains drug use does not have a large scope; that is, a theory with a good scope explains a broad phenomenon. Lastly, a theory that has parsimony will concisely exhibit as few concepts as possible to explain the largest amount of crime. The more concepts included in a theory, the more confusion can arise and make it difficult to test.

This leads into the next quality of a good theory: **testability**. In order to call it a scientific theory, it must be testable and supported by repeated evidence. If it cannot be tested, it is more abstract thought and has no scientific value. Also, it must be open to **empirical falsification**, which allows us to consider evidence that disproves a theory. According to Stinchcombe (1968), a theory that cannot be falsified cannot be tested. Theories that cannot be tested can have a few potential issues. First, the concepts in a theory may be a **tautology**, which involves circular reasoning and can never be fully explained. A theory's propositions may be extremely open-ended. Lastly, a theory may be untestable because the hypotheses cannot be measured by observable events (Akers & Sellers, 2013).

A good theory must also be demonstrate **usefulness** and be able to provide **policy implications**. Findings from theory testing should be used to develop punishments, treatments, and programs to benefit the criminal justice system. If a theory has been supported and validated, then it should produce good policy implications. However, theoretical notions that are ill-supported and not understood will face difficulty when attempts are made to form policies from them.

Sources of Crime Data

There is no way of knowing exactly how much crime occurs across the globe. However, when attempting to predict and explain criminal behavior using theories, scholars often use known empirical data of criminal behavior, which is collected by government agencies, private industry, or academic institutions. This section will discuss a few of the more mainstream sources of crime data.

Uniform Crime Report and National Incident Based Reporting System

Every year since 1930, a statistical summary of crime reported from local agencies to the FBI is compiled into the **Uniform Crime Report (UCR)**. Twenty-nine categories of crime, only eight of which are major crimes, are listed on the UCR (Schmalleger, 2014). The definitions of these crimes are created by the FBI and not legal statute. Participation in the UCR is voluntary for law enforcement agencies, so not all departments report, and what is reported may not be an accurate representation of what actually occurred.

The crimes measured by the UCR are divided into two categories: Index 1 and Index 2. Index 1 offenses include murder, forcible rape, robbery, aggravated assault, burglary, larceny-theft, and motor vehicle theft. Index 2 offenses involve crimes such as shoplifting, drug sale or use, and prostitution and are only counted if a person has been arrested and charged with the crime (Maxfield & Babbie, 2006).

There are validity issues with the UCR and the way this information is presented. No white-collar or high-technology crimes are reported since they often go undiscovered, and the accuracy of the reports vary to an unknown extent as reporting is voluntary for law enforcement (Schmalleger, 2014). Only the most serious crime in a series of events is reported based on the hierarchy rule, so many criminal events are not reported to the FBI (Maxfield & Babbie, 2006). Lastly, uncompleted or "attempted" acts are reported as completed, which is an issue of reliable reporting (Schmalleger, 2014).

In order to close the gap on missing data reporting criminal activity from the UCR, the **National Incident Based Reporting System** (NIBRS) required all agencies to report their crime statistics annually and to give a brief summary of each act or arrest as well as to provide information about the victim and the offender. Forty-six different categories of crime are included, and the data recorded in NIBRS includes: nature/type of event, characteristics of victim and offender, types and value of property stolen/recovered, and characteristics of the arrest (Federal Bureau of Investigation, 2013).

National Crime Victimization Survey

Started in 1972, redesigned in 1992, and piloted by the Census Bureau, the **National Crime Victimization Survey** collects data from 42,000 households randomly chosen in the United States and includes individuals within those households that are 12 years of age or older (Schmalleger, 2014). Interviews and surveys are conducted twice a year for up to three years and new households are rotated into the sample regularly. Crimes measured include personal and property crimes that have happened to the residents and are reported with a profile of the victim, relation to offender, context of the crime, and the extent of the injury (Schmalleger, 2014).

Self-Report Surveys

Self-report surveys will ask subjects to describe their own victimization, as well as offending behaviors. This is yet another way of discovering information not reported to the police that would therefore not show up in official reports (Maxfield & Babbie, 2006). Well-known self-report surveys are used nationally to question youth about drug and alcohol use and other delinquent behaviors. However, these types of surveys are also used quite often on college campuses and other public institutions to get a better sense of criminality.

 # Outline of the Book

In this book, we will consider the value of several main theoretical schools of thought and provide discussion of several components of each theory. First, we will discuss the history of the theories and the main contributors to each school of thought. Further, each chapter will examine the empirical research (often using the data sources discussed above) supporting or disproving each theory, as well as the policy implications resulting from usage of the theory. The criminological theories examined in this book are as follows:

- Chapter 2: Classical School Theories
- Chapter 3: Biological and Psychological Theories
- Chapter 4: Social Disorganization Theory
- Chapter 5: Strain Theories
- Chapter 6: Social Learning Theory
- Chapter 7: Control Theories
- Chapter 8: Labeling Theories

- Chapter 9: Conflict and Critical Theories
- Chapter 10: Feminist Theory
- Chapter 11: Integrative Theory

We would like to invite the reader to critically analyze each theory for the positives and negatives. Is a theory testable? Is it empirically valid? And most importantly, do you as the reader feel as if it provides a logical explanation for criminal behavior? All academics support and favor certain theories and disagree with the tenets of others. We expect the same from each reader of this text.

REFERENCES

Akers, R. (1968). Problems in the sociology of deviance: Social definitions and behavior. *Social Forces, 46*, 455-465.

Akers, R. (1985). *Deviant behavior: A social learning approach* (3rd ed.). Belmont, CA: Wadsworth.

Akers, R. & Sellers, C. (2013). *Criminological theories: Introduction, evaluation, and application* (6th ed.). New York, NY: Oxford University Press.

Maxfield, M., & Babbie, E. (2006). Concepts, operationalization, and measurement. In *Basics of research methods for criminal justice and criminology* (pp. 110-116). Belmont, CA: Thomson/ Wadsworth.

Schmalleger, F. (2014). *Criminal justice today: An introductory text for the 21st century.* Upper Saddle River, NJ: Pearson.

Classical School Theories

CHAPTER OUTLINE

Introduction

Early Classical School

Modern Deterrence Theory
Case Study 2.1: Speedy Trials as a Method of Deterrence
Empirical Tests of Deterrence

Neoclassical School
Rational Choice Theory

Routine Activities Theory

Policy Implications of Classical School Theories
Case Study 2.2: Countering Classical School
Case Study 2.3: Target Hardening in Cyberspace

Summary

Discussion Questions

References

Key Words and Concepts

Age of Enlightenment
Capital Punishment
Classical School
Celerity
Certain
Cost Benefit Analysis
Crime Prevention Through
   Environmental Design
Defensible Space

Demonology
Determinism
Deterrence
Direct File
Drift Theory
Due Process Model of Justice
Felicity (or Hedonistic)
   Calculus
Free Will

General Deterrence
Hedonistic
Hot Spots
Informal Deterrence
Just Deserts
Justified Punishments
Lack of Capable Guardian

(continued)

Mandatory Minimums
Mass Incarceration
Motivated Offender
Neoclassical School
Objective Measures of
    Deterrence
Perceptual Measures of
    Deterrence

Rational Choice/Situational
    Choice Theory
Routine Activities
    Theory
Sentencing Guidelines
Severity
Social Contract
Soft Determinism

Specific Deterrence
Suitable Target
Target Hardening
Thoughtfully Reflective
    Decision Making
    (TRDM)
Three Strikes Laws
Utilitarianism

 # Introduction

Prior to the emergence of criminological theory in the 18th century, all human behavior was viewed as a function of **determinism**. In other words, actions and reactions were already predetermined by a higher and/or otherworldly power and not a matter of choice by the individual. Categorized by the European Church as the school of **demonology**, criminal behavior was a result of demon possession or witchcraft rather than a matter of rational decision making. Known in several forms, such as "the spiritual explanation" (Vold & Bernard, 1986) or "the prescientific view" (Barnes & Teeters, 1943), the basic idea of demonology was that the natural progression of life was interfered on by demonic forces. During the pre-Christian era, the source of deviant behavior was said to be the tormented souls of mothers who died during childbirth or suicide victims. However, after the development of Christian theology, the demon beings were workers of Satan (the Devil).

Demonologists believed that all humans were vulnerable to evil forces, which resulted in participation in nonconforming behavior. Behavior violating social norms was considered to be a result of temptation or possession. Temptations were a result of a lack of faith in God and succumbing to worldly desires and pleasures. Individuals who gave in to these pleasures were said to have made a pact with the Devil in exchange for the goods (Pfohl, 1985) and were declared witches. Possession, on the other hand, was the seizure of a human's soul against his will by dark forces, which resulted in involuntary allegiance to the dark world. Alleviation of either a possession or a temptation was through protection by spells or charms or an exorcism of demons (Einstadter & Henry, 2006).

During this period of demonological thought, specifically in the 13th century, St. Thomas Aquinas broached the concept of law and its role in criminal behavior.

Aquinas asserted that there was a natural law granted by God, and that people were generally more inclined to do good rather than evil. Those who committed crime violated the natural law and also committed a sin. Thomas Hobbes (1588-1678) later asserted that humans were actually very self-consumed and solely pursued their own self-interests without concern of the welfare of others. However, being that humans are rational enough to recognize that this line of thought would result in constant warfare, the human race agrees to commit to a "**social contract**." Individuals agree to give up the right to enforce their own forms of justice against others to the government and in turn receive protection and other benefits. As time progressed, this naturalistic view was widely accepted by scholars such as Locke (1632-1704), Voltaire (1694-1778), and Rousseau (1712-1778), but not supported by those in political power (Vold, Bernard & Snipes, 2012). Yet by the mid-1700s, the fathers of criminological thought produced a groundbreaking reaction based on the concept of the social contract.

In this chapter, we present the basic premises of the classical quest for understanding criminal behavior. We outline the historical context that the premise originates. Next, we provide illustrative examples and contemporary studies of the classical perspective of criminology. We evaluate these findings and assumptions. Finally, we suggest policy implications that may be fruitful in understanding this particular premise.

Early Classical School

As we progressed into the late-1700s, the historical period of the Dark (or Middle) Ages subsided to become the **Age of Enlightenment.** As its label indicates, this was a period of time that the proverbial "light bulb" turned on and scholars considered new intellectual philosophies, many countering the long-accepted beliefs of the Catholic Church. Thinkers like Voltaire, Issac Newton, and Immanuel Kant introduced new ideas and inventions. Also during the historical time period of the Enlightenment, Cesare Beccaria produced a radical essay titled *Dei deliti e delle pene*, otherwise known as *On Crimes and Punishment* (1764). The 26-year-old protest writer birthed the "**Classical School**" of criminology, which focused on penal and judicial reform. At the time, the criminal justice system in most European countries was based on arbitrary and biased judicial decisions. It was not unusual for torture to be used to coerce confessions or for cruel punishments to be used for petty crimes. Classical criminologists placed an importance on **justified punishments**. In other words, the punishment should fit the crime, and cruel and unusual forms of treatment to offenders should be abolished. Based on the Old Testament views of "eye for an eye, tooth for a tooth," this theory advocates for equality and fairness in punishment.

Beccaria recognized that in order for an act to be a crime, a law must be passed to identify harm done to society. In other words, no act can be criminal until a law states the behavior is wrong. He believed laws to be important, as they prevented men from "encroaching upon the freedom of one another as defined by the laws" (Monachesi, 1955). He went on to further describe three categories of crime based on the seriousness of harm: (1) crimes against the state; (2) crimes that injure the property of others; and (3) crimes against public order. Further, Beccaria asserted that laws should be impartial and applied equally to all persons despite status. During this period of time, punishments for the same crime were issued differently depending on the offender's sex, race, religion, or simply the mood of the punisher. Beccaria felt that this not only was unfair but also made the criminal justice process ineffective. Further, in court, judges should only be instruments of the law and not interpret it on a case-by-case basis.

Classical criminology was shaped around the premise that humans were rational beings who could make choices with **free will**. When individuals make a choice to violate the law, they do it by calculating the risk of pain compared to the potential benefit of pleasure that would be accomplished from performing the act. In other words, crime is committed because the offender sees the pleasure he would receive from the act (e.g., money, sex, power) to outweigh the potential pain he might receive if caught. The perceived pain would come in the form of a legal penalty as a result of apprehension.

In order for this assumed rationality to proceed successfully, Beccaria (1764) asserted that punishment must be three things: swift, certain, and severe. Further, the first two components were of utmost importance in order for punishment to be effective. Swiftness, or **celerity**, is the rate that punishment is administered after the commission of a crime. Beccaria determined that a punishment given as immediately as possible after a criminal act would be more useful and just, as the association between the crime and punishment would resonate with the offender. A **certain** punishment is one that would be guaranteed to occur after the commission of a crime. Perception of punishment is not as impactful if the individual believes there is a chance he or she will avoid it (as it is not certain). Lastly, **severity** of punishment is based on the proportionality concept: The punishment must fit the crime. If a punishment is too severe or too lenient based on the behavior, it will not impact the rational decision-making process; therefore, the punishment must be just severe enough that the perceived pleasure obtained from the crime is not worth the risk of the punishment. Essentially, Beccaria (1764) believed that the purpose of punishment should be to deter individuals from committing a crime. This is especially applicable to individuals who have already committed crimes, as they are aware of the punishment that can be received for future recidivism.

Beccaria (1764) had specific views on what constituted appropriate treatment of offenders and punishment. He advocated for time limitations on case preparation by prosecution and defense. He did not support the use of torture during interrogation, nor did Beccaria agree with incarceration of persons not yet convicted of crimes. Prisons and jails were often very filthy, inhumane places where the accused sometimes died before trial due to the horrible conditions. Further, Beccaria supported the use of corporal punishment for offenders who committed particularly violent personal crimes, but generally opposed the use of capital punishment. He did not feel as if the state had the right to take another person's life (Beirne, 2006).

Jeremy Bentham (1765) furthered Beccaria's assertion by delving into the effect of pleasure on humans. Early classical theorists believed that humans were rational, reasoning, and independent decision makers who were in control of their own destiny. Furthermore, they were **hedonistic** and motivated by their own self-interest. In other words, classical theorists were confident that humans were on the constant search for pleasurable activities and focused on what made them feel the best. Bentham asserted that there were four sources of pain and pleasure: physical, political, moral, and religious. Sensations from the ordinary course of nature are physical, while occurrences based on the decisions of a state representative are political. Important or popular individuals in a community can cause moral pleasure or pain, and the experiences attributed to a higher power are religious. Bentham also stated that these pleasures and pains vary in intensity, duration, or certainty, which causes them to have a varied effect on individuals.

It is this variance of pleasures and pains that influence the rational decision making of individuals. Bentham (1765) asserted that in order to make choices, humans participate in **felicity (or hedonistic) calculus**, which is simply the weighing of the pleasures and pains of an act to make a determination of how to proceed. In other words, before a person decides to commit a crime, he or she weighs the potential outcomes (both positive and negative) and then proceeds to what fulfills his or her best interests. If the benefit of robbing a bank is outweighed by the potential incarceration period, the person will choose not to commit that act.

According to Bentham, utilizing a law to define an act as a crime was based on the intent of happiness of the community. In other words, legislators develop laws to protect the individuals in the community and ensure their safety. Bentham was concerned with the "collective human rights of society," rather than protecting certain social interest groups (Galliher, 1989). This concept, otherwise known as **utilitarianism**, not only focused on the importance of law, but also on making punishments as specific as possible. This way, potential offenders could make rational calculations when determining whether to break the law, as the consequences were painful. He further expanded Beccaria's categories of crime by describing five (instead of three) categories of crime: (1) public offenses; (2) semi-public offenses; (3) offenses against the state; (4) offenses harmful only to the offender; and (5) abnormal offenses.

In addition to these major concepts produced by Beccaria and Bentham, classical thinkers stressed the importance of a **due process model of justice**. This rational system of justice should have clearly defined principles and be systematic in delivering justice (Young, 1981). In other words, due process means delivering justice in a fair way to all offenders with bias or prejudice. According to Packer (1968), the due process model should contain several components. First, it should protect the privacy and security of an individual. We should be protected against unwarranted punishment before conviction. Second, the legislative and judiciary bodies should remain separate entities, and the arbitrary power exercised by each should be limited. The system should be based on rules regarding arrest, investigation, search and seizure, and the trial process so that an abuse of discretion would not be used. Furthermore, an adversarial trial system should be used that allowed an accused judgment by jury of his or her peers, rather than one individual (a judge) with large amounts of discretion. Next, accusations and investigations should be public and not in secret. Lastly, punishment should be certain and administered quickly after conviction. In summary, Packer argued that in order for the criminal justice system to be effective in its administration of justice and have impact when doing so, the rights of the accused should be upheld.

Modern Deterrence Theory

As classical theory has evolved, modern interpretations have indicated that crime prevention is a matter of **deterrence**. Potential offenders are aware of the punishment that will present itself for committing a crime—the "**just deserts**"—and are in turn swayed from participating in the behavior. According to Zimring (1971), there are two forms of deterrence. **General deterrence** occurs when the state's punishment for a crime serves as an example to everyone in the general population who has not yet committed a crime. In other words, individuals will avoid committing a crime for fear of the consequences. Second, convicted and punished offenders will refrain from repeating crimes as they are aware of the punishment. This form, termed **specific deterrence**, focuses on those individuals who have already participated in criminal behavior at least once.

Over the past few decades, deterrence has remained a concept of focus in the public eye in a few different ways. During the War on Crime and War on Drugs in the 1980s and 1990s, when criminal legislation was more punitive and conservative, deterrence fueled the development of sentencing policies (i.e., mandatory minimums, three strikes laws) that had the underlying goal of deterring future criminality because of the harshness associated with the punishments. Punishments targeted at drunk drivers and drug offenders were administered with the hopes of deterring this behavior. For example, conviction of a drunken driving offense could equate in suspension of a driver's license, or possession of cocaine meant a mandatory amount of time in prison. Both punishments were undesired and inconvenient for offenders, and therefore, under the principle of deterrence, should keep the general population from committing those offenses based on awareness of the punishment. In addition, an offender who has already been punished for a crime will refrain from doing it again.

CASE STUDY 2.1
SPEEDY TRIALS AS A METHOD OF DETERRENCE

A problem with the concept of deterrence is that our criminal justice system does not proceed with swiftness, as proscribed by Beccaria. Speedy trial laws have been enacted on the federal level, as well as in many states, to address this issue. The Sixth Amendment guarantees an offender a speedy and public trial. However, the Supreme Court developed a standard to determine if the speedy trial clause had been violated in the case *Barker v. Wingo* (1972). In 1958, Willie Barker and Silas Manning were accused of the murder of an elderly couple in Kentucky. Prosecution believed the case against Manning was the strongest and his testimony was necessary to convict Barker. The government had a very difficult time convicting Manning, and it was not until 1962 that he was convicted of one of the murders. The lengthy trial involved 16 continuances, and it was during the 12th, 15th, and 16th continuances that Barker's counsel filed a motion to dismiss on speedy trial grounds. All motions were dismissed and Barker was finally convicted of murder and given a life sentence in 1963, five years after the original arrest.

After affirmation of the conviction by lower appeals courts, the Supreme Court issued a writ of certiorari in 1972. The specific circumstances of the Barker case did receive an affirmation of his conviction by the Court. However, they did state that in order to determine if a defendant has been prejudiced by lack of speedy trial, four factors must be considered:

1. Reason of delay;
2. Length of delay;
3. Time and manner that defendant asserted his or her right to speedy trial; and
4. Degree of prejudice delay caused.

The Court asserted that Barker was not prejudiced by the delay as none of his witnesses were harmed, nor did he want a speedy trial. Yet, this case has been extremely important for future cases in determining bias of speedy trial initiation.

Empirical Tests of Deterrence

Despite its importance and long-standing presence in criminology, empirical tests of deterrence theory were few until the late 1960s. The first studies published mainly focused on comparing states that utilized the death penalty as punishment for first degree homicide and those that had no death penalty. These studies generally indicated that the death penalty had no effect on homicide rates (Sellin, 1959; Bedau, 1964). More recent research has continued to support these findings and generally indicates that the death penalty is not an effective deterrent (Radelet & Akers, 1996). There has also been testing of the deterrent effect of police, with support indicating that law enforcement presence may deter without actual apprehension (Apel & Nagin, 2011). It is the threat of apprehension that deters offenders, so policing is more of a form of general deterrence.

Very recently, Akers and Sellers (2013) categorized measures of deterrence into two categories: **objective and perceptual measures of deterrence**. Objective approaches use official criminal justice statistics to measure the severity and certainty of certain punishments as a deterrent. Certainty is measured by arrest rate or proportion of offenders convicted in court. Severity can be measured by maximum sentence provided by law for a crime or examining the proportion of offenders who are incarcerated for a crime rather than some form of community corrections. Deterrence theorists assert that there should be an inverse relationship between the two measures and the crime rate. In other words, when the certainty and severity of criminal punishments are high, the crime rate should be low (Gibbs, 1975; Pratt et al., 2006).

On the other hand, the perceptual measure of deterrence is to investigate individuals' subjective perceptions of criminal punishments. An objective threat of punishment is ineffective if an individual is not aware of the punishment or believes the risk of being caught and penalized is low. Scheider (2001) stated that a person's perceptions of criminal sanctions are based on the objective knowledge of the sanction. In other words, humans often have limited knowledge of legal penalties and make inaccurate estimations of the likelihood of apprehension and related punishment.

Research of both objective and perceptual deterrence have found negative correlations between certainty of punishment and the rate of criminal behavior, but the correlations are low (D'Alessio & Stolzenberg, 1998; Tonry, 2008). Severity of punishment has even less of an effect (Smith & Akers, 1993; Weisburd, Waring & Chayet, 1995), while celerity has little to no effect (Nagin & Pogarsky, 2001). Further, a meta-analysis performed by Pratt et al. (2006) determined that deterrence factors were consistently the weakest predictors of crime in macro-level tests. In fact, these studies have indicated that most people under most circumstances do not commit crime not because of fear of punishment (i.e., deterrence theory) but because of their moral values. The socialization we have received from family, friends, church, and other sources have indicated it is the accepted norm not to commit crime, and that is our main influential factor (Gibbs, 1975; Pratt et al., 2006).

Paternoster, Saltzman, Waldo, and Chiricos (1983) asserted that prior behavior on perceptions of certainty of punishment, otherwise known as the experiential effect, was a stronger influence compared to the deterrent effect. Those individuals who had lower levels of experience with committing an offense had high levels of certainty of punishment and vice versa. While their original assertion was attempting to disprove specific deterrence, Akers and Sellers (2013) argued that this is not necessarily the case and, in fact, may support this concept. Specific deterrence operates based on a person's experience with getting caught and punished. If an offender has committed crimes and is not caught, his or her perception of certainty of punishment is low and he or she will not be deterred. As Paternoster et al. (1983) did not question respondents on experiences with arrest and punishment, the extent of their findings cannot be determined. However, Helland and Tabarrok (2007) examined the deterrent effect of California's "Three Strikes and You're Out" law. They examined the individuals with two strike offenses compared to those who had been convicted of only one strike offense (this group also included persons who had been tried for a second strike offense but were ultimately convicted of a non-strike offense). The two groups were comparable in regard to several factors, such as age, race, and length of time incarcerated. Yet, results indicated that arrest rates were 20 percent lower for the two strike group, assuming the indication that offenders were aware of the greatly enhanced sentence at the third strike and were in turn deterred.

Other scholars, such as Grasmick and Bursick (1990) and Pratt et al. (2006), examined the effect of deterrence beyond those strictly formal sanctions. **Informal deterrence**, the anticipated or actual social consequences of crime that prevent occurrence, was shown to have more of an effect compared to arrest or actual legal penalties (Nagin & Pogarsky, 2001). These social consequences could be disapproval by friends or family (or the ceasing of relationships with these individuals), loss of a job, or removal of a valued privilege in a person's life. In addition, there is a potential relationship between formal punishments and informal social sanctions. Zimring and Hawkins (1973) and Williams and Hawkins (1989) asserted that some individuals may refrain from criminality because of the perception that their intimate peer groups (the informal social sanction) have on the repercussions of the crime (formal sanction). For example, a juvenile may refrain from participating in vandalism of a car for fear of his parent's reaction to an arrest for the vandalism.

Neoclassical School

Although the classical school was the first formal criminological theory, it and made massive contributions to the field as a whole, as time passed and more theories were introduced, its assertions became dated and at times an invalid explanation of criminal behavior. In the late 1970s, theorists realized that no criminological theory solely relied on free will. Matza's (1964) **drift theory** was possibly the closest relative to the original classical school assertions, as he introduced will as a contributing factor of committing deviance. However, Matza did not claim that individuals made calculated decisions with every act. Instead, he asserted it was a matter of **soft determinism** that explained criminality, which would lie in the continuum between free will and hard determinism. This new theoretical explanation of crime, called the **neoclassical school**, asserted that the following factors affected decision making: 1) character of a person; 2) dynamics of character development; and 3) rational choices made when presented with opportunities for criminal activity (Schmalleger, 2012). With these amendments to the original classical school, new theories have emerged to provide a contemporary explanation of criminal behavior: rational choice theory and routine activities theory.

Rational Choice Theory

The expansion of deterrence theory has been linked with the introduction of **rational choice theory**, a more contemporary version of classical criminology. Clarke and Cornish (1983) developed rational or **situational choice theory**, where criminal behavior is a result of rational decision making based on the situation and the opportunities presented at that time. As described in basic classical criminology, an individual weighs the benefits and detriments of performing a crime. This **cost-benefit analysis** is affected by an individual's preferences, estimations of criminal opportunity and the consequences, and attitudes toward criminal behavior. However, classical criminology was developed as a result of reaction to the law, while rational choice theory was created in economic theory.

Cornish and Clarke (2005) assume that decisions are made with purpose rather than with senselessness. This rationality is limited as it is made as a situational decision, or the "best I can do at the time," rather than seeking the maximum outcome for the future. Because of this, Cornish and Clarke asserted that criminal behavior cannot be studied in the abstract but rather specifically. In other words, crime itself cannot be explained as a whole, but rather by looking separately at homicide, motor vehicle theft, or shoplifting.

Empirical studies have provided some support for rational choice theory, even if it was only partial support (Cromwell, Olson, & Avary, 1991; De Haan & Voss,

2003). These studies have demonstrated that humans do go through a rational decision-making process when choosing to commit crime, but there are generally other influential factors. McCarthy (2002) agreed that human beings do weigh information before making choices, but this thought process is not always maximal or thorough. Secondly, the concept of human agency also plays a role in decision making. Individuals do make the decision to commit or refrain from criminal behavior, but degrees of social control and learning also play a part in the decision making. For example, humans may choose to commit crime because a friend is also doing it or they have no emotional connection to the person or object victimized.

Paternoster and Pogarsky (2009) recently introduced the idea of **thoughtfully reflective decision making (TRDM)**. TRDM is a process that involves the following steps:

1. Compiling information;
2. Carefully considering the information for possible solutions;
3. Consideration of alternative solutions; and
4. Reflection on the positives and negatives of the outcomes of the choice.

This decision making is thoughtful because individuals who use this process are deliberate and careful with the way they collect and use information when applying it to a problem. Reflection occurs when the individual can objectively remove personal feelings from the situation and evaluate how well he or she made the decision, as well as what can be learned from it. Paternoster and Pogarsky asserted that when individuals make decisions deliberately and thoughtfully, they are also considering the impact of the decision on human agency (i.e., society as a whole). Furthermore, they generally make better decisions in both the short term and the long term.

Routine Activities Theory

Hindelang, Gottfredson, and Garofalo (1978) developed what is commonly termed "lifestyle/exposure theory," which was based on correlation between lifestyle choices and victimization. Variance in victimization risk is related to differences in lifestyle choices, which are the daily activities of a person's life, such as work, school, and extracurricular activities. Choices made by individuals influence their exposure to different persons and places. Exposure to some persons and places may increase exposure to criminal behavior, which also influences one's own risk of victimization (Hindelang et al., 1978).

Routine activities theory is somewhat similar to lifestyle/exposure theory (Messner & Tardiff, 1985). Cohen and Felson sought to expand and improve lifestyle theory by incorporating ecological concepts, specifically Hawley's (1950) components of temporal organization: rhythm, tempo, and timing. Rhythm is the regularity with which events occur, while tempo is the number of events that occur per unit of time. Finally, timing is the duration and recurrence of the events. The inclusion of these three components improves the explanation of how and why criminal activity is performed. While Cohen and Felson (1979) agreed with the assertion of Hindelang et al. (1978) that the routine activities of certain groups expose them to greater risks of victimization, they also argued that societal changes have provided motivated offenders with more opportunities to commit crime (Felson, 1986). As a result of changes in people's routine activities, the number of available targets has increased and the presence of capable guardianship has decreased. After World War II and the Women's Liberation Movement, there was a shift in the amount of routine activities that were performed outside the home. With more individuals working outside the home, those places were more frequently left unguarded during the day.

The currently recognized routine activities theory states that there are three components necessary in a situation in order for a crime to occur: a **suitable target,** a **lack of a capable guardian,** and a **motivated offender** (Cohen & Cantor, 1980; Cohen & Felson, 1979; Cohen & Felson, 1981; Felson, 1986; Felson, 1987). Moreover, crime is not a random occurrence but, rather, follows regular patterns that require these three components. Target suitability is based on a person's availability as a victim, as well as his or her attractiveness to the offender. Guardianship is the ability of persons and objects to prevent a crime from occurring (Garofalo & Clark, 1992; Meier & Miethe, 1993; Tseloni et al., 2004) and can take two forms: social and physical. Social guardianship can exist through such factors as household composition, lifestyle, or marital status. Physical guardianship refers to self-protective measures taken by a person, such as locked gates and outside lighting. Finally, a motivated offender is a person who is willing to commit a crime when opportunities are presented through the presence and absence of the other two components (Cohen & Felson, 1979; Mustaine & Tewksbury, 2002).

Routine activities theory was quite the contribution to theoretical criminology as it attempted to explain victimization rather than offending behaviors. Cohen and Felson (1979) were quick to emphasize that an individual's routine activities were those that occurred through the natural and most prevalent activities of a person's life, such as going to work and school, maintaining romantic relationships, or social interaction. For example, a burglar could take notice that the victim is gone every Monday and Wednesday from 10:00 a.m. to 5:00 p.m. for undergraduate coursework at the local university, which leaves his house unguarded. Or, a rapist takes note that a single female walks home from her job at the bar every night at 3:00 a.m. in a poorly lit alley. Furthermore, agents of the government (i.e., law enforcement) are not the only capable guardians, as it could be friends or family, installation of a front porch light, or adoption of a large German Shepherd. Policies built from this theory (further discussed in the next section) essentially address limiting opportunities to commit crime and increasing guardianship. For example, **crime prevention through environmental design (CPTED)** advocates for altering the physical construction of a community to deter criminal behavior. These spaces should be clearly seen at all times.

There has been generous support for routine activities theory in the decades' worth of empirical studies. Macro-level studies have shown that lack of guardianship in areas with large amounts of transiency was shown to produce a significant effect on crime rates in neighborhoods (LaGrange, 1999; Roncek & Bell, 1981; Roncek & Maier, 1991). Further, lack of guardianship and risky lifestyles of city residents have been shown to have a significant relationship with victimization (Cao & Maume, 1993; Forde & Kennedy, 1997). Micro-level studies allow for analysis of factors that specifically apply to individuals. Personal and property crime victimization studies suggested a person's routine activities significantly increase the likelihood of victimization (Arnold et al., 2005; Cohen & Cantor, 1980; Gaetz, 2004; Spano & Nagy, 2005; Tewksbury & Mustaine, 2000; Woolredge et al., 1992). Also, current studies revealed that drug and alcohol consumption is a significant predictor of sexual victimization of females (Mustaine & Tewksbury, 2002; Schwartz et al., 2001).

Policy Implications of Classical School Theories

The classical school is based on the premise that in order for punishment to be effective and serve as a deterrent, it must be swift, certain, and severe. As the most emphasis is placed on the latter, there is justification for the "tough on crime" policies developed since the 1970s (Pratt et al., 2006; Webster, Doob, & Zimring, 2006). Policy implications such as the reduction of use of parole and indeterminate sentencing, as a well as reducing good time for prison inmates, are a retributive form of punishment. The ultimate punishment, **capital punishment**, is still ever-present in the United States as it is still used by 33 states and the federal government. As mentioned previously, early classical theorists did not support the use of capital punishment. Bentham considered it too harsh because the pain is greater than its purpose (Geis, 1960), and in order for punishment to be effective it must not be overly harsh. Beccaria believed it to be unnecessary and brutal, unless the execution of an inmate would improve the security of a nation. Specifically, Beccaria supported the use of capital punishment if (1) an incarcerated individual still poses a threat to society, (2) his existence could produce a revolution, or (3) the execution deters others from criminality (Beirne, 1991).

There have been mixed findings that have made it difficult to produce a consensus on whether deterrent effects are present with the death penalty. Dezhbakhsh, Rubin, and Shepherd (2003) and Mocan and Gittings (2003) have found strong deterrent effects with capital punishment. In addition, Shepherd (2005) stated that capital punishment deterred homicides if executions exceeded an empirically identified threshold, as a small amount of executions actually raises murder rates. These findings have been challenged by scholars such as Fagan (2006) and Cohen-Cole et al. (2009), stating that these strong deterrent effects are fragile and could easily be reversed by changes in the model. Furthermore, Katz, Levitt, and Shustorovich (2003) stated that since executions are infrequent, prison mortality rates are the deterrent and not capital punishment. Interestingly, several states have recently abolished the use of the death penalty. Most recently, New Mexico (in 2009) and Connecticut (in 2012) repealed the use of the death penalty but, as it was not retroactive, there were still individuals left on death row.

Despite the slow decrease in the crime rate in the United States, several sentencing policies have increased the number of inmates incarcerated. **Mandatory minimum sentencing** (laws requiring a specific amount of time for the violation of state and federal laws) and **three strikes laws** (requirement of harsh penalties, often 25 years to life sentences, for commission of three felonies in a state) have increased sentence lengths for career criminals, most often drug and violent offenders. Many states mandate a sentence enhancement if a firearm is used in the commission of a felony such as a robbery. In addition, the use of **sentencing guidelines** (uniform sentencing policies implemented by the federal government and multiple states) has also contributed to the large number of offenders incarcerated. While implemented with the original intention of decreasing judicial discretion, it has actually caused more of a problem. The sentencing grid provides suggested incarceration lengths by comparing the seriousness of the current offense and the criminal offense history. The federal sentencing guidelines have received much criticism, especially with their effect on disparity in the prison population due to drug crimes. The 20 states that use the guidelines have attempted to separate themselves as much as possible from them.

CASE STUDY 2.2
COUNTERING CLASSICAL SCHOOL

Families Against Mandatory Minimums (FAMM) is a nonprofit organization that is fighting against mandatory minimums and promoting legislation that does not rely on incarceration. They advocate for community corrections and programs that lessen overcrowding in prison and allow offenders to reintegrate into society. They are directing projects in Florida, Massachusetts, and on the federal level to change sentencing legislation, often those targeted at low-level drug offenders. Currently, they are working on amending federal guidelines that consider financial loss as the guideline for sentencing for economic crimes. FAMM believes it should be one of four things considered, and not the sole basis of a sentence.

The treatment of juvenile offenders has also changed based on classical school concepts. For instance, the use of direct file has increased. **Direct file** is the prosecutor's discretion to file a juvenile case in juvenile or adult court (Steiner & Wright, 2006). By processing juveniles in adult court for particularly serious crimes, they are in turn sentenced more seriously. Despite the empirical evidence that scared straight programs and shock incarceration is ineffective, their appealing premise has convinced many that their implementation should effectively deter adolescents. Furthermore, the usage of boot camps for juveniles and adults became popular in the 1980s and are still used as a sentencing option (Peters, Thomas, & Zamberian, 1997). Although participants are able to maintain good behavior during their time in the camp due to the strict discipline and militaristic style, they are not able to reduce recidivism (MacKenzie & Piquero, 1994; Jensen & Rojek, 1998; Zhang, 2000).

The most obvious effect of get tough policies is the continued overcrowding of our adult incarceration system. Beginning with President Regan's War on Crime and continuing with the War on Drugs, the 1990s began the expansion of the prison system. The "**mass incarceration**" phenomenon (Clear, 2007) has caused prisons and jails to go beyond capacity in regard to inmate population. By the end of 2011, approximately 6,977,700 were under some form of correctional supervision in the United States (Glaze & Parks, 2012). While this was a 1.4% decrease from the previous year, this was largely due to a drop in the probation population. Further, 1 out of 107 adults in the United States was either in prison or jail. Incarceration is an extremely pressing problem for minority communities. According to Raphael and Stoll (2009), approximately one-third of the black males between the ages of 26 to 35 who did not graduate high school were incarcerated on any given day.

Policies based on routine activities theory or rational choice theory are based more on influencing what happens before a crime occurs. The concept of **target hardening** makes targets less appealing for victimization by tightening security. Measures such as surveillance, locks, and other environmental management tools are examples. Furthermore, target hardening strategies have demonstrated effectiveness in reducing crime in digital locations (Marcum, 2009). The uses of password protection and encryption software are target hardening strategies that can be used online. Situational crime measures focus on the concept of **defensible space**, which is architecture developed to reduce criminal behavior. Also, improved lighting, closed-circuit television, and even steering column locks can decrease the likelihood of crime occurring (Clarke & Cornish, 1983). In summary, Felson and Boba (2010) referred to these techniques as "designing out crime" or "environmental design," as they are changes in an environment that can change the decision-making process of a potential offender.

We see the above-referenced techniques used in policing. **Hot spots**, or small geographic areas identified by law enforcement as a high-crime areas in a community or city, are targets for problem-oriented policing. Multiple studies have indicated that these small areas, generally city blocks or neighborhoods, are the source of the majority of police calls (Sherman et al., 1989; Weisburd et al., 2006). Despite the findings of the Kansas City Patrol Experiment in the 1970s, efforts have been made by police departments to increase police presence and response time in these areas. Based on Braga's (2008) review of the literature, many cities have found success via crime reduction in these hot spot areas.

CASE STUDY 2.3
TARGET HARDENING IN CYBERSPACE

Target hardening practices makes targets less appealing for victimization by tightening security. These methods of protection can be applied online to make it more difficult for an individual to access information or websites. It addresses the patterns of the user online that can often leave an individual wide open for victimization. Many Internet users will use the same password for important accounts as it is easy to remember, and this makes identity theft or hacking easy for offenders who steal the password. Simply changing your passwords regularly and not having the same password for your accounts, email, and social networking websites will prevent this victimization.

 Summary

The classical school of criminology was met with resistance as it completely challenged the belief of the causes of human behavior from centuries past. For hundreds of years, scholars based studies on the premise that human behavior was predetermined by a higher power. Classical criminologists fully disagreed, stating that humans made decisions with their own free will. These decisions were made rationally and after consideration of the benefits and costs of the behavior. Therefore, individuals who chose to commit crime found it to be more beneficial to them compared to the potential consequence. As time progressed, classical criminology proved to be the basis for the due process model of crime, a model that focused on the rights of the accused and fair processing through the criminal justice system.

Classical theorists also examined the concept of effective punishment and determined it was necessary for criminal sanctions to be equal to the crime. Punishments that were too lenient or too harsh would not be effective, nor serve as a deterrent for the future. Furthermore, punishments must be administered swiftly and with certainty. Modern day sanctions have revolved around this retributive or "just deserts" basis and have advocated for the punishment of the offender to the fullest extent of the law. Changes in sentencing policies have caused a boom in the offender population and stretched our corrections system.

Modern day theoretical applications of classical theory have also focused on the routine activities of an individual and the situations they put themselves in during their daily activities. These theories assert that victimization occurs based on the attributes of an individual's daily routine and lifestyle. Preventative measures, called target hardening strategies or defensible space architecture, are implemented to better protect an individual and decrease opportunities for victimization.

Critics of the classical school have argued that the theory has a limited explanation of criminality, as not all individuals have the capacity to make rational decisions without the influence of other factors (e.g., peer influences, environmental factors, and psychological dispositions). As we move through this book exploring various theoretical explanations, each school of thought will assert its superiority over others and attempt to provide a better explanation of criminality.

Discussion Questions

1. Does our criminal justice system effectively apply Beccaria's concepts of an effective punishment?
2. How do you see the classical school applied at your college or university in regard to academic dishonesty or other deviant behaviors? Do you feel as if those measures work as an effective deterrent?
3. What type of target hardening techniques could you implement in your own life to decrease your likelihood of victimization?

REFERENCES

Akers, R. & Sellers, C. (2013). *Criminological theories: Introduction, evaluation, and application* (6th ed.). New York, NY: Oxford University Press.

Arnold, R., Keane, C., & Baron, S. (2005). Assessing risk of victimization through epidemiological concepts: An alternative analytic strategy applied to routine activities theory. *Canadian Review of Sociology & Anthropology, 42(3)*, 345-364.

Barker v. Wingo (1972). 407 U.S. 514.

Barnes, H. & Teeters, N. (1943). *New horizons in criminology: The American crime problem.* New York: Prentice Hall.

Beccaria, C. (1764). *On crimes and punishment,* trans. Henry Paolucci. Indianapolis: Bobbs-Merrill, 1964.

Bedau, H. (1964). *The death penalty in America.* New York: Anchor.

Beirne, P. (1991). Inventing criminology: The science of man in Cesare Beccaria's *dei delitte e delle pene* (1764). *Criminology, 29,* 777-820.

Beirne, P. (2006). Free will and determinism? Reading Beccaria's *Of crimes and punishments* (1764) as a text of enlightenment. In S. Henry & M. Lanier (Eds.), *The essential criminology reader* (pp. 3-17). Boulder, CO: Westview Press.

Bentham, J. (1765). 1970. In J.H. Burns and H.L.A. Hart (Eds.), *An introduction to the principles of morals and legislation.* London: The Athlone Press, University of London.

Braga, A., & Bond, B. (2008). Policing crime and disorder hot spots: A randomized controlled trial. *Criminology, 46,* 577-607.

Cao, L., & Maume, D. (1993). Urbanization, inequality, lifestyles, and robbery: A comprehensive model. *Sociological Focus, 26(1),* 11-26.

Clarke, R., & Cornish, R. (1983). *Crime control in Britain: A review of policy and research.* Albany: State University of New York Press.

Clear, T. (2007). *Imprisoning communities: How mass incarceration makes disadvantaged places worse.* New York: Oxford.

Cohen, L., & Cantor, D. (1980). The determinants of larceny: An empirical and theoretical study. *Journal of Research in Crime and Delinquency, 17(2),* 140-159.

Cohen, L., & Felson, M. (1979). Social change and crime rate trends: A routine activity approach. *American Sociological Review, 44,* 588-608.

Cohen, L., & Felson, M. (1981). Modeling crime trends: A criminal opportunity perspective. *Journal of Research in Crime and Delinquency, 18,* 138-164.

Cohen-Cole, E., Durlauf, S., Fagan, J., & Nagin, D. (2009). Model uncertainty and the deterrent effect of capital punishment. *American Law and Economics Review, 11,* 335-369.

Cornish, R., & Clarke, R. (2005). The rational choice perspective. In S. Henry and M. Lanier (Eds.), *The essential criminology reader* (pp. 18-29). Boulder, CO: Westview Press.

Cromwell, P., Olson, J., & Avary, D. (1991). *Breaking and entering: An ethnographic analysis of burglary.* Newbury Park, CA: Sage.

D'Alessio, D. & Stolzenberg, L. (1998). Crime, arrests, and pretrial jail incarceration: An examination of the deterrence thesis. *Criminology, 36,* 735-762.

De Haan, W., & Vos, J. (2003). A crying shame: The overrationalized conception of main in the rational choice perspective. *Theoretical Criminology, 7,* 29-54.

Dezhbakhsh, H., Rubin, P., & Shepherd, J. (2003). Does capital punishment have a deterrent effect? New evidence from post moratorium panel data. *American Law and Economics Review, 5,* 344-376.

Einstadter, W., & Henry, S. (2006). *Criminological theory: An analysis of its underlying assumptions* (2nd ed.). Lanham, MD: Rowman & Littlefield Publishing Group.

Fagan, J. (2006). Death and deterrence redux: Science, law, and causal reasoning on capital punishment. *Ohio State Journal of Criminal Law, 4,* 255-319.

Felson, M. (1986). Linking criminal choices, routine activities, informal social control, and criminal outcomes. In D. Cornish and R. Clarke (Eds.), *The reasoning criminal* (pp. 119-128). New York: Springer-Verlag.

Felson, M. (1987). Routine activities and crime prevention in the developing metropolis. *Criminology, 25,* 911-932.

Felson, M., & Boba, R. (2010). *Crime and everyday life* (4th ed.). Los Angeles: Sage.

Forde, D., & Kennedy, L. (1997). Risky lifestyles, routine activities, and the general theory of crime. *Justice Quarterly, 14(2),* 265-289.

Galliher, J. (1989). *Criminology: Human rights, criminal law, and crime.* Englewood Cliffs, NJ: Prentice Hall.

Geis, G. (1972). Jeremy Bentham 1748-1832. In. H. Mannheim (Ed.), *Pioneers in criminology,* (pp. 51-68). Montclair, NJ: Patterson Smith.

Gibbs, J. (1975). *Crime, punishment and deterrence.* New York: Elsevier.

Glaze, L., & Parks, E. (2012, November). *Correctional Populations in the United States, 2011.* U.S. Department of Justice, NCJ 239972. Washington, DC.

Grasmick, H., & Bursik, R. (1990). Conscience, significant others, and rational choice: Extending the deterrence model. *Law and Society Review, 24,* 837-862.

Hawley, A. (1950). *Human ecology.* New York: The Ronald Press Company.

Helland, E., & Tabarrok, A. (2007). Does three strikes deter? A nonparametric estimation. *Journal of Human Resources, 42,* 309-330.

Hindelang, M., Gottfredson, M., & Garofalo, J. (1978). *Victims of personal crime: An empirical foundation for a theory of personal victimization.* Cambridge, MA: Ballinger Publishing Company.

Jensen, G., & Rojek, D. (1998). *Delinquency and youth crime* (3rd ed.). Prospect Heights, IL: Waveland.

Katz, L., Levitt, S., & Shustorovich, E. (2003). Prison conditions, capital punishment, and deterrence. *American Law and Economics Review, 5,* 318-343.

LaGrange, T. (1999). The impact of neighborhoods, schools, and malls on the spatial distribution of property damage. *Journal of Research in Crime and Delinquency, 36(4),* 393-422.

MacKenzie, D., & Piquero, A. (1994). The impact of shock incarceration programs on prison crowding. *Crime and Delinquency, 40,* 222-249.

Marcum, C.D. (2009). Identifying potential factors of adolescent online victimization in high school seniors. *International Journal of Cyber Criminology, 2(2),* 346-367.

McCarthy, B. (2002). New economics of sociological criminology. *Annual Review of Sociology, 28,* 417-442.

Meier, R. & Miethe, T. (1993). Understanding theories of criminal victimization. In M. Tonry (Ed.), *Crime and justice: An annual review of research* (pp. 459-499). Chicago: University of Chicago Press.

Messner, S. & Tardiff, K. (1985). The social ecology of urban homicide: An application of the routine activities approach. *Criminology, 23(2),* 241-267.

Mocan, N., & Gittings, R. (2003). Getting off death row: Commuted sentences and the deterrent effect of capital punishment. *Journal of Law and Economics, 46,* 453-478.

Monachesi, E. (1955). Cesare Beccaria. *Journal of Criminal Law Criminology and Police Science, 46,* 439-449.

Mustaine, E., & Tewksbury, R. (2002). Sexual assault of college women: A feminist interpretation of a routine activities analysis. *Criminal Justice Review, 27(1),* 89-123.

Nagin, D. & Pogarsky, G. (2001). Integrating celerity, impulsivity, and extralegal sanction threats into a model of general deterrence: Theory and evidence. *Criminology, 39,* 865-892.

Packer, H. (1968). *The limits of the criminal sanction.* Stanford, CA: Stanford University Press.

Paternoster, R. & Pogarsky, G. (2009). Rational choice, agency and thoughtfully reflective decision making: The short and long term consequences of making good choices. *Journal of Quantitative Criminology, 25,* 103-127.

Paternoster, R., Saltzman, L., Waldo, G., & Chiricos, T. (1983). Perceived risk and social control: Do sanctions really deter? *Law and Society Review, 17,* 457-480.

Peters, M., Thomas, D., & Zamberian, C. (1997). Boot camps for juvenile offenders: Program summary. Washington, DC: U.S. Department of Justice, Office of Juvenile Justice and Delinquency Prevention.

Pfohl, S. (1985). *Images of deviance and social control: A sociological history.* New York: McGraw-Hill.

Pratt, T., Cullen, F., Blevins, K., Daigle, L., & Madensen, T. (2006). The empirical status of deterrence: A meta-analysis. In T. Cullen, J. Wright, and K. Blevins (Eds.). *Taking stock: The status of criminological theory. Advance in criminological theory* (pp. 367-396). New Brunswick, NJ: Transaction Publishers.

Radelet, M. & Akers, R. (1996). Deterrence and the death penalty: The view of the experts. *Journal of Criminal Law and Criminology, 87,* 1-16.

Raphael, S., & Stoll, M. (2009). Why are so many Americans in prison? In S. Raphael & M. Stoll (Eds.), *Do prisons make us safer?* (pp. 27-72). New York: Russell Sage Foundation.

Roncek, D., & Bell, R. (1981). Bars, blocks, and crimes. *Journal of Environmental Systems, 11,* 35-47.

Roncek, D., & Maier, P. (1991). Bars, blocks, and crimes revisited: Linking the theory of routine activities to the empiricism of "hot spots." *Criminology, 29(4),* 725-753.

Scheider, M. (2001). Deterrence and the base rate fallacy: An application of expectancy theory. *Justice Quarterly, 18,* 63-86.

Sellin, T. (1959). *The death penalty.* Philadelphia: American Law Institute.

Shepherd, J. (2005). Deterrence versus brutalization: Capital punishment's differing impacts among states. *Michigan Law Review, 104,* 203-255.

Sherman, L., Gartin, P., & Buerger, M. (1989). Hot spots of predatory crime: Routine activities and criminology of place. *Criminology, 27(1),* 27-55.

Smith, L, & Akers, L. (1993). A research note on racial disparity in sentencing to prison or community control. Unpublished paper, Department of Criminology, University of South Florida.

Spano, R. & Nagy, S. (2005). Social guardianship and social isolation: An application and extension of lifestyle/routine activities theory to rural adolescents. *Rural Sociology, 70(3),* 414-437.

Steiner, B. & Wright, E. (2006). Assessing the effects of relative state direct file waiver laws on violent juvenile crime: Deterrence or irrelevance. *Journal of Criminal Law and Criminology, 96(4),* 1451-1478.

Tewksbury, R. & Mustaine, E. (2000). Routine activities and vandalism: A theoretical and empirical study. *Journal of Crime & Justice, 23(1),* 81-110.

Tonry, M. (2008). Learning from the limitations of deterrence research. *Crime and Justice, 37,* 279-311.

Tseloni, A., Wittebrood, K., Farrell, G., & Pease, K. (2004). Burglary victimization in England and Wales, the United States and the Netherlands. *The British Journal of Criminology, 44(1),* 66-91.

Vold, G., & Bernard, T. (1986). *Theoretical criminology* (3rd ed.). New York: Oxford University Press.

Vold, G., Bernard, T., & Snipes, J. (2012). *Theoretical criminology* (6th ed.). New York: Oxford University Press.

Webster, C., Doob, A., & Zimring, F. (2006). Proposition 8 and crime rates in California: The case of the disappearing deterrent. *Criminology & Public Policy, 5,* 417-448.

Weisburd, D., Waring, E., & Chayet, E. (1995). Specific deterrence in a sample of offenders convicted of white collar crimes. *Criminology, 33,* 587-607.

Weisburd, D., Wyckoff, L., Ready, J., Eck, J., Hinkle, J., & Gajewski, F. (2006). Does crime just move around the corner? A controlled study of spatial displacement and diffusion of crime control benefits. *Criminology, 44,* 549-592.

Williams, K. & Hawkins, R. (1989). The meaning of arrest for wife assault. *Criminology, 27,* 163-181.

Young, J. (1981). Thinking seriously about crime: Some models of criminology. In M. Fitzgerald, G. McLennan, & J. Pawson, *Crime and society: Readings in history and society* (pp. 248-309). London: Routledge and Kegan Paul.

Zhang, S. (2000). An evaluation of the Los Angeles County probation juvenile drug treatment boot camp. San Marcos, CA: California State University.

Zimring, F. (1971). Perspectives on deterrence. NIMH Monograph Series on Crime and Delinquency Issues. Washington, DC: U.S. Government Printing Office.

Zimring, F., & Hawkins, G. (1973). *Deterrence.* Chicago: University of Chicago Press.

Biological and Psychological Theories

CHAPTER OUTLINE

Introduction

Biological Theory of Crime Assumptions

Biology to Understand the Criminal
Lombroso
Ferri
Garofalo
Dugdale
Hooten
Sheldon
Biosocial Criminology
Case Study 3.1: The Kray Twins

Policy Implications of the Biological School

Psychology and Crime

Assumptions of Psychological Theories of Crime

Progression Through Psychological Theory
Freud
Personality Theories
Cognitive Theory

Policy Implications

Summary

Discussion Questions

References

Key Words and Concepts

Adoption Studies	Criminal Act	Epileptoid
Atavism	Criminal by Passion	Endomorphs
Biosocial Criminology	Criminaloid	Eros
Born Criminal	Development	Eugenics
Conditional Free Will	Ectomorphs	
Criminal Actor	Ego	*(continued)*

Genes   Neurotransmitters   Socialization
Habitual Criminal   Occasional Criminal   Superego
Id   Positivism   Thanatos
Insane Criminal   Pseudo Criminal   Twin Studies
Mesomorphs   Reaction Formation

Introduction

Biological theories have generally been known as predisposition theories. The central thesis of biological theories is that crime and other traits are inherited. Biology has been used to explain criminal behavior since the 16th century. Baptiste della Porte (1535-1615) used cadavers of criminals to study facial features to determine a link between crime and biology. Other accounts of biology in crime did not come until much later. In the 1760s, Lavater (1741-1801) argued that he had found a connection between facial structure and behavior. Gall (1810) wrote volumes on the connection between biology and behavior. In his writings, he argued that crime was a behavioral function that was controlled by a portion of the brain. This led to him arguing that phrenology was able to explain criminal behavior. Within phrenology, Gall suggested that feeling the bumps on a person's head would be an indicator of potential criminal behavior. With true advances in modern science and medicine, biology did not become central to explanations of criminal behavior until the late 1800s.

In this chapter, we present the basic premises, as well as the historical context, of the biological quest for understanding criminal behavior. Next, we provide illustrative examples and contemporary studies of the biological perspective of criminology and evaluate these findings and assumptions. We suggest policy implications that may be fruitful in understanding this particular premise. In addition, we discuss the psychological perspective of crime.

The mind has long been an area of interest in criminology. The mind houses an individual's thoughts and processes. The mind may also become diseased, leading to mental health problems. Victims and offenders could need diagnosis and treatment. It is critical that criminologists understand the assumptions of psychological theories of crime; this understanding will provide the foundation for research methods and policy implications. This chapter searches for psychological explanations of crime by providing an understanding of the basic premises, illustrations of functions, and a critique of the findings from research.

Biological Theory of Crime Assumptions

In order to understand biological theories, we believe that it is important to understand the assumption that the perspective makes about human behavior. The major emphasis of this perspective was that humans have predisposition for criminal behavior. These predispositions interact with the environment, and under the proper conditions, they will lead to criminal behavior. This means that something within an individual will drive him or her to criminal behavior under the correct conditions. For instance, some people may behave in a normal manner most of the time, but when they are in a store they may not be able to control the urge to shoplift. For others, the use of alcohol or drugs may send them into violent rages.

In early biological thought, the emphasis was changed. To clarify, biological theorists and philosophers were not satisfied with the idea of examining the **criminal act**. They felt that this did not provide a clear enough link between the actor and the behavior. Therefore, they felt it important to study the criminal actor instead. This allowed biological theorists and philosophers to study the types of people that would likely commit crime.

Biological theorists were, then, forced to develop methods for collecting the proper data about the **criminal actor**. To determine the types of people who would likely commit crime required information that came from rigorous methods that provided careful observation. The biological theorists applied the positivist approach to study crime. **Positivism** was the application of the scientific method in studying biological characteristics of crime (Williams & McShane, 2010). This approach provided detailed direct observation, experimentation, and use of controlled samples to identify individuals that were predisposed to crime. This version of positivism was not confined to this era, but is engrained in many criminological theories today.

Early biological theorists were known as criminological anthropologists. They followed the view that criminal behavior could be explained by physical laws that hindered or thwarted free will. These early biological theorists claimed that they could explain crime based on physical appearance. The physical features that were most often studied were body type, shape of head, genes, eyes, and physiological imbalances. The problem with early biological theory was that methods were crude and flawed, so the results that came from these early efforts were discounted. These early biological efforts are still able to provide ample instruction to assist in understanding the growth of the scientific method in criminology and the development of contemporary biological explanations of criminal behavior.

The late 19th century was important for the development of biological explanations of behavior. During this period, there was a movement toward science over theology, which led to the use of the scientific method to arrive at results that could be used to better understand societal problems. The development of a different way of thinking about evolutionary psychology came about during this period. Darwin (1809-1882) developed and presented his theory in his book *On the Origin of Species*. In his theory, he suggested that that the development of any species changes and grows through the variance among offspring. Darwin (1859) argued that the weakest of the offspring would not likely adapt to their environment, which would make it impossible for them to reproduce and survive. He further argued that the stronger offspring would adapt to their environment, reproduce, survive, and dominate the species at a more advanced state. Researchers from the Italian School of Criminology (Ceasar Lombroso, Enrico Ferri, and Rafaele Garofalo) applied these ideas to criminal behavior. This application put the Italian school of criminological thought at odds with the classical school of thought, which originated with Beccaria. The Italian school of thought viewed the classical school as an overreliance on free will in behavioral choices (versus determinism). To clarify, the Italian school's view of crime was that individuals were different from one another in some appreciable way that made them prone to criminal behavior, rather than criminal behavior being a product of rationality or self-interest.

The early biological view of criminal behavior gave rise to new scientific methods of collecting data. One of the more valued methods was the experimental method. This method was used to develop key knowledge and empirically arrive at facts. This view suggested that knowledge was to accumulate over time through systematic observation. Examining criminal behavior in this manner was the only way to provide enough information; that is, this new scientific method would take time to develop facts and potential remedies of criminal behavior.

 ## Biology to Understand the Criminal

Understanding the growth of biological explanations required an appreciation of the scientific method being viewed as a "new religion." This method would provide valuable information that would help alleviate a number of social ills. Lombroso was one of the leaders of developing and using the scientific method in criminology. This led him to some of his famous works. For instance, Lombroso, with Ferri, Garofalo, and Lombroso-Ferraro, examined the differences between noncriminals and criminals. He would argue that with this work he could arrive at an explanation of crime.

Lombroso

Lombroso's work was published in his 1876 book, *The Criminal Man*, in which he based his theory on Darwinian ideas. He focused on ideas of humans in their worse states and argued that this was a reversion back to savage states (Darwin, 1856). This led Lombroso to hone the term "atavism." **Atavism** is the reappearance of a characteristic or trait after it has been dormant or absent for many generations. This meant that criminals were nothing more than evolutionary or hereditary throwbacks to previous generations that were less developed. Discoveries of this nature came from the examination of the skulls of cadavers.

The throwback nature of criminals allowed Lombroso to develop an identification tool: *stigmata*. Stigmata referred to the visible physical abnormalities of criminals. These abnormalities may be a number of characteristics such as asymmetry of the face; additional nipples, fingers, or toes; enormous jaws; or deformed ears. Lombroso argued that possessing 5 or more of the 18 stigmata was evidence of atavism and could explain criminal behavior.

Through a number of editions of his book, Lombroso seemed to suggest that atavism was not the only way to categorize individuals. In fact, by the fourth edition of his book, Lombroso had developed four typologies to explain criminal behavior. The first typology was the **born criminal.** The born criminal was atavistic, responsible for the most serious offenses, and was likely to recidivate. In Lombroso's eyes, under this typology, people were responsible for one third of their criminal behavior. Their biological push for criminal behavior made them incorrigible and dangerous. The people in this typology were not afflicted with one anomaly, but they had a number of anomalies that contributed to their identification and ultimate criminal behavior.

The second typology was the **criminal by passion**. These people would commit crime to relieve social injustice. Criminals by passion had such a strong belief in a cause that they became emotional, and the strength of that emotion would push them toward criminal behavior.

The third typology was the **insane criminal**. These people were mentally ill. They had issues with their ability to distinguish between right and wrong. Distinguishing between right and wrong was not based on free will. This distinction was interrupted by severe problems with the brain, which did not function in a way that allowed the individual to see the consequences of his or her actions.

The fourth typology was the **occasional criminal**. The occasional criminal typology was complex. This typology involved the following four subtypes:

1. The **criminaloid,** who was weak in nature and swayed by others. This person had some Darwinian remnants that suggested he or she might not survive.
2. The **epileptoid,** who suffered from epilepsy.
3. The **habitual criminal,** who was a career criminal.
4. The **psuedo-criminal,** who committed crime by accident.

(Williams & McShane, 2010)

As with the development and evolution of humans, Lombroso's theories and ideas continued to develop and evolve. In his last book, it became clear that Lombroso's ideas about criminals had shifted. The shift was closer to that of an environmental criminologist; that is, Lombroso was moving away from the idea that biology was the only cause of crime. In this book, Lombroso acknowledged that environmental factors were integral in the production of criminal behavior. While this was the case, he firmly established that criminals were different from noncriminals. Although Lombroso's theories have been soundly disproven, criminology owes a debt of gratitude to him. He was the forerunner for the use of the scientific method of criminology and provided the foundation for examining biological explanations of criminal behavior.

Ferri

Following Lombroso's lead, Ferri (1901) embraced environmental factors of criminal behavior but held onto the idea that biology was integral in the commission of crime. Ferri used his statistical training to examine crime in France, where he showed that crime was related to a number of factors. The factors were physical (e.g., climate, race, geography), anthropological (e.g., age, gender, psychology), and social (e.g., population density, religion, customs, economic conditions). This was groundbreaking work, and it remains a cornerstone of criminological work today.

Ferri's views were costly for his career. Ultimately, he lost his university position because he did not follow the view of classical theorists. Ferri's ideas about environment and biology shaped his views on behavior and criminal justice policy. He believed that juries of laypeople were not appropriate. In essence, laypeople were not capable of understanding the complexities of the links between environment and biology in the context of crime. Therefore, juries were to be comprised of scientists. Scientists had the proper training to understand these links. Further, Ferri argued that retribution was not important or necessary, but the focus should be on prevention by protecting the state through minimizing the causes of crime. This would require environmental changes and therapy (e.g., surgery or, in some situations, death). Ferri used the scientific method and applied statistics to bring about a more balanced and complete understanding of crime.

Garofalo

Garofalo was a student of Lombroso. He focused on the view that biology was the reason for criminal behavior. Garofalo was not moved by environmental factors like Lombroso or Ferri. Further, Garofalo rejected the idea that avatism was the central cause of criminal behavior. Garofalo proffered that criminal behavior was due to problems with adaption. Using Darwin's ideas of adaption, he suggested that people are criminal because they are not able to adapt to their environment in key prosocial ways (Vold & Bernard, 1986). This lack of adaption allowed Garofalo to develop harsh and direct forms of criminal justice policy (e.g., death, long-term or life imprisonment, or enforced reparations) that would be consistent with nature's evolutionary process.

At the time of their writing, the theoretical premises were groundbreaking. Presently, the theories have been discounted and are only mentioned for their historical value. The methods used to develop the theories were flawed, which has allowed others to disprove them. The historical value of the theories is the use and development of the scientific method. The scientific method moves from data collection to the use of statistics. Further, the theories held value because of the acknowledgement that the scientific method would require a substantial amount of time for results to become fact. In addition to the rise of the use of the scientific method, the theories were valuable because they provided the foundation for new theories.

Biological theories of criminal behavior were not just European products. The United States had biological theorists as well. Early biosocial criminologists followed the **eugenics** perspective of biological theory. Coming from Galton, this perspective describes the science of improving the human race through better "breeding." Scientists that followed this line of thought believed that individuals' mental, moral, and physical characteristics were inherited. Further, this view suggested that the instant in which an individual committed a crime, that the criminal behavior was encoded into his or her blood that could then be transmitted to his or her offspring.

Dugdale

Operating from the eugenics tradition, Richard Dugdale (1877) was an early U.S. biological theorist. Dugdale (1877) followed the history of a Dutch family—the Jukes—during a study for the New York State Prison Association. The family had criminals in six generations. Examining this family, Dugdale was able to trace a number of paupers, prostitutes, habitual thieves, murderers, and other criminals. This led Dugdale to conclude that the burden of crime was found in unmarried family lines; the oldest child was more likely to be criminal; and males were more likely to be criminal than females.

Hooten

Later, Hooten (1939) took up the charge in examining biology and criminal behavior. Hooten made use of advances in research methods (e.g., large samples and control groups). Using 17,000 people (14,000 prisoners and 3,000 civilians), Hooten showed that criminals were "organically inferior." He argued that the inferiority was probably due to inherited features. With such bold statements, Hooten's results were challenged in a number of ways. First, his control group used a number of people that were firefighters or police officers, but their service in these jobs was due to their physical size. Second, Hooten found small differences between the two groups, and there were greater differences among the prisoners than the prisoners and the civilians. This was likely because of the unbalanced sample size between prisoners and civilians.

Sheldon

Although there was a general decline in the study between biology and crime, Sheldon and his colleagues developed a body typology and crime. They built their typology on the foundation of somatatyping (Kretschmer, 1925). Sheldon and colleagues observed three different types of people. Their first typology was **endomorphs.** These were people that were medium height with round, soft bodies and thick necks. The second typology was **mesomorphs.** These were muscular and strong people with wide shoulders and thin waists. The third typology was **ectomorphs.** These people had thin, frail bodies and sensitive personality types. Suggesting the no one typology will explain all criminal behavior, Sheldon and colleagues argued that each type had a different personality. These different personalities may have created a different view or desire for criminal behavior. The endomorph was an extroverted person that was motivated by his gut, so Sheldon and his colleagues proffered that delinquency was likely in this group, but it would more likely be fraud. The mesomorph was insensitive to others, making the types of criminal offenses that he or she would perform physical in nature (e.g., robbery, homicide, or violence). The ectomorph was sensitive in nature, and would be an occasional thief. These assertions did not go without some level of support. Sheldon and Eleanor Glueck (1950) performed a study that examined these assertions. In their study, the Gluecks used 500 incarcerated delinquent boys and 500 nondelinquent boys. They found that 31 percent of the nondelinquent boys were mesomorphs, but 60 percent of the delinquent boys were mesomorphs. The Gluecks also found that a number of environmental factors were relevant in the delinquent group (e.g., parenting), leading them to conclude that body type was only one of many factors that contributed to delinquency.

Unfortunately, these studies had major methodological flaws. The studies did not include the proper sampling devices, making their samples unrepresentative. In addition, they did not provide much information in the area of stereotypes based on race or gender. The studies did not always include women in their samples. Because the theories emphasized prisoners or those incarcerated, the studies did not provide much information about the causes of crime rather than criminal justice processing. With these problems understood, they provided the foundation for a new and exciting study of *biosocial* criminology, which deserves serious consideration.

In addition to the methodological flaws, research in this area provided a foundation for a number of improper policies and legislation. One form of legislation that came from this research made interracial marriage illegal. In addition, immigration legislation was passed that did not allow individuals to move about the country because of their "inferior nature." Further, sterilization was a practice that was imposed on individuals who were considered mentally ill, feebleminded, or chronic criminal offenders. The manner in which biological theorists presented their subjects (e.g., hunchbacks), methodological flaws, and the resulting forms of improper policy and legislation pushed biological theories away from mainstream criminology.

Biosocial Criminology

Criminologists that have worked to develop the understanding between crime and biology have changed the name of the topical area. The current manner of thinking in the shared arena of biology and crime utilizes the term **biosocial criminology**. Changing the name gives the topical area a fresh start in the criminological world. This fresh start rests on a few principles. The term biosocial criminology inherently makes the assumption that biology and the social environment interact with one another. In addition, the term biosocial criminology does not rest upon a specific theoretical premise (e.g., self-control theory or social learning theory), but is part of an integration of different fields of study including psychology, psychiatry, behavioral genetics, pediatrics, molecular genetics, and related fields. Using the term biosocial criminology also moves the thought process away from specific physical appearances and moves criminology to consider the roles of traits, behaviors, personality and cognitive features, hormones, physiological factors, genetic factors, and brain functioning. In the end, biosocial criminology is attempting to provide an understanding of how nature and nurture work to produce human behavior, focusing on biology and social environment.

Biosocial criminology has survived the methodological shortcomings and has grown with the use of the scientific method. The development of better technology and statistical methods have allowed for better measurement and analysis of biological data. This has allowed for a better understanding of genetics, especially in mapping genes. **Genes** have been shown to have an important link with chromosomes. In 1952, a major discovery occurred that showed that genes were made up of chemicals. The chemicals allowed researchers to make the connection that they could be shared. The sharing of chemicals provided the explanation of how heritability may occur. Some have written that by 1959, genes had been used to explain all parts of life; however, this was an over exaggeration.

The development of the genetic theory of crime came from evidence from **twin studies** and **adoption studies**. The central thesis of this perspective was relatively simple. If crime or factors contributing to crime were heritable, we should find that crime was prevalent among the identical twin (monozygotic) groups rather than fraternal twin (dizygotic) groups or siblings. This is because monozygotic (MZ) twins share 100 percent of the same genes. Dizygotic (DZ) twins share 50 percent of the same genes, and they are genetically the same as siblings born at different times. The percentage of genes indicates that MZs are fertilized from the same egg; hence, they are always the same biological sex. Further, this shows that DZs are fertilized from two different eggs at the same time; thus, they can take on different biological sexes.

CASE STUDY 3.1
THE KRAY TWINS

Known as the most notorious identical set of thugs, the Kray twins, born in 1933, ran deadly mafia-style operations in London's East End throughout the 50s and 60s. Though they started off as amateur boxers, Reggie and Ronnie Kray moved on to extortion, armed robbery, arson, hijacking, assault, torture, and murder. "In gang fights they seemed to be telepathic, as if they were one," wrote John Pearson, author of *The Cult of Violence: The Untold Story of the Krays*. The reason that they seemed almost telepathic is due to their biological nature and socialization (CITE).

Research that examined this premise provided some interesting results. The estimates of heritability vary widely among the studies. Most of this research has provided heritability estimates between 40 and 60 percent (Beaver et al., 2009; Rowe, 1986; Lyons et al., 1995; Miles & Carey, 1997; Rhee & Waldman, 2002; Moffitt, 2005). The differences between these studies were influenced by different methodologies and measurements of behavior.

Two factors were found to be relevant moderators of the link between genetics and criminal behavior. The first factor was age. Researchers have shown that the link between genetics and criminal behavior varies across the lifespan (Goldman & Ducci, 2007). To clarify, the genetic link with crime appears to be low in adolescence, but the environmental influence is high (Jacobson, Prescott, & Kendler, 2002). However, the genetic link with crime across the lifespan appears to increase, while the environmental influence is low (Goldman & Ducci, 2007).

The second factor was the type of crime the person committed. For instance, violent or aggressive forms of crime appear to heritable (Eley, Lictenstein, & Moffitt, 2003). Nonaggressive forms of behavior appear to be influenced more by the shared environmental factors (Moffitt, 2005). Overall, this suggests that genetics is not the only factor that has a link with crime, but an interaction with age improves the link with crime.

Consideration needs to be given to the types of studies that were performed and their methodologies. Studies that only have non-adoption twin studies may not be able to show a reasonable effect of the shared and non-shared environment. The two main factors above may not have much of a moderation effect. A way to eliminate this issue was to perform adoption twin studies. These studies proposed that twins raised by non-biological parents or guardians would carry their criminal predispositions with them. Studies of this type tend to show that criminal behavior is genetically shared. However, these studies have been criticized due to selectivity of sample and prenatal and perinatal factors. On the surface, using these types of methods provides some evidence of a genetic influence, but they ultimately raise more questions than they answer.

Biosocial criminologists (i.e., a criminologist who studies the link between biology and crime) use a specific logic to understand the link between biology and crime. Importantly, they agree that genetics is not the sole factor in understanding criminal behavior. Instead, biosocial criminologists believe that there is an interaction between biology and the environment in which criminal behavior is produced. Fishbein (1997) argued that crime was not heritable, but that how someone responded to the environment in a criminal way was heritable.

Contemporary biosocial criminologists are inclusive (rather than exclusive) to classical criminological thought. For instance, these criminologists do not abandon the ideas of free will as Lombroso and his colleagues did. Rather, they modified this logic to fit their needs. For instance, biosocial criminologists would argue that they use **conditional free will** as an acknowledgement of the factors that impede or guide decision making.

A number of theories have used this view of conditional free will. For instance, the chromosome theory of crime attributes violent male criminality to an extra Y chromosome. The additional Y chromosome was to turn males into "super males" that would be violent. This theory has been soundly discarded.

Others have examined the link between genes and **neurotransmitters.** For instance, Caspi and colleagues (2002) conducted a study that examined the link between monoamine oxidase (MOA) and childhood maltreatment in the context of four outcomes: conduct disorder, violence, antisocial behavior, and criminal conviction for a violent offense. Their results showed that the interaction between MOA and child maltreatment had relevant links with all four of these outcomes. In other words, when childhood maltreatment was not present, the link between the MOA and these outcomes was not present.

Other theories that came from this perspective included attention deficit disorder (ADD). The ADD view of crime was that the inability to control oneself due to hyperactivity was more likely to lead one to commit crime. Those that had this disorder were more likely to be loners and not to perform well in school. This would lead to poor job skills that would increase the likelihood of future criminal behavior (Moffitt & Silva, 1988).

Hormones and neurotransmitters have also been implicated as causes of criminal behavior. Hormones are described as molecules that have been released into the bloodstream making their way to various tissues in the body. Two common types of hormones that have been shown to have a link with crime are cortisol and testosterone. Cortisol is described as a hormone that is activated when the body senses stress. This hormone provides energy in times of stress. Researchers have shown that low levels of cortisol are present in antisocial, criminal, and delinquent children (Loney et al., 2006; van Goozen et al., 1998; Virkkunen, 1985). Testosterone has been described as a hormone that has a link with aggressive behavior and violence. Results from numerous studies show that the link between these two is mixed (Banks & Dabbs, 1996). Regardless, hormones have been hypothesized to have a link with criminal behavior.

Neurotransmitters are described as molecules that travel between neurons and the central nervous system. Neurotransmitters send signals from one neuron to another, creating a chain of signals. One neurotransmitter that has been hypothesized to have a link with criminal behavior is serotonin. Serotonin levels have been shown to have a link with violent behavior (Moore, Scarpa, & Raine, 2002). This suggest that neurotransmitters have shown links with criminal behavior.

In summary, the research evidence is clear that the link between biology and crime is uncertain. While many research efforts have shown a link between the two, the research is not without flaws and is in need of replication.

A number of studies have examined the link between biology and crime; however, the studies are unable to provide clear evidence that biology is the sole reason for criminal behavior. In fact, contemporary biosocial criminologists acknowledge that biology alone is not the only cause of criminal behavior. They acknowledge that environment is integral to understanding criminal behavior. This casts some doubt as to the role of biology in crime. To date, this line of research continues to prompt questions rather than provide answers. For instance, how many different ways can biology be used in a study to find a link? Without some type of standardization in how biology is captured in a study, doubt will be cast on the perspective. Another limit to this line of research is the ability to distinguish between sporadic criminals and those that are persistent criminals. Sporadic criminals may be taking advantage of opportunities that are present rather than acting on biological stimuli.

Presenting these limits is not designed to reduce the importance or development of this research. In fact, the intention is just the opposite. Casting a light on these limits draws attention to the development of biosocial research that examined the link between the environment, biology, and psychology.

Policy Implications of the Biological School

Biological explanations of criminal behavior have some policy implications. At the heart of this perspective was the idea that the individual was different based upon genetics, chromosomes, hormones, or chemical imbalances in the brain. The policy implications include identification of these individuals and some sort of treatment for offending rather than punishment. A person with biological problems that make him or her prone to criminal behavior should receive a sentence that would be commiserate with the proper treatment that fits the diagnosis. From a correctional perspective, this means indeterminate sentencing may be best.

Other policies involved come at different points of life. For instance, one prevention policy was the development of prenatal and postnatal care. This type of care would include nutritional programs, neurological examinations for brain injuries, examinations for lead, and examinations for learning disabilities. This would assist families so that they could have children without biological issues.

Because the environment was found to be a moderating factor with biology, the environment may be an area that can be manipulated. The issue here is that the environment needs to be manipulated in a way that provides the same physiological high as performing crimes. This may be accomplished in a number of ways: competitive sports, skydiving, or other pro-social risk-taking activities.

Psychology and Crime

The mind has been a source of abnormal behavior. Psychologists consider crime an abnormal behavior. Early psychologists believed that crime was a release of pathology. The pathology allowed the individual to become violent and, for some, remain consistently violent. Keep in mind that psychosis was thought of as biological. This places pathology and psychosis within biological theory. The issue with placing psychological theories with biological theories is that it may give the impression that mentally ill individuals are determined to commit crime. The reality is that mentally ill individuals are no more likely or determined to commit crime as individuals that are mentally healthy. At this point, we should examine the idea that crime was not caused by mental illness, but that some psychological processes in any mind could lead to criminal behavior. Psychology is a way to study this phenomenon.

Psychologists begin with the idea that crime is abnormal. The abnormality comes from thought processes that develop over many years. Because of the development of thought, multiple approaches are possible for understanding psychology and criminal behavior.

Assumptions of Psychological Theories of Crime

Although psychological theories may have varied explanations of criminal behavior, they tend to share a number of assumptions. Psychological theories are microlevel; the theories assume that individuals commit criminal behavior. By using different explanations, the theories try to find differences in the predispositions for criminal behavior.

Central to psychological theories are the ideas of socialization and development, and this emphasis on socialization divorced psychological theories from biological theories. **Socialization** refers to the acquisition of values and norms. This may take place in a number of ways. First, the environment in which someone lives may provide a set of values and norms that someone could acquire. In psychological theories, the environment generally consists of peers or nonfamily others. Interaction with these individuals provides the exchange of values and norms. Second, family (i.e., parents and other family members) provides socialization. The close nature within family provides the values and norms for survival.

Development refers to an individual progressing through a number of mental, moral, and sexual stages of life. The development of individuals may be interrupted. Interruptions may come from abnormal experiences early in life or traumatic events, and the personality may be reshaped by disorders and psychological disturbances. The disorders and disturbances are not external but reside in the mind. While these disorders and disturbances are internal, a number of social or environmental factors serve as stimuli for deviant or criminal behavior. Additional traumatic experiences are another factor.

Psychologists use a number of instruments in their work. These instruments are called scales, inventories, or questionnaires. These instruments allow psychologists to quickly understand the symptoms that an individual may possess. Understanding these symptoms provides an easy and quick method of diagnosing the disturbances that an individual suffers. This makes measurement an important part of the diagnostic process.

Psychologists' assumption that criminal behavior is abnormal has implications for policy. Psychologists tend to advocate treatment rather than long sentences. Treatment is thought to be able to balance the psychological disturbances that an individual possesses. These basic assumptions are rooted in every psychological theory, but this is the only set of similarities that are present.

Progression Through Psychological Theory

Rather than being a cohesive collection of theories, psychological theory development was a movement. The beginning of the movement was the discovery of the hidden unconscious within the mind. After this discovery, there was an increased recognition that the environment was influential in criminal behavior. This led to the idea that learning behavior was more complex than had been previously understood. Our journey through psychological theories begins with Sigmund Freud.

Freud

Freud wrote and developed psychoanalytic theory. The theory was very complex and difficult to empirically verify. To date, a number of the assumptions that Freud provided have never been empirically verified. The central thesis of the theory was that crime came from the internal conflicts that arose from trauma and deprivations in childhood. From Freud's view, trauma that occurred in childhood did not stay in isolation. Rather, the trauma was something that the individual carried throughout life. The trauma would bury itself in the unconscious.

Freud's view was that the human mind had conscious and unconscious components. The conscious contained the **ego**. The ego was the portion of the mind that contained reality. Within the ego, the individual made an effort to rationally mediate between the conflicting demands of unconscious desires. The unconscious contained two additional pieces of the mind. First, the unconscious contained the **id**. The id followed the pleasure principle. The pleasure principle was with an individual since birth and was biologically based. The id governed the sexual energy of an individual (i.e., the libido). In addition, the id controlled the **eros** (i.e., the life instinct) and the **thanatos** (i.e., death instinct). Overall, the id controlled the area of the mind that suggested if an act was pleasurable it was acceptable to perform. Second, the unconscious contained the **superego**. The superego contained an individual's socialization that resulted in control of the individual's morality. The superego was a reflection and summarization of an individual's experiences. In addition, the superego provided self-criticism and a source of guilt. The ego balanced the id and superego.

While Freud emphasized the conscious and the unconscious, the consequences toward behaviors were made clear. For Freud, deterrence for a behavior fell under the purview of guilt. An individual experienced a number of drives, but the guilt of the drives was what kept the individual from performing a number of behaviors. Freud provided two important ways that individuals made their decisions to perform a behavior using the interplay between desires and guilt. First, sublimation was used to avert the desires to a prosocial behavior to reduce the amount of guilt that an individual feels. Second, repression was when an individual denied a desire from the id.

These two reactions did not just occur, but they occurred through a process. One part of the process was **reaction formation**. Reaction formation was when an individual repressed his or her thoughts and desires. For instance, an individual who had a traumatic sexual experience as a child may repress that experience, and it could manifest in the individual by being prudish toward sexual behavior later in life. Another part of the process was projection. Projection was when someone would see his or her desires in someone else's behavior.

The interplay between the id, ego, and superego and the reactions to the interplay were considered conflicts. The conflicts occurred at different developmental stages of life, but Freud (1915, 1950) took particular interest in childhood. Freud argued that childhood was fraught with developmental stages. These stages revolved around drives and sexuality. Specifically, Freud argued that the developmental stages were centered around oral, anal, phallic, latent, and genital drives. These drives were sequential, and becoming "stuck" in one of these stages would be problematic because of some type of trauma. The guilt that arrived from the various stages had to be properly handled by the ego to avoid a negative personality later in life.

While Freud (1915, 1950) only spoke briefly about crime, he suggested that the guilt complex resulted in crime. Crime resulting from guilt did not come from singularity. Crime resulted in a number of ways. First, crime came from an over-developed superego. In other words, crime was a relief from the pressure that came from the superego. Second, the lack of proper socialization resulted in an under-developed ego and superego. This put the child in a position of being unable to control himself or herself. Third, repressed desires were the cause of frustration. These views were important because they provided some perspective about the complexity of crime.

Overall, criminologists have discredited psychoanalytic theory, which has limits that are important to understand. One important limit is that the theory is tautological; that is, the theory involves circular reasoning. Psychoanalytic theory interpretations were viewed as "after the fact." This means that a problem was not present until after the problem occurred, which makes the theoretical perspective untestable. The lack of testability was considered a problem because it was really a series of interrelated concepts rather than a theoretical whole. In addition, most of the concepts rested in the unconscious, making it impossible to confirm or deny their existence.

Psychoanalytic theory has to overcome a clinical bias before it can be accepted in criminology. Most of the time, the evaluation of psychoanalytic theory occurs in a clinical setting. These settings have a small number of individuals participating. This makes it impossible for comparisons to be made with the healthy population.

With the lack of support in the psychological world for Freud's theory, psychology took very different paths. One path that psychologists took was to develop personality theory, and this path was led by Gordon Allport (1937). Another path that was taken was to study behavioral or situational learning theories that used Pavolv's (1967) ideas of conditioning. These two paths have been brought together in a number of applications to criminal behavior, such as Eysenck's (1964) version of criminal personality theory and Wilson and Herrnstein's (1985) integrated theory that combined genetics and social learning.

Personality Theories

Personality theories were different from psychoanalytic theories. The differences between the two theories begin with where the theories assume criminal behavior comes from. Personality theories assume that criminal behavior comes from the personality, and psychoanalytic theories assume that criminal behavior comes from unconscious causes. Central to personalities are traits. Traits refer to consistent characteristics that are relevant to a variety of behaviors (Caspi et al., 1994). Personality theorists criticized Freud's psychoanalytic theory and behavioral conditioning. The definition of personality made this clear. Personality referred to the dynamic organization of an individual's psychophysical system in response to certain environmental stimuli (Allport, 1937). Central to the survival of personality trait theories as an explanation of behavior was the measurement of these various traits in different people and their effects.

Personality trait theories operate using a number of assumptions. For instance, criminal behavior is a manifestation of an underlying trait. In criminology, personality traits have been examined extensively. For instance, criminologists have examined the link between impulsivity, aggression, extroversion, neuroticism, thrill seeking, hostility, and emotions and crime.

A number of versions of personality theory exist, but Eysenck (1977) provided a popular approach to examining crime. Eysenck (1977) argued that there were three personality dimensions: psychoticism, extraversion, and neuroticism. Criminal behavior had been shown to have a link with all three versions of personality, but some types of crime may be linked to the personality in different ways. Age seemed to influence the link between the three personality dimensions and crime. Younger criminals tended to be more extraverted rather than neurotic. Older criminals tended to show high levels of neuroticism. No matter the age group, the psychotic personality was always linked with criminal behavior. Eysenck (1977) found these results across a number of countries and behaviors that include smoking and other criminal behavior. He developed his theory to contain a conscience and through a learning process he termed conditioning. Eysenck (1977) argued that there was a high need for external stimulation. The conditioning process was one of the areas that distinguished criminals from non-criminals. Criminals tended to condition poorly, and this forced them to develop their conscience slowly.

Cognitive Theory

Walters and White (1989) provided important information concerning cognitive theory and criminology. They argued that criminology had neglected the role of cognitive theory in explaining criminal behavior. Specifically, the issue was that social and environmental conditions placed limits on individual options rather than determine behavior. Walters and White (1989) argued that the social and environmental conditions were the place where the decisions take place, and these factors influence or pattern the activities.

Walters and White argued that criminal behavior was the product of poor thought. They deny that environmental factors determine criminal behavior, but are clear that environmental factors limit options. When examining career criminals, Walters and White observed that they were mostly irresponsible and self-indulgent individuals. The career criminal was thought to be slow to mature and resembled an adolescent that had little concept of responsibility and self-discipline. The slow maturity or lack of development in cognition placed these individuals into a "high risk" situation for failure. When the career criminal failed, it was not solely in the area of crime, but it was also in other areas: school, work, and relationships. When considering age, the career criminal showed issues with management problems. Because of the lack of maturity, the career criminal rationalized his or her behavior and was preoccupied with short-term gains.

Policy Implications

The policy implications for psychological theories were varied. The variance was due to the different assumptions that were made by the theorists. For instance, the main policy implication for psychoanalytic theory was therapy. The therapy was specific: psychoanalysis. Psychoanalysis was a process in which the patient would discuss anything that came to mind. In conjunction with a therapist, the patient would begin to make connections with issues that were being discussed. This would reveal the unconscious and the potential problems that were present.

In addition to psychoanalysis, Freud (1915, 1950) discussed another form of therapy: transference. Transference was a process that required the patient and the therapist. The patient would describe a troubled relationship and the therapist would role play the other person(s) involved in the troubled relationship. It would be up to the therapist to assist in redeveloping the relationship so that it would not be troubled anymore. While transference and psychoanalysis were important in understanding problems, the main way that psychoanalysis would be useful to a patient would be if the therapist assisted him or her in overcoming problems. Unfortunately, this particular treatment does not seem to provide much help to patients.

Policy implications can come from learning theories. For instance, an individual is capable of learning pro-social behavior through reinforcement or observation. Reinforcement may be necessary for the development of pro-social behavior, especially in younger children. Further, those that seem to be taking an antisocial or criminal path may be able to change their behavior by observing others doing the same.

Finally, treatment that includes parts of cognition is important in the criminal justice system. The reason that cognition is important is because it provides a clear distinction between those that are criminal and those that are non-criminal. To date, many policymakers do not subscribe to psychologists' notion that treatment is central, but some are willing to place individuals into correctional facilities so that the individuals may reflect and change their thinking,

Summary

The early biological theories have been largely discredited. The empirical results of these theories did not support them. While these theories provided insight into the scientific method, early studies of these theories were not methodologically sound. Regardless, these theories inspired research into this area while they promoted the scientific method.

Contemporary biological theories have mixed validity. The mixed validity comes from the perspective that biology was not shown to be the only cause of crime. The environment was shown to be important in the development of criminal behavior. While the research methods have been improving, they are still suspect. At best, biological factors appear to be part of an indirect cause of criminal behavior. This means that biology is best served as a part of an integrated theory with self-control, social learning, and the social environment to understand criminal behavior.

Discussion Questions

1. Consider an instance where you have noticed traits or behaviors that were similar to those of other family members. Did you think that these traits or behaviors were inherited?
2. Which theorist best explains biosocial criminology, and why?

3. Biosocial criminology suggests that traits and behaviors interact with the environment. Why?

4. Consider how individuals think. Have you had an instance where you may have acted without thinking? Is this bad thinking?

5. What are the differences between the id, ego, and superego? How do they work together?

REFERENCES

Allport, G. (1937). *Personality : A psychological explanation*. New York, NY: Holt.

Banks, T., & Dabbs, J. M. (1996). Salivary testosterone and cortisol in delinquent and violent urban subculture. *Journal of Social Psychology, 136*, 49-56.

Beaver, K. M., Delisi, M., Wright, J. P., & Vaughn, M. G. (2009). Gene environment interplay and delinquent involvement: Evidence of direct and indirect, and interactive effects. *Journal of Adolescent Research, 24*, 147-168.

Caspi, A., Moffitt, T. E., Silva, P. A., Stouthamer-Loeber, M., Kruega, R. F., & Schmutte, P.S. (1994). Are some people crime-prone? Replications of the personality crime relationship across countries, genders, races, and methods. *Criminology, 32*, 163-195.

Darwin, C. R. (1859). *On the origin of species*. New York, NY: Penguin.

Dugdale, R. L. (1877). *The jukes: A study in crime, pauperism, disease, and heredity* (3rd ed.). New York, NY: G. P. Putnam.

Eley, T. C., Lichtenstein, P., & Moffitt, T. E. (2003). A longitudinal behavioral genetic analysis of the etiology of aggressive and non-aggressive antisocial behavior. *Developmental and Psychopathology, 15*, 383-402.

Eysenck, H. J. (1964). *Crime and personality* (2nd ed.). London: Routledge and Kegan Paul.

Ferri, E. (1901). *Criminal sociology*. New York, NY: D. Appleton.

Fishbein, D. (1997). Biological perspective in criminology. In Stuart Henry and Werner Einstadter (eds.), *The criminological theory reader*. New York, NY: New York University Press.

Freud, S. (1915). *Der Verbrecher aus Schuldbewusstsein* Gesammelte Schriften, v. 10. Vienna: Internationaler. Psychoanalytsischer Verlag.

Freud, S. (1950). Criminals from a sense of guilt. In *Gesammelte werke*, v. 14 (pp. 332-333).

Goldman, D., & Ducci, F. (2007). The genetics of psychopathic disorders. In Alan R. Felthous and Henning Sass (Eds.), *International handbook of psychopathic disorders and the law*, v. 1. West Sussex, UK: Wiley.

Glueck, S., & Glueck, E. (1950). *Unraveling juvenile delinquency*. New York, NY: Commonwealth Fund.

Hooten, E. A. (1939). *The American criminal: An anthroplogical study*. Cambridge, MA: Harvard University Press.

Jacobson, K. C., Prescott, C. A., & Kendler, K. S. (2002). Sex differences in the genetic and environmental influences on the development of antisocial behavior. *Development and Psychopathology, 14*, 395-416.

Kretschmer, E. (1925). *Physique and character*. New York, NY: Harcourt, Brace.

Lombroso, C. (1876). *L'uomo delinquente*. Milan: Hoepli.

Loney, B. R., Butler, M. A., Lima, E. N., Counts, C. A., & Ec., L. A. (2006). The relation between salivary cortisol, callous-unemotional traits, and conduct problems in an adolescent non-referred sample. *Journal of Child Psychology and Psychiatry, 47*, 30-36.

Lyons, M. J., True, W. J., Eisen, S. A., Goldberg, J., Meyer, J. M., Faraone, S. V., Eaves, L. J., and Tsuang, M. T. (1995). Differential heredity of adult and juvenile traits. *Archives of General Psychiatry, 52*, 906-15.

Miles, D. R., & Carey, G. (1997). Genetic and environmental architecture of human aggression. *Journal of Personality and Social Psychology, 72,* 207-217.

Moffitt, T. E. (2005). The new look of behavioral genetics in developmental psychopathology: Gene-environment interplay in antisocial behavior. *Psychological Bulletin, 131,* 533-554.

Moffitt, T. E., & Silva, P. A. (1988). Self-reported delinquency, neuropsychological deficit, and history of attention deficit disorder. *Journal of Abnormal Psychology, 16,* 553-569.

Moore, T. M., Scarpa, A., & Raine, A. (2002). A meta-analysis of serotonin metabolite 5-HIAA and antisocial behavior. *Aggressive Behavior, 28,* 299-316.

Rhee, S. H., & Waldman, I. D. (2002). Genetic and environmental influences or antisocial Behavior: a meta-analysis of twin and adoption studies. *Psychological Bulletin,* 128, 490-529.

Rowe, D. C. (1986). Genetic and environmental components of antisocial behavior: A study of 265 twin pairs. *Criminology, 24,* 513-532.

Walters, G., & White, T. (1989). Heredity and crime: Bad genes or bad research. *Criminology, 27,* 455-486.

Williams, F. P., & McShane, M. (2010). *Criminological theory.* Upper Saddle River, NJ: Prentice Hall.

Wilson, J. Q., & Herrnstein, R. (1985). *Crime and human nature.* New York, NY: Simon Schuster.

van Goozen, S. H. M., Matthys, W., Cohen-Kettenis, P. T., Thijssen, J. H. H., van Engelan, H. (1998). Adrenal androgens and aggression in conduct disorder prepubertal boys and normal controls. *Biological Psychiatry, 43,* 156-158.

Vikkunen, M (1985). Urinary free cortisol secretion in habitually violent offenders. *Acta Psychiatrica Scandinavica, 72,* 40-44.

Vold, G. B., & Bernard, T. J. (1986). *Theoretical criminology* (3rd ed.). New York, NY: Oxford University Press.

Social Disorganization Theory

CHAPTER OUTLINE

Introduction

Origins of Social Disorganization
The Criminological Element

Revisions of Social Disorganization Theory
Empirical Research

Policy Implications

Case Study 4.1: Too Tough to Fix Broken Windows?

Case Study 4.2: Mobilization of Youth

Summary

Discussion Questions

References

Key Words and Concepts

Broken Windows Theory
Collective Efficacy
Concentric Zone Theory
Endogenous Community
Macro-Level Theory

Micro-Level Theory
Mobilization of Youth
Racial Heterogeneity
Residential Mobility
Social Capital

Social Disorganization
  Theory
Social Ecology
Socioeconomic Status
Zone of Transition

Introduction

In 1892, the first department of sociology was formed at the University of Chicago. Termed the "Chicago School," this group of academics made impressive contributions to the sociology field over several decades. Their study of **social ecology**, or the study of the behavior and relationships of individuals in a specific environment, was influenced by the historical events going on at the time of their development. Between 1898 and 1930, Chicago doubled in population due to the waves of immigrants flooding the city (Cressey, 1938). These immigrants were drawn to large cities as industrial growth was booming and cheap labor was needed for the factories. However, when technology began replacing human labor, many unskilled laborers became displaced and were forced to move into low income areas.

The melting pot of immigrants searching for the American dream was now overflowing out of small, cramped apartments in low socioeconomic areas. Sanitation, homelessness, and cultural conflicts became huge issues. With multiple cultures thrown together in an urban nightmare, it became extremely difficult to establish any type of social norm. These areas became extremely disorganized, and it was impossible to form a sense of community amongst the residents. Further, this lack of acceptance of customs and norms became a problem for law enforcement as property and personal crimes began to escalate in these areas. The purpose of this chapter is to examine the historical roots of **social disorganization theory**, a criminological theory resulting from the historical happenings involving the unsuccessful merging of immigrant culture in urban areas.

In this chapter, we present the basic premises of the social disorganization understanding of criminal behavior. We outline the historical context that the premise originates. Next, we provide illustrative examples and contemporary studies of this perspective. We evaluate these findings and assumptions. Finally, we suggest policy implications that may be fruitful in understanding this particular premise.

Origins of Social Disorganization

The origins of the social disorganization theory of crime actually originated with sociologists who were investigating urban crime and delinquency. Robert E. Park, a sociologist at the University of Chicago from 1914 to 1933, compared the city of Chicago to a plant or animal community invaded by a new species. With this invasion came changes, competition for resources, and eventually a dominating group that maintained the space while the others migrated to a new location. Park (1936) asserted that human communities react the same way with invasion, especially when industries begin to expand and invade residential areas. The residents are pushed out of communities and into outer edges of the city.

Along with colleague Ernest W. Burgess of the University of Chicago, Park developed the theory of urban growth. This theory asserted that cities do not just expand at the outmost edges, but expand radially in specific areas which place pressure on other areas to expand (Burgess, 1925). Burgess' theory described the city of Chicago as a target consisting of concentric rings, with each ring (or zone) serving a different function. The **concentric zone theory** stated that as the city expands, every inner ring invades the ring surrounding it, activating a process of invasion and domination, as explained by Park.

According to Burgess (1925), there are five different zones of a city. The bullseye of the target, or Zone I, is the business district. Zone I is comprised of retail stores, office buildings, city government, and industry. Zone II is the "**zone of transition**," an area of continuous change due to the moving in and out of immigrants. This zone contains lower income housing and dilapidated communities due to the closeness of industry from Zone I. Further, as this zone has a continual change in residents as immigrants from all over the world will move out as soon as financially able, there are a lack of norms, values, and customs. In other words, Zone II is a revolving door of culture that is unable to give stability to its residents.

The remaining three zones gradually increase in financial stability and space for its residents. Zone III is the residential area of the working man, where skilled workers employed in the factories live (often former residents of Zone II). Zone IV is the "commuter zone" and Zone V is the "residential zone." White collar workers live in these areas and there is more privacy for the financially stable residents.

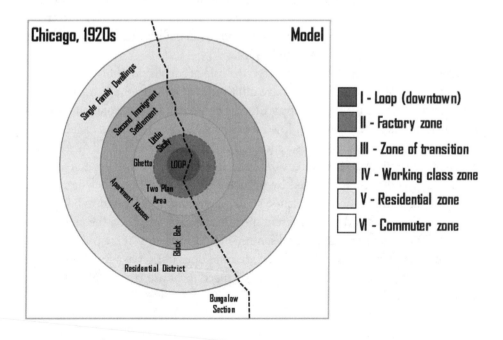

The Criminological Element

Clifford Shaw and Henry McKay (student of Parks and Burgess) are most noted for their examination of delinquency in the city of Chicago through application of the concentric zone theory. In their study, they noted the differences between the levels of economic success in the communities and how it would affect criminality in juveniles (Shaw & McKay, 1942). They proposed that areas with high economic status had low rates of delinquency due to consistent beliefs of the residents in regard to child rearing, abiding the law, and community care. They invest more time on health and education programs for children and assert the importance of respecting the law and following the rules to their children. In addition, people in these communities make time to clean up litter, organize neighborhood watches, and do other activities to promote the well-being of the community. These residents advocate for education, legitimate employment, and a crime-free lifestyle (Shaw & McKay, 1942).

Conversely, areas with low economic status in the city of Chicago had high rates of delinquency due to their approach to community and family, which was less consistent and uniform than that of the more wealthy communities (Shaw & McKay, 1942). In other words, the residents in poorer communities are not supportive of adhering to the law, becoming involved in community organizations, or maintaining strict supervision and guidance for their children. These areas do not reflect the conventional beliefs supported by high income areas. Although money and power are important, use of skill, aggression, and criminal acts are completely acceptable to achieve these status symbols. Youth living in this type of environment are exposed to a disorganized community with contradictory assertions of what is acceptable behavior. For example, a young female may get adjudicated of delinquency in a juvenile court and receive punishment for her act but receive praise and support from the members of her community for participating in behavior deemed acceptable. Further, she sees a large portion of adults in her area fully immersed into the criminal lifestyle (Shaw & McKay, 1942).

Shaw and McKay (1942) also discussed the role of social and public institutions in communities. High income areas have multitudes of athletic and extracurricular outlets for the juvenile residents, supporting the conforming beliefs of their parents. Social institutions (often found in low income areas) are sometimes called "non-indigenous philanthropic agencies," such as the YMCA and Boys and Girls Club. They provide services and resources to youth in order to provide positive outlets and mentors, and they are funded by private agencies. On the other hand, tax-supported public institutions like schools and playgrounds are found in both high and low income areas and have different meanings depending upon the perception of the residents. If it supports the local sentiment of community, it is a positive place to interact. However, if it is in an isolated area and does not serve a function within the community, it may become an informal place to house truants and deviants (Shaw & McKay, 1942).

Using the concentric zone theory, Clifford Shaw and Henry McKay examined the distribution of delinquent boys across the city of Chicago (Shaw & McKay, 1969). They collected the addresses of boys under age 17 who had been arrested by the police, in juvenile court, and/or in a juvenile facility during three time periods (1900-1906, 1917-1923, and 1927-1933). They also collected and plotted geographical data on truants, infant mortality rates, mental disorder, population changes, and other economic indicators.

Shaw and McKay (1942; 1969) found that the rates of juvenile delinquency were highest near the inner city and declined as the city extended into the wealthier areas. Further, no matter the time period of composition of the population, the zone of transition always had the highest crime rates compared to all other zones. The zone of transition exhibited characteristics of physical decay, lower income housing of poor quality, single parent households, and high rates of illegitimate births. Individuals who lived in this zone had low education levels, menial to no employment, and high rates of drug and alcohol abuse.

The delinquency pattern for the zones was the same for all racial and ethnic groups. In other words, Shaw and McKay's (1942; 1969) findings indicated that being a certain race or ethnicity was not a predictive factor for criminality. Instead, participation in criminal behavior was based on the organization and income level of your neighborhood. Individuals who reside in more disorganized areas are more likely to commit crimes compared to more organized, affluent neighborhoods.

Shaw and McKay (1942) addressed the importance and role of family in the shaping of a child in these disorganized neighborhoods. Families are generally the symbol of conventional values and organization. However, when a member of the family is earning a living in illegal practices, or simply enjoys the committing of crime, the appeal to juveniles to participate in delinquent behavior overruns the family values. During the period of Shaw and McKay's research, immigrant parents represented the conservative views of the "Old World" or "Old Country" and were not reflective of the contemporary views of youth. So even if their European-born parents were law-abiding, juveniles felt allegiance to their delinquent groups that were more "Americanized." This rejection of parents continues to happen in present day as teenagers of every generation generally consider their parents to be old-fashioned regarding behavior, dress, music, etc.

Lastly, another reason family may be ineffective in directing a juvenile toward conventional goals and values are the new problems associated with the generation of the juvenile. Shaw and McKay (1942) discussed the concept of leisure time, as individuals from the Old World began work at an early age and rarely had any down time. However, those juveniles in their study did not go to work until later ages, and this continues to be true today. Presently, today's youth are dealing with the constant presence of the Internet in their lives, which was not an issue for their parents. This generation is constantly "plugged in" and providing more and more personal information and photographs to this international online community.

While the Internet can be a positive, resourceful place, it is also congested with predators targeting young people.

Revisions of Social Disorganization Theory

Once this theory was introduced, it was extremely influential for policies and program development in the 1950s and 1960s (Pratt & Gau, 2010). However, closer to 1970, the theory started to lose popularity as there was a trend to use **individual (micro)-level** theories rather than **aggregate (macro)-level** (Bursik & Grasmic, 1993) theories. Second, there was criticism of the theory's assertion that community dynamics are stable, when in actuality they are constantly changing (Pratt & Gau, 2010). As the majority of criminological research was cross-sectional at that time, it was difficult to truly capture community dynamics with that form of research design. In addition, only census data was used to measure disorganization as collecting direct measures was extremely difficult at the time. Lastly, critics of social disorganization theory believed it to be racist, as racial minority groups tended to populate the areas termed "disorganized" or low income in the studies (Matsueda & Heimer, 1987).

Despite the popularity of the theory as a potential explanation of crime on the macro-level, there have been multiple questions and criticisms regarding the methodological and measurement perspectives (Kubrin & Weitzer, 2003). Robinson (1950) raised concern over the relationship between social disorganization, crime, and the appropriate unit of analysis to use in the models, which was echoed by multiple researchers (Bursik, 1988; Hipp, 2007; Kubrin & Weitzer, 2003). Creating a definition for the concept "neighborhood" can be difficult. Census blocks, block groups, and tracts are the most common boundaries used in social disorganization research (Hart & Waller, 2013). However, Sampson, Morenoff, and Gannon-Rowley argue that official census data is not always appropriate for forming boundaries for study in research as a neighborhood is more of a perception of community members. Wooldredge (2002) further echoed this sentiment by stating that when defining neighborhoods in administrative boundaries, results from research may be biased because different sized "neighborhoods" will generate issues in empirical relationships.

After Kornhauser's (1978) widely seen criticism of social disorganization theory, several theorists have reframed the theory and applied it with better success. Robert Bursik (1988) asserted that Shaw and McKay were not suggesting that economic conditions and rapid social changes were the cause of crime. He believed they were asserting that social disorganization causes a weakened social control in an area, allowing for high rates of crime to occur. Further, he combined the concepts of social disorganization with those of social control theory and routine activities theory to better explain criminality in disorganized geographic areas.

Sampson and Groves (1989) agreed with Bursik's claims on the true assertions of social disorganization theory in regard to predicting criminality. By testing data from British communities, they found that external factors affecting social disorganization were related to criminal victimization. These external factors included residential mobility, family disruption, and lack of teenage supervision. As a side note, Veysey and Messner (1999) revisited this data and did find that some of the external factors were stronger predictors of crime compared to the social disorganization variables.

Sampson, Raudenbush, and Earls (1997) made further contribution to the theory by adding in the concept of **collective efficacy**, the perceived ability of residents in a geographic area to enforce social control, as a contributing factor to crime rates in an area. Collective efficacy is composed of two parts: social cohesion and shared expectations of social control. Sampson and colleagues further asserted that when urban areas have weak ties of collective efficacy (i.e., less motivation to invoke social control methods), crime rates increase.

Using data from the Project on Human Development in Chicago Neighborhoods, Sampson et al. (1997) measured collective efficacy by surveying urban residents regarding their perceptions of the willingness of their neighbors to enforce social control. Hypothetical scenarios involving delinquent acts by juveniles (e.g., truancy, fighting, and vandalism) were described to the residents, and they were asked to respond on the hypothesized reaction of the community. Findings revealed that low collective efficacy was related to homicide and violent behaviors, and future research studies (many using the same data set) found similar support to the theory's ability to predict crime (Morenoff, Sampson, & Raudenbush, 2001; Kirk & Matsuda, 2011; Wright & Benson, 2011).

As collective efficacy can be difficult to conceptualize and measure, some studies have utilized the related concept of **social capital** to predict social disorganization and crime. Social capital is defined as the relationships among people who live and work together that allow a society to operate efficiently. Strong networks of people have value and can positively contribute to maintaining a peaceful society. Deprivation of resources and large populations can diminish the social capital of a neighborhood (Messner, Baumer, & Rosenfeld, 2004). Neighbors are less likely to trust each other, and the cohesiveness of a community declines.

Empirical Research

Published tests of the theory generally include three measures of social disorganization. First, **socioeconomic status (SES)** of a neighborhood is either a single variable, a scale of economic variables (Sampson & Groves, 1989; Sampson, Raudenbusch &

Earls, 1997), or a combination of income level and unemployment rates (Bursik, 1986; Sampson, 1986). Second, racial composition, or **racial heterogeneity**, is either measured by percent of blacks in a neighborhood (Sampson, 1986) or the percent of nonwhites in a neighborhood (Bursik, 1986). Lastly, **residential mobility** (movement) of the residents examines the number of residents who have resided in the same dwelling for the past five years (Sampson, 1986; Sampson et al., 1997).

Sampson (1986) asserted that a large portion of the published studies using social disorganization theory failed to apply the impact of other important variables, such as family structure and stability. He believed that social disorganization theory was linked to control and routine activities theory, as a family disruption can remove important social controls over youth and create opportunities for victimization (parents are not there supervising the young people). Sampson advocated for measuring family structure in three ways:

1. Percentage of residents who were married or divorced;
2. Percentage of homes with a female head of household; and
3. Households with only one primary head.

Recent research has combined concepts of social disorganization theory and control theories to demonstrate the link between parental monitoring and criminal behavior (Pratt & Cullen, 2000; Pratt, Turner & Piquero, 2004).

The majority of research indicating support for social disorganization theory has involved the examination of correlations between crime rates in common areas (i.e., neighborhoods, cities, states) and indicators of economic conditions. Studies have looked at a wide array of economic factors and their relationship with criminality. Currently, a large body of literature indicates that disadvantage, racial heterogeneity, residential stability, and familial disruption are all associated with crime in neighborhoods (Boggess & Hipp, 2010; Hipp, 2007, 2010; Lowenkamp, Cullen, & Pratt, 2003; Veysey & Messner, 1999). Further, according to Pratt and Cullen (2005), most of the economic indicators are significantly related to violent crime more often than property crime (with the exception of absolute poverty).

Two recent studies testing social disorganization theory are unique compared to most research as they examined areas outside metropolitan areas. Osgood and Chambers (2000) tested the theory with a sample of 264 counties in Florida, Georgia, South Carolina, and Nebraska through the examination of juvenile violence. They indicated that disrupting formal and informal controls in a community is a significant indicator of high crime rates despite the type of geographic area. Further, as early studies on urban ecology had indicated, rapid population growth in rural areas weakened social ties. Results indicated that juvenile violence was significantly associated with residential mobility, family disruption, and ethnic heterogeneity, but not poverty variables. A similar study by Bouffard and Muftic (2006) used a sample of 221 non-metropolitan counties in the Midwest and found that violence offenses were also significantly related to residential mobility and family disruption, but not heterogeneity and poverty.

In the past few decades, **endogenous community** dynamics such as social control, social capital, and collective efficacy have been used in social disorganization models to better examine crime (Sampson & Groves, 1989). Measurement of social disorganization through collective efficacy and social capital has also produced varied results. Collective efficacy measures trust amongst neighbors by including resident intervention in deviant activities, such as calling the police if juveniles are vandalizing property or breaking up a physical altercation between two people. Social capital measurement includes participation in civic activities, such as volunteer organizations or political campaigns (Rosenfeld et al., 2001; Messner et al., 2004). Social capital has been significantly correlated with lower rates of crime, but social disorganization measurements generally have a direct relationship with crime rates and not with social capital (Rosenfeld et al., 2001; Hawdon & Ryan, 2004).

Policy Implications

Potentially the most notable policy implication of social disorganization theory is the Chicago Area Project (CAP), a large-scale urban delinquency project developed in the 1930s. CAP was developed in several of the lower class neighborhoods in Chicago with the intention to institute social control and organization in the communities. Another goal of the program was to combat the influence of delinquent peers and criminal adults who resided in the neighborhood. A wide variety of efforts were made to achieve these goals. Sanitation, physical improvements, and traffic control were implemented. Law-abiding adults ran recreational programs, camps, athletic teams, and other positive activities for youth. Social workers identified delinquent gang members and attempted to engage them in alternative behaviors (Kobrin, 1959; Lundman, 1993).

Assessments of the CAP were performed 25 years (Kobrin, 1959), 30 years (Finestone, 1976), and 50 years (Schlossman & Sedlak, 1983) after initiation of the project. Results indicated various levels of success. The overall plan was successfully implemented in some of the neighborhoods, but there was variation on how well the programs were organized based on each area. Professionals involved in the project criticized the volunteer effectiveness, and volunteers argued that the professionals were undermining the efforts of the parents, schools, and churches. Finestone (1976) indicated that some neighborhoods had reduced delinquency rates. Follow up by Scholssman et al. (1984) found that four of the six areas measured had lower delinquency rates than expected.

Broken windows theory, introduced by Wilson and Kelling (1982), has been closely linked with social disorganization theory based on its push for order maintenance in communities in order to decrease crime. The theory indicated that dilapidated neighborhoods marked with broken windows, graffiti, litter, and other signs of decay indicated communities with lack of care and concern by the members for the physical area. These areas are overrun by low-level thieves and drug dealers, prostitutes, and loiterers. Any law-abiding residents hide in their homes for fear of harassment and lack of social control. Serious criminals also begin to make their homes in these areas and the crime rate rises (Wilson & Kelling, 1982).

Broken windows theory and social disorganization theory focus on the stability of a neighborhood and how various levels of social control can affect the delinquency rates of its youth. The major difference between the two theories is that social disorganization theory is macro-level (neighborhoods, communities), while broken windows theory focuses on individuals and individual behavior. However, the benefit of combining the two is that police could justify focusing on one of their main missions: order maintenance. In 1994, Mayor Rudolph Giuliani appointed William Bratton as Chief of the New York City Police Department and began initiating multiple broken windows-based policing methods. Multiple studies indicated that these changes in law enforcement were the reason for the drastic reduction in crime rate in the city (Bratton & Knobler, 1998; Kelling & Coles, 1996; Kelling & Sousa, 2001). Programs with a broken windows basis are still used today on smaller levels, such as enforcement of civil ordinances (Mazerolle, Roehl, & Kadleck, 1998), and in larger efforts, such as community policing programs (Brunson, 2007).

CASE STUDY 4.1
TOO TOUGH TO FIX BROKEN WINDOWS?

In November 2014, Michael Greenberg wrote an online article called "'Broken Windows' and the New York police." Greenberg asserted that the contemporary uses of broken windows policies are more extreme than 30 years ago and not nearly as effective. William Bratton, still Chief of Police in New York City, worked with Mayor Bloomberg to initiate and heavily use the "stop and frisk," which essentially permitted New York City police officers to stop and frisk anyone on the street exhibiting suspicious behavior. In 2011, Judge Shira Scheindlin of the United States District Court ruled this to be an indirect form of racial profiling, and critics of the "stop and frisk" initiative asserted that the majority of those stopped were in fact minorities.

Greenberg goes on to state that the chokehold death of Eric Garner is another extreme example of the use of broken windows policing. Garner was approached by police for selling loose cigarettes by the Staten Island ferry. After resisting arrest, he was put in a chokehold by officers and died from the interaction. His screams of "I can't breathe!" became the protest rally for through chants, t-shirts, and other forms of media. The grand jury decided not to indict the officer involved in the incident, causing increased reaction from communities in New York City who argued that individuals arrested for small, "rule-breaking" crimes, like Garner, were generally nonviolent minorities who were being targeted due to their race.

Do you feel as if these modern-day examples are in fact biased broken windows policing?

There has been a large push for the implementation of programs in socially disorganized, low income areas that provide role models for at risk and delinquent youth. A famous national example, the Big Brothers/Big Sisters mentoring program, provide positive, older adolescents for young boys and girls who need guidance. This program, as well as similar regional and neighborhood initiatives, not only provides role models but also after school activities as an alternative to delinquent behaviors.

Police-sponsored programs such as Neighborhood Watch and community policing initiatives are credited as preventative crime measures based off social disorganization theory. Neighborhood Watch brings citizens together to monitor neighborhoods for criminal activity and produce community cohesion. While some of these programs have had some impact on crime reduction, it is difficult to estimate the impact based on research design flaws (Bennett, Holloway, & Farrington, 2006). Reisig (2010) indicated that community policing has had a positive impact on crime reduction; however, a lack of research fails to determine which specific community policing programs are more effective than others.

CASE STUDY 4.2
MOBILIZATION OF YOUTH

Living in the Lower East Side of New York City in the 1950s was especially difficult for residents because of the clash of cultures. Soldiers had returned from war suffering from mental anxieties and stresses, and gang activity and drug use became prevalent. Living conditions were unhealthy due to lack of enough income to maintain acceptable housing for families. During a Henry Street Settlement House Board of Directors meeting in 1957, members were concerned with juvenile delinquency in the neighborhood and asserted the need for a solution. In 1962, funding was acquired to initiate the **Mobilization of Youth** program (Abraham et al., 2007).

The program was developed on unique principles regarding the cause of juvenile delinquency. Delinquency was not blamed on the person, but instead the lack of opportunities for persons in low income areas. Advocates for Mobilization of Youth believed it was society's responsibility to provide programs for education, life skills, and employment opportunities. Essentially, the program wanted to revitalize neighborhoods and bring back a feeling of community bond. Despite multiple struggles, including lack of funding support and accusations of criminal behavior by administration, the program was deemed a success by the federal government. Over 6,500 youth were provided job training and educational services to better the outlook of their futures (Abraham et al., 2007).

Summary

Social disorganization theory made a unique contribution to the field of criminological theory at the time it was introduced. Rather than placing the blame for criminal behavior on the individual, it indicated responsibility in the organization of the environment and opportunities present (or lack thereof) for the individual. In addition, Roh and Choo (2008) asserted the importance of recognizing the connection between crime rates and mobility. They believed that high crime rates could be explained by long residencies of disadvantaged people in disorganized areas. If given the opportunity and resources to relocate into more cohesive areas, criminal activity by such people would decline.

While this theory has its flaws, it did allow the academic community to consider other explanations of high crime rates in concentrated areas. Preventative measures that provide resources, opportunities, and alternative avenues to criminal behavior are effective in these areas and helpful for the residents. Options are given and, for academics and residents, this is a new concept. Continued consideration of the effect of a disorganized neighborhood on the behavior of its residents would suggest rehabilitative programming rather than more punitive measures for offenders.

Discussion Questions

1. Many scholars assert that social disorganization theory is unique as it does not indicate that race or sex is a predictor of criminal behavior, but rather environment. Conversely, critics of the theory believe it to be racist and sexist. Why would critics take this position?
2. Is this theory only useful in explaining crime in urban areas or in all geographical categories (urban, rural, and suburban)? Why or why not?
3. Would programs like Mobilization of Youth work in all areas?

REFERENCES

Abraham, S., Bede, S., Jerney, J., & Schomberg, M. (2007). *Mobilization for youth: A revolution in youth work.* University of Minnesota, Organizational Approaches to Youth Development. Retrieved from http://shaina.saaricreated.com/wp-content/uploads/2010/09/Abraham-MFY-11-2007.pdf

Bennett, T., Holloway, K., & Farrington, D. (2006). Does neighborhood watch reduce crime? A systematic review and meta-analysis. *Journal of Experimental Criminology, 2,* 437-458.

Boggess, L.N. & Hipp, J.R. (2010). Violent crime, residential instability and mobility: Does the relationship differ in minority neighborhoods? *Journal of Quantitative Criminology.*

Bouffard, L.A., & Muftic, L.R. (2006). The "rural mystique": Social disorganization and violence beyond urban areas. *Western Criminology Review, 7*(3), 56-66.

Bratton, W.J. & Knobler, P. (1998). *Turnaround: How America's top cop reversed the crime epidemic.* New York: Random House.

Brunson, R.K. (2007). Police like black people: African-American young men's accumulated police experiences. *Criminology & Public Policy, 6,* 71-102.

Burgess, E. (1925). The growth of the city: An introduction to a research project. In R. Park, E. Burgess & R. McKenzie (Eds.). *The city,* (pp. 47-62). Chicago: University of Chicago Press.

Bursik, R.J. (1986). Ecological stability and the dynamics of delinquency. In A.J. Reiss & M. Tonry (Eds.), *Communities and crime* (pp. 35-66). Chicago: University of Chicago Press.

Bursik, R.J. (1988). Social disorganization and theories of crime and delinquency: Problems and prospects. *Criminology, 26*(4), 519-552.

Bursik, R.J., & Grasmick, H. (1993). *Neighborhoods and crime: The dimensions of effective community control.* New York: Lexington Books.

Cressey, P.F. (1938). Population succession in Chicago: 1898-1930, *American Journal of Sociology, 44 (1),* 59-69.

Finestone, H. (1976). *Victims of change.* Wesport, CT: Greenwood.

Hart, T. & Waller, J. (2013). Neighborhood boundaries and structural determinants of social disorganization: Examining the validity of commonly used measures. *Western Criminology Review, 14(3),* 16-33.

Hawdon, J. & Ryan, J. (2004). Social capital, social control, and changes in victimization rates. *Crime and Delinquency, 55,* 526-549.

Hipp, J.R. (2007). Income inequality, race, and place: Does the distribution of race and class within neighborhoods affect crime rates? *Criminology, 45*(3), 665-697.

Hipp, J. (2010). The role of crime in housing unit racial/ethnic transition. *Criminology, 48(3),* 683-723.

Kelling, G.L. & Coles, C.M. (1996). *Fixing broken windows.* New York: Simon & Schuster.

Kelling, G.L. & Sousa, W.H. (2001). *Do police matter? An analysis of the impact of New York City's police reforms.* New York: The Manhattan Institute.

Kirk, D.S., & Matsuda, M. (2011). Legal cynicism, collective efficacy, and the ecology of arrest. *Criminology, 49*(2), 443–472.

Kobrin, S. (1959). The Chicago Area Project—25 year assessment. *Annals of the American Academy of Political and Social Science, 322,* 19-29.

Kornhauser, R. (1978). *Social sources of delinquency.* Chicago: University of Chicago Press.

Kubrin, C. & Weitzer, R. (2003). New directions in social disorganization theory. *Journal of Research in Crime & Delinquency. 40,* 374-402.

Lowenkamp, C.T., Cullen, F.T., & Pratt, T.C. (2003). Replicating Sampson and Groves's test of social disorganization theory: Revisiting a criminological classic. *Journal of Research in Crime and Delinquency, 40,* 351-373.

Lundman, R. (1993). *Prevention and control of juvenile delinquency* (2nd ed). New York: Oxford University Press.

Mazerolle, L.G., Roehl, J., & Kadleck, C. (1998). Controlling social disorder using civil remedies: Results from a randomized field experiment in Oakland, CA. In L.G. Mazerolle & J. Roehl (Eds.), *Crime preventions studies* (pp. 141-159). Monsey, NY: Criminal Justice Press.

Messner, S.F., Baumer, E.P. & Rosenfeld, R. (2004). Dimensions of social capital and rates of criminal homicide. *American Sociological Review, 69*, 882-903.

Morenoff, J.D., Sampson, R.J., & Raudenbush, S.W. (2001). Neighborhood inequality, collective efficacy, and the spatial dynamics of urban violence. *Criminology, 39*, 517-560.

Osgood, D.W., & Chambers, J.M. (2000). Social disorganization outside the metropolis: An analysis of rural youth violence. *Criminology, 38*(1), 81-116.

Park, R. (1936). Human ecology. *American Journal of Sociology, 42*, 3-49.

Pratt, T.C., & Cullen, F.T. (2000). The empirical status of Gottfredson and Hirschi's general theory of crime: A meta-analysis. *Criminology, 38*, 931-964.

Pratt, T.C., & Cullen, F.T. (2005). Assessing macro-level predictors and theories of crime: A meta-analysis. In M. Tonry (Ed.), *Crime and justice: A review of research*, Vol. 12, 373-450. Chicago, IL: University of Chicago Press.

Pratt, T. & Gau, J. (2010). Social disorganization theory. In H. Copes & V. Topalli (Eds.), *Criminological theory: Readings and retrospectives* (pp.104-113). New York, NY: McGraw-Hill.

Pratt, T.C., Turner, M.G., & Piquero, A.R. (2000). Parental socialization and community context: A longitudinal analysis of the structural sources of low self-control. *Journal of Research in Crime and Delinquency, 41*, 219-243.

Raudenbush, S.W. & Sampson, R.J. (1999). Ecometrics: Toward a science of assessing ecological settings, with application to the systematic social observations of neighborhoods. *Sociological Methodology, 29*, 1-41.

Reisig, M. (2010). *Does punishment deter? Policy backgrounder No. 148*. Washington, DC: National Center for Policy Analysis.

Robinson, W. (1950). Ecological correlation and the behavior of individuals. *American Sociological Review, 15*, 351-357.

Rosenfeld, R., Messner, S. & Baumber, E. (2001). Social capital and homicide. *Social Forces, 80*, 283-310.

Sampson, R.J. (1986). Neighborhood family structure and the risk of personal victimization. In R.J. Sampson & J.M. Byrne (Eds.), *The social ecology of crime* (pp. 25-46). New York: Springer-Verlag.

Sampson, R.J. and Groves, B.W. (1989). Community structure and crime: Testing social-disorganization theory. *American Journal of Sociology, 94*, 774-802.

Sampson, R.J., Raudenbusch, S., & Earls, F. (1997). Neighborhoods and violent crime: A multilevel study of collective efficacy. *Science, 227*, 918-924.

Schlossman, S. & Sedlak, M. (1983). The Chicago Area Project revisited. *Crime and Delinquency, 29*, 398-462.

Schlossman, S., Shavelson, R., & Sedlak, M., & Cobb, J. (1984). *Delinquency prevention in South Chicago: A fifty year assessment of the Chicago area*. Santa Monica, CA: Rand Corporation.

Shaw, C.R. & McKay, H.D. (1942). *Juvenile delinquency in urban areas*. Chicago: University of Chicago Press.

Veysey, B.M. & Messner, S.F. (1999). Further testing of social disorganization theory: An elaboration of Sampson and Grove's "community structure and crime." *J. Res. Crime Delinq., 36*, 156-174.

Wilson, J.Q., & Kelling, G. (1982). The police and neighborhood safety: Broken windows. *The Atlantic Monthly*, 29-38.

Wooldredge, J. (2002). Examining the irrelevance of aggregation bias for multilevel studies of neighborhoods and crime with an example comparing census tracts to official neighborhoods in Cincinnati. *Criminology, 40*(3), 681-710.

Wright, E.M. & Benson, M.L. (2011). Clarifying the effects of neighborhood context on violence "behind closed doors." *Justice Quarterly, 28*(5), 775-798.

Strain Theories

CHAPTER OUTLINE

Introduction

Progression of Strain Theory
Merton
Case Study 5.1: Bernie Madoff
Cohen
Miller
Cloward and Ohlin
Agnew
Messner and Rosenfeld

Empirical Research

Policy Implications
Case Study 5.2: STARR

Summary

Discussion Questions

References

Key Words and Concepts

Achievement Orientation
Anomie
Anticipated Strain
Autonomy
Behavioral Coping Strategies
Belonging
Cognitive Coping Strategies

Conflict Subculture
Conformity
Confrontation with
   Negative/Noxious Stimuli
Criminal Subculture
Delinquent Subculture
Deregulation

Differential Opportunity
Disjuncture Between
   Aspirations and
   Expectations/
   Achievement

(continued)

Disjuncture Between Expectations and Reality

Disjuncture Between Fair Outcomes and Actual Outcomes

Double Failures

Emotional Coping Strategies

Excitement

Failure to Achieve Positively Valued Goals

Fatalism

Fetishism of Money

Focal Concerns

Individualism

Innovation

Institutional Balance of Power

Learning Environments

Mechanical Society

Middle-Class Expectations

Objective Strain

One-Sex Peer Unit

Organic Society

Reaction Formation

Rebellion

Removal of Positively Valued Stimuli

Retreatism

Retreatist Subcultures

Ritualism

Serial Monogamy

Smartness

Status

Status Frustration

Strain

Subjective Strain

Toughness

Trouble

Universalism

Vicarious Strain

Introduction

Anomie/strain theory was strongly influenced by sociologist Emile Durkheim's (1893) concept of **deregulation** occurring in society, as discussed in his book, *The Division of Labor in Society*. According to Durkheim, the expectations and rules of society in regard to appropriate behavior towards one another have fragmented, and individuals do not know how to behave. This feeling of normlessness, or deregulation, leads to criminal behavior. This concept of deregulation was applied to his central thesis of the book, which stated that societies evolve from simple forms (**mechanical society**) to complex, highly specialized forms (**organic society**). In a mechanical society, all members share the same values and morals, in turn behaving similarly. Further, as they all work toward the same goals, they perform very similar tasks. As a society evolves into an organic society, individuals begin to specialize in their work and develop separate goals. Complex relationships are created based on the person's skills that can be offered. As a result, individuals vary in value to the society.

As an expansion of his first work, Durkheim developed the concept of **anomie** in his book, *Suicide: A Study in Sociology* (1897/1951), referring to it as a deregulated condition where people have lessened moral controls over their behavior (Olsen, 1965). He asserted that people who struggle with striving for success and how to treat people during this drive suffer from anomie. Individuals have a difficult time finding their role in a society and adjusting to life conditions. Since Durkheim's initial contributions, his concept of anomie has been used by more contemporary theorists to explain criminality.

In this chapter, we present the basic premises of anomie and strain theories. We outline the historical context that the premise originates. Next, we provide illustrative examples and contemporary studies of the anomie and strain perspective of criminology. We evaluate these findings and assumptions. Finally, we suggest policy implications that may be fruitful in understanding this particular premise.

Progression of Strain Theory

Merton

Robert Merton (1938) utilized Durkheim's concept of anomie to explain modern industrial societies and the adaptation of individuals to the struggle for success. He discussed the effects of pressure placed on members of a society to behave in a certain manner and achieve certain goals. In other words, "fitting in" involves conforming to the standard social structure sets, or socially acceptable goals. In addition, society also develops acceptable standards, or means, of achieving these goals. Not only do we state what behaviors are legal or illegal, we also categorize what is acceptable and not acceptable. Legal, or legitimate means, are not always supported by the culture as the acceptable way to obtain a goal.

Merton (1938) asserted that complex society members attempt to maintain a balance between socially acceptable goals and the legitimate means to obtain them, but this often results in a tug-of-war between the two. In other words, it can be difficult for both to occur simultaneously for many individuals in difficult situations. There is a strong cultural emphasis on success, or the "American Dream," which entails education, career, and financial and personal success (marriage, children, etc.). Even members of the lowest economic class are socialized to want these things. With that being said, there is often a discrepancy between obtaining these successes and the appropriate ways to get them. Merton argued that Americans are more concerned with success and money and less concerned with the cost. While "The American Dream" asserts that we all have equal opportunities, lower economic classes and disadvantaged persons often do not have legitimate opportunities; therefore, the **strain** (pressure) placed on these groups to take advantage of whatever is necessary to obtain success (legitimate or illegitimate) is present.

Merton (1938) proposed that individuals adapt to the disjuncture between socially acceptable goals and legitimate means to obtain them (i.e., anomie) in

TABLE 5.1	MERTON'S ADAPTATIONS TO DISJUNCTURE BETWEEN SOCIALLY ACCEPTABLE GOALS AND LEGITIMATE MEANS TO OBTAIN THEM

Adaptation	Use of Societally Acceptable Norms	Use of Legitimate Means
Conformity	+	+
Innovation	+	-
Ritualism	-	+
Retreatism	-	-
Rebellion	+-	+-

five possible ways. The most common response, **conformity**, occurs when an individual accepts societal rules and reaches goals through legitimate means. This conventional behavior is geared toward the values of a group, while rule **innovation**, the second adaptation, is the most common deviant response of the remaining four adaptations. Individuals still strive for the socially acceptable goals, but do not use legitimate means to obtain them. For example, a person may sell drugs to earn money to buy a nice car or home. **Ritualism** is not adhering to societal norms, but still using legitimate means to live life. In other words, these persons do not necessarily support socially accepted norms, but still participate in the means to obtain them as it is what is expected (i.e., going through the motions). For instance, people who do not believe in God but still attend church (as it is a socially acceptable norm to be religious and attend services) are examples of ritualists. The fourth (and likely last) type of adaptation, **retreatism**, involves an escapist response to life. Essentially, these are societal dropouts and are often addicts, alcoholics, or vagrants. Lastly, **rebellion** entails completely rejecting the means and ends and attempting to violently overthrow the system. An individual who participates in rebellion is frustrated with the current social order and wants new standards for society (Merton, 1938).

It is important to understand the reasons individuals adapt in certain ways. Persons may participate in antisocial (criminal) behavior due to lack of access to legitimate means. Although a person may support and invest in The American Dream, he may not have the financial opportunities to get an education, which leads to a better paying job. Merton (1938) stated it is difficult to legitimately "transcend class lines" when society puts up boundaries to prevent an individual from doing so. In addition, a person may not morally invest in the rigid standards society has set to equate success. For example, although a female high school graduate may have the legitimate means (i.e., money, parental support) to obtain a college degree, she may have no desire to pursue an education and would rather live in her parents' basement and stay unemployed. She may want to rebel against what her parents expect of her or simply explore other deviant options of survival (i.e., theft).

CASE STUDY 5.1
BERNIE MADOFF

Bernie Madoff, one of America's most notorious Ponzi scheme artists of the 21st century, is a classic example of Merton's Innovator. Using money he earned as a lifeguard, he began his own investment company. By the year 2000, Madoff was a billionaire and managing the money of celebrities and European royalty. However, he was not truly investing the money for them; instead, he was involved in a complicated financial scheme of theft. In 2009, the 71-year-old was sentenced to 150 years in prison for his crimes, but left personal lives in devastation and was the indirect cause of suicides and ruined relationships. Madoff's criminal behavior was rooted in one simple desire: greed.

Cohen

Albert Cohen (1955) supplemented Merton's assertions regarding strain and criminal adaptations by further exploring the effect of a **delinquent subculture** on adolescent males in the lower class. Cohen was not necessarily concerned with explaining individual behavior or even why the subculture continued to exist over time. He wanted to explore why the delinquent subculture originated.

Cohen (1955) also supported Merton's notion that deviance is produced by strain caused by blocked goals. However, he believed the strain was a result of the inability to earn acceptance in society and to achieve a status, which is achieved by acclimating to society's standards of acceptable behaviors, intellectual abilities, clothing, etc. The individuals who represent these accepted standards are the middle class, as they exhibit the above-referenced characteristics. Specifically, in regard to adolescents as a whole, Cohen asserted that they all strived for **middle-class expectations** as these are the standards not only imposed by society but also by teachers. Wearing the right clothes, demonstrating good manners, making good grades, and participation in extracurricular activities are all ways students can gain approval from teachers and status in the community.

According to Cohen (1955), it is easy for middle-class students to meet these expectations and gain status because they have the support of middle-class parents. Lower-class youth, on the other hand, have a more difficult time meeting these standards (especially if they are males). Not only do they not have the educational background, they also lack the social skills. As a result of not meeting the middle-class standards, Cohen asserted that they experience **status frustration**. Boys who collectively experience this feeling of frustration form a delinquent subculture that has its own values and standards revolving around malicious behavior and negative concepts. This **reaction formation** of a new delinquent subculture stresses the importance of aggression and contempt for academic achievement. In other words, the boys who are unable to excel in conventional standards rebel and create their own acceptable achievements that revolve around criminal enterprise.

In his book, *Delinquent Boys,* Cohen (1955) discusses how reaction formation is a process experienced by working and lower class boys who are often raised in a family in which the mother is the primary caregiver and socializer. The mother is the head of household, possibly due to a neglectful or absent father. Boys develop their own concept of masculinity by doing the opposite of female behaviors, which are sensitive, nurturing, and caring. As an alternative, these boys believe masculinity equates to deviance and aggression.

Miller

Following the work of Cohen regarding the delinquency of male gangs in lower class neighborhoods, and agreeing with the assertion that delinquency is a result of an attempt for success, Walter Miller (1958) asserted that delinquency is an adaptation to lower class culture, and that by committing criminal acts, these young people will be embraced by the culture. According to Miller, the term "lower class" is a distinctive cultural system that is becoming increasingly large. Their way of life is characterized by issues that demand constant attention and have a large degree of emotional involvement, otherwise known as **focal concerns**. Juveniles learn to behave in accordance with the focal concerns of the adults in the neighborhood and perform these values in an embellished way. In other words, their behavior is influenced by cultural forces in their neighborhood in the manner of which the juvenile perceives these forces and their meaning.

Miller (1958) and his team collected data during a three-year service research project focusing on gang delinquency. The seven social workers maintained contact with the corner gangs (21 total) in a low income district in a large city in the East. The contact lasted between 10 to 30 months. Members of the gangs were black and white, male and female, and varied in ages from early to late adolescence. After review of the data, Miller identified six focal concerns of the lower class culture.

Trouble is commitment to breaking the law and being a problem for other people. It is a dominant feature for the lower class and can refer to getting into trouble or staying out of trouble. Male trouble can include use of aggression, or fighting, as well as drunken sexual escapades. Female trouble usually involves a sexual involvement that results in unwanted consequences (pregnancy, disease).

However, getting into trouble can be associated with law-violating behavior, which often equates to prestige and status in a gang (Miller, 1958).

Toughness is the demonstration of physical power, courage, and machismo. Toughness, or masculinity, is demonstrated not only by physical strength, but also by athleticism. Males who are tough can be identified by tattoos, have an uncaring and insensitive attitude, and see women as sexual conquests. In addition, there is an underlying current of fear of homosexuality or being perceived as gay. "Queers" or "fags" are often treated with violence to demonstrate the masculinity of the attacker (Miller, 1958).

The next focal concern does not indicate the intelligence of an individual but instead the ability to outwit persons of lesser abilities. Those who exhibit **smartness** have the ability to con and manipulate others, as well as to obtain material goods and status. The media portrays "smart" people as card sharks or con artists, not nerdy academics. Smartness is also earned through incessant teasing from your associated corner gang. Often referred to as the "the dirty dozen" or "playing house," young members are teased to sharpen their abilities to respond with equally assertive comments or quips (Miller, 1958).

Miller (1958) stated that the fourth focal concern, **excitement**, is the quest for risk, danger, and thrills. Seeking excitement often involves consumption of alcohol and prowling for the opposite sex. Members of the gang will go "bar hopping" to find attractive members of the opposite sex, continue to drink, and often end up in fights. This is a part of normal life for these individuals, with fighting occurring at least once a week and often penal consequences following.

Fatalism is the focus on luck or fate. Members of the lower class often feel as if they have little to no control over their lives, not due to religious beliefs, but more related to the concept of destiny. They are big advocates of performing rituals to change their fate and are extremely superstitious (Miller, 1958).

Lastly, **autonomy** is freedom from authority, or independence. Members of the lower class often resent authority figures and restrictions on their own behavior. In other words, control by someone else or an organization is not well received. Miller (1958) stated that these individuals strongly felt the need to be in control of their own lives and decisions.

Miller (1958) also makes a specific point of indicating the role of **serial monogamy** as an influence of lower class juvenile behavior. In many lower-class households, children are often raised by single mothers who live with other females of child-bearing age. These mothers have multiple short-term relationships with men, which do not allow youth to develop a bond with a father figure. The lack of male role models is an issue for young men trying to learn appropriate adult behavior. Membership in a gang often fills this gap, specifically gangs Miller (1958) called a **one-sex peer unit**. As the majority of male youth members come from single-parent homes (generally females), they desire the membership and tutelage of other boys.

Recruiting members to adolescent male gangs is a selective process. There is a huge need for group solidarity, so members must often give up their own selfish interests for the betterment of the group. Further, members must be accepting of the possibility of receipt of sanctions for deviant behavior, as punishment is part of the lifestyle. The reward for gang membership is fulfillment of two focal concerns Miller (1958) stated were unique to adolescents: **belonging** and **status**. Belonging is acceptance into a group and the feeling of involvement. Status is a ranking, or pecking order, of group membership. Adolescents have an intense desire to be seen as an adult, rather than an immature child, and demonstration of the focal concerns discussed earlier earns a person status.

Cloward and Ohlin

Continuing to draw on the work of Merton, Richard Cloward and Lloyd Ohlin (1960) created a theory indicating how **differential opportunity** explained delinquency. Their theory not only used some of Merton and Cohen's assertions on strain but also the concepts of Shaw and McKay's social disorganization and Sutherland's differential association theories. Cloward and Ohlin believed that Merton was incorrect with his assertion that lower-class persons automatically have access to illegitimate opportunities when denied legitimate opportunities. Instead, they focused on the different adaptations explained by the types of opportunities available. They stated that a main purpose of norms is to create boundaries between legal and illegal practices so we as a society know what is right and wrong. Further, Cloward and Ohlin believed that criminologists who believed that crime could be explained simply by examining a person's readiness to commit the crime were overlooking a host of other explanations. For example, what illegal alternatives are available to a person? Just because a person decides to be a successful criminal does not mean it automatically happens; he or she must utilize the avenues available to him or her to become a criminal (Cohen, 1955). Sutherland (1937) reinforced their beliefs with his work, *The Professional Thief*, by stating that an inclination to steal does not make a person a professional thief. A person must be tutored by professionals in the field as well as accepted by those who are already professional thieves.

According to Cloward and Ohlin (1960), motivation and desire to succeed do not solely explain behavior. Instead, persons must be in **learning environments** that allow a person to learn and perform skills that are either conforming or deviant. However, they noted that just because legitimate opportunities are blocked does not mean that illegitimate opportunities are automatically available, and vice versa. In turn, the delinquent behaviors that boys who are deprived of legitimate opportunities participate in depend on options available in their communities. Boys from racial and ethnic minorities are most likely to be deprived of legitimate opportunities in regard to education and employment, especially those in lower income neighborhoods. The subculture they adopt is dependent on the social organization of the area where they live, and Cloward and Ohlin believe these subcultures can be divided into three categories.

A **criminal subculture** corresponds with Merton's innovation adaptation, as these are youth gangs organized to commit income-producing crimes. These gangs are located in lower-class ethnic neighborhoods and learn from the corresponding adult gangs how to commit fraud, theft, and extortion. These adults are generally successful and are role models for the juveniles.

The second delinquent subculture, the **conflict subculture**, is a label affiliated with violent, aggressive gangs. These groups earn respect and status by their abilities to physically fight. While also in socially disorganized neighborhoods, they have few illegitimate opportunities to replace legitimate opportunities that are missing. Adult role models and economic success opportunities are void from the lifestyle of these juveniles, and therefore they turn to violence as criminal expression.

Lastly, Cloward and Ohlin (1960) identified the **retreatist subculture** as the third and final type of juvenile delinquent subculture. These individuals focus on drug and alcohol use and have given up both legitimate and illegitimate goals and means, much like Merton's idea of retreatism. They did not categorize these individuals in a physical neighborhood, but instead termed them **double failures** as they do not do well academically or occupationally. Their only goals are to hustle for drugs and get high with fellow retreatist friends.

Agnew

Robert Agnew (1985; 1992) tackled strain theory from a micro-level perspective by examining the sources of strain. This theory is written at a social-psychological level, as it focuses on the social environment of an individual. He believed that crime is an adaptation or coping mechanism to stress, no matter the source. However, he identified three main types of strain that produce deviance.

The first category of strain, **failure to achieve positively valued goals**, can actually be broken down into three subcategories (Agnew, 1985; 1992). First, strain can be a **disjuncture between aspirations and expectations or actual achievements**. In other words, our society encourages individuals to pursue ideals of financial success and all the trappings of a middle-class status. A person may have an ideal goal (aspiration), such as becoming a doctor or lawyer and an expectation of high income and wealth that goes along with it. However, individuals (often in the lower class) are sometimes unable to reach a lofty goal due to lack of opportunity. Strain can also involve the **disjuncture between expectation and reality**. For instance, many physicians often struggle financially for years after graduation from medical school due to student loans, when their expectation was instant wealth and success.

Lastly, failure to achieve positively valued goals can include the **disjuncture between fair outcomes and actual outcomes** (Agnew, 1985; 1992). In other words, a person may feel as if the reward received is not comparable to the actual effort put forth. For example, a person may not be paid enough for a labor-intensive project and become frustrated with the unfair nature of the compensation. If individuals are in a situation of inequality between what is perceived to be a fair outcome and the actual outcome, they may choose a delinquent path. They may commit criminal behavior to increase outcomes (i.e., earn money in other ways), lower their efforts (e.g., skip school or work), devalue the outcome of others (via theft or graffiti), or increase the work performed by others (i.e., behave in an inappropriate way).

Agnew's (1985; 1992) second identified source of strain is **removal of positively valued stimuli**. These strains typically involve the loss of someone or something of great worth. For adults, this might be a valued job or a spouse. Juveniles may experience this type of strain due to lack of a girlfriend or boyfriend, suspension from an athletic team, or relocation. Finally, **confrontation with negative/noxious stimuli** is the last source of strain identified by Agnew. Noxious stimuli can include abuse by a significant other or parent or bullying at school. Essentially, these are negative actions performed by others.

Agnew asserted that deviant or criminal behavior is not a direct result of strain but an individual's management of emotions that are caused by strain. If legitimate coping skills are used, a person may choose other outlets to deal with the strain. Further, Agnew does not limit strain to **objective strain** (universal stressors) and **subjective strain** (stressful to a particular person). Strain can also be **vicarious strain**, which is witnessing another person's experiences with strain, or **anticipated strain**, which is an assessment of future stress.

Agnew (1985; 1992) also discussed the adaptations that individuals can perform as a result of strain. Individuals can create **cognitive coping strategies**, or methods of dealing with the strain, by minimizing the stress associated with it. For example, when a strain is encountered, a person can cope by thinking, "It's not that bad," or "It's not that important." Cognitive coping strategies can involve maximizing the positive of a situation, minimizing the negative of a situation, and/or accepting one's responsibility for the situation. **Behavioral coping strategies**, the second adaptation method, involve two different methods. First, maximizing positive outcomes and minimizing negative outcomes can be performed legitimately or illegitimately. For example, if a person does not like her job, she can either find another job (legitimate) or skip work without notice (illegitimate). Behavioral coping strategies can also involve vengeful behavior or taking revenge on a person or entity. Lastly, Agnew (1985; 1992) described **emotional coping strategies**, which can also be legitimate or illegitimate. For instance, a person can meditate or seek counseling (legitimate) or take illicit drugs or drink alcohol excessively (illegitimate).

Messner and Rosenfeld

The last derivation of strain theory, specifically feeding from Merton's concepts of strain, are Messner and Rosenfeld's (1994; 2007) institutional-anomie theory. Specifically, they discussed their definition of "The American Dream," which is conducive to criminal behavior in four ways based on its achievement. First, **achievement orientation** places emphasis on valuing individuals based on what they possess or achieve. Without reaching a certain standard of achievement, individuals are viewed as not contributing positively to society. Second, **individualism** creates competitiveness between individuals to succeed rather than to work together. **Universalism** develops the expectation that all members of society are striving for the same goals. Lastly, **fetishism of money** attributes stockpiling money as the end all of success, even above possessions or power resulting from the money.

Essentially, Messner and Rosenfeld (1994; 2007) asserted that the constant strive for "The American Dream" is supported by various institutions, with the economic institution being the most important. Together with the political, familial, and educational institutions, the dominating economic institution plays a vital role in the **institutional balance of power**. First, non-economic institutions are not valued as much as the economic powers, giving precedence to the almighty dollar. Second, non-economic institutions function at the whim of the economic institutions. Schools base their curriculum on economic demands, and governments often operate according to corporate interest. Lastly, economic expectations of normalcy infiltrate non-economic institutions. Corporate models of operation are pressed to families and schools as the acceptable way to function.

Messner and Rosenfeld (2007) stated these powerful economic institutions weaken the positive social control of the other institutions. Educational institutions press the need for careers that guarantee financial success. Economic institutions also endorse financial success but do not promote the use of solely legitimate methods to obtain money. In other words, businesses and corporate entities press the importance of having money but do not instruct that it has to be made through non-criminal activities. When the credibility of the family and educational institutions that place importance on legitimate methods of earning financial success are devalued, their ability to exert social control is diminished. Large schools that are unable to properly supervise students or parents who do not provide consistent discipline are unable to direct youth toward socially approved goals in a positive way (Messner & Rosenfeld, 2007).

The theorists go on to state that institution imbalance is an international issue and not just one in the United States. Societies that are economically dominant produce crimes that focus on material gain. Political dominance creates cynicism against the moral majority and produces corruption. Further, societies controlled by extreme religious beliefs may develop vigilantism and hate crimes (Messner & Rosenfeld, 2001). After studying 45 nations, they asserted that if a society can teach its members to be more independent and less reliant on the economy, the crime rate will decrease (Messner & Rosenfeld, 1997).

Empirical Research

In empirical studies, strain theories stress the performance of crime and delinquency among lower class and minority populations as they are the most deprived of legitimate opportunities. Older studies have examined criminality of these groups as applied to different strain theorists' propositions. For example, testing the assertions of Cohen and Cloward and Ohlin, Short, and Strodtbeck (1965) found that lower class, minority gang members perceive less legitimate opportunities compared to middle class, white individuals who are not a member of a gang. Elliott and Voss (1974) found some support specifically for Cohen's (1955) version of strain by determining that individuals who drop out of school due to strain are less likely to commit delinquent acts as the stress is not removed. However, Thornberry, Morre, and Christenson (1985) found the exact opposite for high school dropouts.

There have also been a multitude of studies that have demonstrated that strain in an adolescent's life is related to a high risk of delinquency (Brezina, 1996; Broidy, 2001; Drapela, 2006; Hay & Evans, 2006; Mazerolle, Burton, Cullen, Evans, & Payne, 2000). Other theories have tested moderating factors, such as self-esteem, with strain and found mixed results. For instance, Hoffman and Miller (1998) found that high self-esteem and delinquency were related, while Agnew (2002) found the opposite. Broidy (2001) collected data from college students and found that experiencing unfair outcomes increases anger, but experiencing blocked goals decreases anger in this population.

More recent empirical studies of the theory have focused on the assertions of general strain theory (GST). Agnew's (2002) concepts of experienced, vicarious, and anticipated strains have been tested at length to explain delinquency. Agnew found independent effects of experienced and vicarious victimization on participation in serious delinquency. In his study, only one measure of anticipated strain was found to have an impact on delinquency: anticipation of being murdered before age 25. Baron (2009) also studied the effect of these types of strains on violent offending by youth and found that all three types were predictors of this category of offending for homeless youth.

Other recent studies have found support for Agnew's work to a variety of forms of criminal behavior. Chen (2010) explored the effect of autonomy on adolescent deviant behavior (e.g., truancy, alcohol and tobacco use, and sexual activity) by performing a longitudinal study of male students in middle to late adolescence. He found that the desire for autonomy had a direct effect on delinquency in school but not outside of school. Further, the indirect effect of the desire for autonomy impacted delinquency through the impact of anger (supporting GST). Related studies looking at the impact of anger and depression on minority racial and ethnic groups have also found a direct relationship on these emotions and delinquency (Kam, Cleveland, & Hecht, 2010; Simons, Chen, Stewart, & Brody, 2003).

GST has been tested and supported in multiple contemporary studies examining not only offending but also victimization. Multiple studies have asserted that negative emotions (feelings of anger, frustration, and sadness) from criminal victimization do increase delinquency (Jang, 2007; Moon et al., 2009; Piquero & Sealock, 2000). However, Hay and Evans (2006) found that anger is more likely to mediate delinquency compared to depression, and those who experience anger from violent victimization are more likely to use drugs and participate in general delinquency. Zavala and Spohn (2013) examined a sample of high school males and found that both vicarious and anticipated strain increased the likelihood of victimization by violent crime. Not surprisingly, past criminal behavior was also a predictor of victimization. Fifty percent of the sample who reported victimization were also offenders, and 54 percent of male youth who reported offending behaviors were also victims of violent crime.

Critics of GST have argued that despite its extensive support, it is unable to explain all aspects of criminality. For instance, it does not provide explanation of middle-class delinquency or why only some strained individuals commit crime. However, most damaging is the limited support of studies focusing on the disjuncture between aspirations and expectations. As a result, current revisions of the theory have investigated youth criminality as a result of not only social class strain, but also looking at attractiveness and athleticism.

There are few studies testing Messner and Rosenfeld's (2001) institutional anomie theory and most are indirect tests of the theory (Kubrin, Stucky & Krohn, 2009). Chamlin and Cochran (1995) found that while poverty potentially affected state rates of property crime, they were also dependent on other measures such as divorce rates and church membership. However, the study did not include any cross-national comparisons, which is a limitation in the testing of this theory (Maume & Lee, 2003; Schoepfer & Piquero, 2006). Bjerregaard and Cochran (2008) found that measures of economic dominance did not have an effect on homicide in 49 nations; however, there was no direct comparison of American society to these other nations.

The main critique of strain theory as a whole is that the link between strain and illegal behaviors is flawed. Strain theorists do not explain why some people get angry with stressful events while others accept it or emotionally withdrawal. Further, there is a question of the origin of aggression: Is it a result of strain or is it present before the stressful event occurs? Krahe (2001) stated that aggression is a stable trait that occurs early in life. Felson (1992) argued that frustration caused by strain did not cause aggression and delinquency, but anger did.

Policy Implications

Policies and programs developed from strain theory focus on changing society to reduce causes of strain rather than making changes in the processes of the criminal justice system. In other words, these changes intervene in social structure and the pressures it presents. In regard to policy implications based on Merton's (1938) strain theory, focus is placed on providing legitimate opportunities to obtain socially desirable goals. This is especially important for individuals who are not given these tools early in life. Interventions that are preventative provide children with tools to be better prepared for school. For example, preschool and head start programs are designed for children who have caregivers with low educational backgrounds and opportunities. These programs are designed to not only to educate children on basic academic skills but also to provide parents and children with positive techniques to deal with stress, social anxieties, and discipline (Webster-Stratton, Reid, & Hammond, 2001).

Programs utilizing both Merton's (1938) and Agnew's (1992) assertions regarding the effect of strain focused on adaptation of coping skills to deal with personal issues. In other words, these programs are designed to affect a person on the individual level and give them positive coping skills to deal with stress rather than act out inappropriately. For example, groups like Narcotics Anonymous (NA) and Alcoholics Anonymous (AA) provide individuals with legitimate coping mechanisms to prevent them from resorting to alcohol or drug abuse. While alcohol abuse is not illegal, a large portion of offenders are under the influence of alcohol and/or drugs at the time of arrest.

Crime control techniques based on strain theory would ideally be nonpunitive (Einstadter & Henry, 2006). Rather than punishing individuals with the most amount of strain and least amount of legitimate opportunities to pursue, these strategies should provide legitimate opportunities for individuals. The Mid-City Project in Boston was developed specifically on Miller's (1958) lower class culture theory. In order to combat delinquency among gangs in the city, the project proposed provided social work services to families, community neighborhood programs, and detached worker programs with juvenile gangs. Unfortunately, only the detached worker program was instituted and the project failed over a conflict of goals and ideologies (Akers & Sellers, 2013).

During the 1960s, several programs were designed based on Cloward and Ohlin's (1960) subcultural strain theory as well as addressing a decline in the community. Job Corps or AmeriCorps offered job training and placement services for individuals in low income neighborhoods. Mobilization of Youth targeted adolescents in impoverished neighbors in New York City by providing educational services and legitimate extracurricular activities. This was particularly aimed at adolescents in gangs to provide them with alternative avenues compared to gang life (Einstadter & Henry, 2006). Much like the Mid-City Project, detached workers were also hired to interact with gang members on the street. Mobilization of Youth also faced political oppression and protesting from community agencies. While it ultimately failed, this program did provide a prototype for future anti-poverty programs such as Job Corps (Bynum & Thompson, 1992).

Cognitive behavioral therapies (CBTs) are likely the most promising programs developed from strain theory. These programs, generally targeted at adolescents, teach social skills, reduce hostile reactions to stressful situations, and demonstrate how to better interact with others. Essentially, they are forms of aggression-reduction and problem-solving therapy. Evaluations have provided support for the use of these programs, stating they were most effective with older children and adolescents (Hollon & Beck, 2003; McCart, Priester, Davies, & Azen, 2006).

CASE STUDY 5.2
STARR

STARR, or Staff Training Aimed at Reducing Rearrest, is a cognitive behavioral therapy program aimed at reducing recidivism rates for offenders on federal probation. Federal probation officers are taught how to instruct their offenders, or clients, on how to learn and utilize different ways to handle stressful situations. In other words, skills are implemented to "rewire the brain" and teach them new, positive methods for managing their lives. The fundamentals of STARR include the Risk-Need-Responsivity model, cognitive-behavioral strategies to improve offender decision making, motivational interviewing, and relationship characteristics such as empathy, autonomy, and collaboration that have been identified as important in working with involuntary offenders. While the program is fairly new, preliminary evaluations of the program in a southeastern state have indicated positive results for offenders.

 Summary

Anomie/strain theories assert that the struggle between an individual's quest for success and obtaining these achievements in legitimate ways is the root of criminality. Further, the inability to conform causes stress, which results in acting out via criminal behaviors. Since the origination of strain in 1938, we have seen multiple derivations of the theory. Merton focused on the effect of anomie on the lower class and their lack of access to legitimate opportunities, indicating the importance of providing these people with better education and job training to pursue legitimate means. Cohen, as well as Cloward and Ohlin, adapted this theory to specifically apply it to the experiences of delinquent gangs. Often gang members are raised in areas where there is an expectation for membership, and other opportunities are not available or even considered an option.

Messner and Rosenfeld explored the effect of the economy and the American institution on monetary success and an imbalance of power in social structure. Their contribution to strain theory did not necessarily solely target the lower income group, but instead demonstrated the power of the economic groups as a method of social control. Further, these financially-driven groups are able to diminish the influence of other positive confederations, such as family and education, supporting the notion that money may be the root of all evil.

Of all the adaptations of Merton's theory, Agnew's general strain theory has most likely received the most formal and informal support. Agnew described strain as a result of several sources that affect our emotions, which in turn affect our criminality. Crime prevention strategies based on this theory target low socioeconomic groups and attempt to provide them with alternative outlets for positive coping and skills to obtain legitimate opportunities for gaining personal success.

Despite the specific assertions of the theorist, there is a resounding push by strain academics to recognize the influence of the desire for success on criminality. Individuals may choose a life of crime simply because they see no other option to obtain financial stability as they have no college degree or job skills. Others may commit criminal acts due to the pressure they experience to succeed—so more or less acting out as a result of stress. This theory, while at times contested, has provided a new perspective of explanation for criminal behavior and has promoted the creation of some moderately successful prevention programs.

Discussion Questions

1. Consider a situation in which you reacted to a strain in your life. Did you act legitimately or illegitimately, and why?
2. Which theorist best explains criminal behavior based on strain, and why?
3. Strain theorists argue that lack of opportunity is often a reason for strain. What types of programs could help alleviate the strain for adolescents who want to attend college but do not have the financial support?

REFERENCES

Agnew, R. (1985). A revised strain theory of delinquency. *Social Forces, 64*, 151-167.

Agnew, Robert. (1992). Foundation for a general strain theory of crime and delinquency. *Criminology. 30*(1), 47-87.

Agnew, R. (2002). Experienced, vicarious, and anticipated strain: An exploratory study on physical victimization and delinquency. *Justice Quarterly, 19*, 603-633.

Baron, S.W. (2009). Street youths' violent responses to violent personal, vicarious, and anticipated strain. *Journal of Criminal Justice, 37*, 442-451.

Bjerregaard, B., & Cochran, J. K. (2008). A cross-national test of institutional anomie theory: do the strength of other social institutions mediate or moderate the effects of the economy on the rate of crime? *Western Criminology Review, 9*(1), 31-48.

Brezina, T. (1996). Adapting to strain: An examination of delinquent coping responses. *Criminology, 34*, 39-60.

Broidy, L. (2001). A test of general strain theory. *Criminology, 39*, 9-35.

Bynum, J. & Thompson, W. (1992). *Juvenile delinquency: A sociological approach.* Boston, MA: Allyn & Bacon.

Chamlin, M.B. & Cochran, J.K. (1995). Assessing Messner and Rosenfeld's institutional anomie theory: A partial test. *Criminology, 33*, 411-429.

Chen, X. (2010). Desire for autonomy and adolescent delinquency: A latent growth curve analysis. *Criminal Justice and Behavior, 37*, 989-1004.

Cloward, R., & Ohlin, L. (1960). *Delinquency and opportunity.* New York: Free Press.

Cohen, A. (1955). *Delinquent boys: The culture of the gang.* Illinois: Free Press.

Drapela, L. (2006). The effect of negative emotion on licit and illicit drug use among high school dropouts: An empirical test of general strain theory. *Journal of Youth and Adolescence, 35*, 755-770.

Durkheim, E. (1893). *The division of labor in society*, (pp. 1-262). Beverly Hills: Sage Publications.

Einstadter, W. J., & Henry, S. (2006). *Criminological theory: An analysis of its underlying assumptions.* Boulder, CO: Rowman and Littlefield.

Elliott, D. & Voss, H. (1974). *Delinquency and dropout.* Lexington, MA: Lexington.

Felson, R. (1992). "Kick'em when they're down": Explanations of the relationship between stress and interpersonal aggression and violence. *The Sociological Quarterly, 33*, 1-16.

Hay, C., & Evans, M. M. (2006). Violent victimization and involvement in delinquency: Examining predictions from general strain theory. *Journal of Criminal Justice, 34*, 261–274.

Hoffman, J. & Miller, A. (1998) A latent variable analysis of general strain theory. *Journal of Quantitative Criminology, 14*, 83-110.

Jang, S. (2007). Gender differences in strain, negative emotions, and coping behaviors: A general strain theory approach. *Justice Quarterly, 24*, 523-553.

Kam, J., Cleveland, M., & Hecht, M. (2010). Applying general strain theory to examine perceived discrimination's indirect relation to Mexican-heritage youth's alcohol, cigarette, and marijuana use. *Prevention Science, 11*, 397-410.

Krahe, B. (2001). *The social psychology of aggression.* New York: Psychology Press.

Kubrin, C., Stucky, T., & Krohn, M. (2009). *Researching theories of crime and deviance.* New York: Oxford University Press.

Maume, M.O. and Matthew, R. L. 2003. Social institutions and violence: A sub-national test of institutional anomie theory. *Criminology. 41*, 1137-1172.

Mazerolle, P., Burton, V., Cullen, F., Evans, T., & Payne, G. (2000). Strain, anger, and delinquent adaptations specifying general strain theory. *Journal of Criminal Justice, 28*, 89-101.

Merton, R. K. (1938). Social structure and anomie. *American Sociological Review, 3*(5), 672-682.

Messner, S., & Rosenfeld, R. (1994). *Crime and the American dream.* Belmont: Wadsworth.

Messner, S. & Rosenfeld, R. (1997). Political restraint of the market and levels of criminal homicide: A cross-national application of institutional anomie theory. *Social Forces 75*, 1393-1416.

Messner, S., & Rosenfeld, R. (2007). *Crime and the American dream.* (4th ed.). Belmont: Wadsworth.

Miller, W. (1958). Lower-class culture as a generating milieu of gang delinquency. *Journal of Social Issues, 14,* 5-19.

Olsen, M. (1965). Durkheim's two concepts of anomie. *The Sociological Quarterly, 6*(1), 37-44.

Piquero, N.L., & Sealock, M.D. (2000). Generalizing general strain theory: An examination of an offending population. *Justice Quarterly, 17,* 449-484.

Schoepfer, A. & Piquero, N.L. (2006). Exploring white-collar crime and the American dream: a test of institutional anomie theory. *Journal of Criminal Justice, 34*(3), 227-235.

Short, J., & Strodtbeck, F. (1964). *Group process and gang delinquency.* Chicago, IL: University of Chicago Press.

Simons, R., Chen, Y., Stewart, E., & Brody, G. (2003). Incidents of discrimination and risk for delinquency: A longitudinal test of strain theory with an African American sample. *Justice Quarterly, 20,* 827-854.

Thornberry, T., Moore, M., & Christenson, R. (1985). The effect of dropping out of high school on subsequent criminal behavior. *Criminology, 23,* 3-18.

Webster-Stratton, C., Reid, M. J., & Hammond, M. (2001). Social skills and problem solving training for children with early-onset conduct problems: Who benefits? *Journal of Child Psychology and Psychiatry, 42*(7), 943-952.

Zavala, E. & Ryan S. (2013). The role of vicarious and anticipated strain on the overlap of violent perpetration and victimization: A test of general strain theory. *American Journal of Criminal Justice. 38,* 119-140.

Social Learning Theory

CHAPTER OUTLINE

Introduction

History of Social Learning Theory

Progression of Social Learning Theory
Pavlov
Skinner
Bandura
Wilson and Herrnstein

Contemporary Social Learning Theory
Sutherland

Burgess and Akers
Akers
Case Study 6.1: Tech Boyz Heist

Policy Implications

Summary

Discussion Questions

References

Key Words and Concepts

Blank Slate
Classical Conditioning
Culture Conflict
Definitions
Differential Associations
Differential
   Reinforcement

Differential Social
   Organization
Imitation
Interaction
Laws of Imitation
Macro-Level
Meso-Level

Negative Reinforcement
Operant Conditioning
Positive Reinforcement
Process
Reinforcement
Role Models
Symbolic Interactionist

Introduction

This chapter explores differential association and social learning theories of criminal behavior. Specifically, these theories emphasize the importance of family, school, peers, and longer-term processes that people use to develop, learn, and integrate social norms into their behavioral choices. This chapter focuses on differential association (Sutherland, 1942), social learning theory (Burgess & Akers, 1966; Akers, 1985, 1998), and social network theory. Because of the potential process that takes place in these interactions, the term "social learning theory" will be used as the larger umbrella for this group of theories.

In criminology, social learning theory focuses on process. The process of concern is that of learning to become criminal or delinquent through socialization. Within social learning theory, the socialization process emphasizes observation, learning, and execution of criminal or delinquent behavioral choices. Two key groups of actors in this theoretical perspective are family and peers; that is, this theory addresses the role family and peers play in criminal and delinquent behavior. Social learning theorists focus on modeling behavior and how interactions among family and peers influence behavioral choices. The numbers of potential social interactions are vast, so social learning theory's explanation of how people learn the values, attitudes, techniques, rationalizations, neutralizations, and motives for criminal and delinquent behavior is why it remains one of the most studied crime theories in criminology.

By the end of this chapter, you should be able to do four things. First, you should be able to understand the history and assumptions of differential association-social learning theory perspectives. Second, you should be able to articulate the problem focus and scope of differential association-social learning theory. Third, you should be able to understand the propositions among the different parts of social learning theory. Fourth, you should be able to explain the practical implications of differential association-social learning theory.

History of Social Learning Theory

Historically, differential association-social learning theories use the ideas of socialization and delinquent peers as pivotal forces for offending. These theories soundly integrate sociological and psychological concepts to explain offending. In addition, the theories address the question: Why do people commit crime? In these explanations, the environment is important in learning offending patterns. Essentially, the macro-environment (i.e., where an individual lives and goes to school) and the micro-environment (i.e., parents or peers) are primary foci for learning offending.

To that end, one of the most consistent findings in criminology is that delinquent peer association has a link with offending (Warr, 2002). This theoretical premise can be traced to Gabriel Tarde's (1902) **laws of imitation**. Sutherland expanded these laws, and Akers expands on Sutherland's views by adding psychological concepts. The basis of these theories is heavily influenced from the Chicago School of Sociology.

While the theories appear to build off one another, they have historical roots in the symbolic-interactionist perspective (Lilly, Cullen, & Ball, 2002). The **symbolic interactionist** perspective suggests that individuals use the way others treat them as the basis for their views of themselves. In other words, interacting with others plays a substantial role in how individuals will interpret the communication (verbal or non-verbal) about themselves. The interpretation process allows the individual to put real or imagined meaning to the communication that may shape their attitudes about themselves or others. These attitudes will have import in shaping their behavior.

Symbolic-interactionism, as well as differential association, is a product of the Chicago School. The Chicago School was the first sociology department that was founded at the University of Chicago in 1892. The Chicago School was home to a number of vigilant researchers that worked to develop and support their theories using quantitative and qualitative data. Many at the Chicago School referred to cities as laboratories for understanding human behavior (Williams & McShane, 2010).

From its inception until the 1950s, the Chicago School remained a force in the development of theory and understanding groups in multiple fields that include criminology. For example, Shaw and McKay (1942) completed their influential work on social disorganization at the Chicago School. During this time, researchers at the Chicago School showed that historical changes in society had profound effects on individuals' attitudes about criminals. For instance, the change in immigration into Chicago was influential in how Chicagoans felt about criminals.

Delving into this issue, the researchers at the Chicago School were able to develop a number of themes. One central theme was that the environment of the city served as a force of "culture shock." The city environment was vastly different than many immigrants' "homeland" environments, making their previous experiences nearly irrelevant. This put a substantial strain on relationships and attitudes, forcing immigrants to restructure their lives and attitudes to fit the new environment. In other words, immigrants had to review previously held norms, either consciously or unconsciously, so that they may be abandoned or restructured. According to Shaw and McKay (1942), this left some neighborhoods more prone to offending than others. In the neighborhoods that were more prone to offending, criminal values and attitudes were transmitted from generation to generation in a process known as cultural transmission.

Sellin's (1938) version of **culture conflict** theory came from the Chicago School. Briefly, Sellin (1938) argued that two forms of conflict—primary and secondary—were present in neighborhoods. Primary conflict refers to when an immigrant's culture is in conflict with society as a whole. An immigrant's religious culture may differ from the dominant culture. For instance, some may view sacrificing animals as religiously acceptable, but the wider religious community does not view these types of sacrifices as being acceptable.

Secondary conflict refers to the development of a subculture. A subculture is a group that has completely different values that differ from society as a whole. The point is that members of the Chicago School were interested in how immigration influenced all parts of life (e.g., work, religion, family, school, neighborhoods, and crime). The stimulus for these interests came from what the researchers were finding in neighborhoods in Chicago. These findings also led to research on individual level social patterns and eventually learning of behavior.

Progression of Social Learning Theory

Before moving into the different criminological versions of social learning theory, a review of some of the tenets of psychological learning theories is instructive. For many of these theorists, the assumption was made that individuals were passive consumers of past experiences and associations. Within these theories, it was also assumed that individuals would make decisions based on their interpretations of past and present experiences.

Pavlov

The passive nature of learning theory was influenced by Pavlov and Skinner. Their view suggested that individuals would make decisions and continue to make the same decisions based on whether they would receive a reward. Pavlov (1967) argued that behavior would continue when it was rewarded. This was known as **classical conditioning**. Pavlov (1967) continued by suggesting that some stimuli would initiate behavior. After a series of opportunities, Pavlov's sample of dogs would consistently salivate when meat was present. This process created a passive learning experience because the dog knew what to expect from the environment.

Skinner

Skinner (1953) provided a theory that had a slight change in activity level. **Operant conditioning** provided that behavior could be controlled through manipulation. Skinner (1953) proposed that this was more active because the individual knew how to manipulate the environment to get what he or she wanted rather than waiting passively. A key issue in operant conditioning was reinforcement. Reinforcement referred to activities that would increase the tendency to behave in a certain manner. **Reinforcement** occurred in two ways: positive or negative. **Positive reinforcement** was the presentation of a reward for an expected behavior. **Negative reinforcement** was the removal or avoidance of an unpleasant experience of a behavior. In the context of crime, a reward or positive reinforcement may be given when the crime is committed (e.g., status or money). Taking drugs to avoid low self-esteem is an example of negative reinforcement.

Bandura

Other versions of learning theory are present in the psychological literature. Bandura (1969, 1973, 1977) presented a version of learning theory that was more complex than Skinner or Pavlov's. Bandura suggested that learning was more involved than mere conditioning. He suggested that learning involved a process of observation and an analysis of situations before a decision to act was made. Using the process of observation brought a social sense to the theory. This was lamented in the theory by Bandura's views that individuals learned using **role models**. The role models performed a behavior, and others would observe this behavior and make a decision to perform the behavior; the motivating factor was not reinforcement. Another way of thinking about this process was that observation and experience would interact to form imitation and instigation of behavior that included criminal behavior.

Wilson and Herrnstein

Others have suggested that learning was even more complex than Bandura's theory proffered. Wilson and Herrnstein (1985) integrated a number of perspectives in an attempt to develop an understanding of learning behavior. They used research from biology, psychology, and other social learning theories to clarify learning criminal behavior. Wilson and Herrnstein (1985) argued that biological and behavioral explanations had been neglected in the study of crime. Their review of the literature showed that criminal behavior was committed by males, young people, and mesomorphs with certain personality traits (e.g., aggressive, impulsive, and cruel). They went on to make a number of assertions about intelligence. Wilson and Herrnstein (1985) argued that African Americans had lower IQ scores than Caucasians, and they argued that those with lower IQ scores committed more crime. Their book generated a large amount of controversy.

From the criminological perspective, learning theories make a number of assumptions as well. For instance, differential association-social learning theorists make a number of assumptions. An essential assumption is that humans are a **blank slate**. This means that individuals have to be taught everything, including attitudes, behaviors, rationalizations, motives, and decision making. In essence, humans are a product of their interactions with others and their learning histories.

Differential association-social learning theorists also assume that humans are able to learn offending behavior. Offending is, simply, a piece of the learning history that a human ascertains through the **interaction** with others that are criminals. It is important to note that these theorists also say that humans interacting with non-criminals are able to avoid offending and obey laws.

Differential association-social learning theorists also assume that offending is positive and determined; that is, these theorists assume that humans are able to make a distinction between acts that are criminal and those that are non-criminal. This process is done by associating with others. Through association, the human is able to elicit information about attitudes and behavior to determine criminal or non-criminal behavior. In addition, the theorists make an assumption that offending is determined. To clarify, the theorists cogently assumed and argued that offending behavior was determined beyond the human's control. This type of determinism is different from psychology and biology because the focus is on social factors (e.g., family, peers, friends, and relatives).

From the assumptions above, differential association-social learning theories are often thought of as social process theories. Social process theories place an emphasis on the general acceptance of right and wrong, but they do not require a complete consensus of right and wrong. This allows the theorists to acknowledge that multiple systems of competing values and norms exist (Williams & McShane, 2010). Certain laws are disputable. For example, some drug laws, at the time of writing, are in flux. In Colorado, medical marijuana is legal, but it remains illegal in many other states.

Finally, these theorists assume that humans are rational. The theorists make the assumption that humans are able to weigh the potential pleasure of an action against the potential pain of an action. When the potential pleasure of an action outweighs the potential pain of an action, the individual is likely to perform the action. The general acceptance of right and wrong provides valuable information in this decision-making process, but the theorists proffer the final choice may be under the influence of the interactions with others. With an explanation of the key assumptions of differential association-social learning theory, the focus now turns to the central question, scope, and level of explanation.

 # Contemporary Social Learning Theory

Differential association-social learning theory is designed to answer a specific question, through various types of scopes and levels of explanation. The question is: Why do people commit crime? This question is not simple to address. The theorists have put a large amount of thought into acquisition of criminal knowledge. For any of these types of theories, in the context of offending, the acquisition comes from the interaction with others that are currently criminal or offenders.

Differential association-social learning theories are designed to provide explanations of behavior at multiple scope levels. The theories are able to provide explanations that come from a single offense or offending in general. For instance, the theories may be able to explain crime or they may be able to explain assault. The choice of scope levels comes from the explanation interest.

These theories are able to explain offending at different levels. The theories are able to accommodate interests that are at the micro- and meso-levels. For instance, differential association is able to explain offending of individuals, and its primary use has been at this level. Akers's (1998) version of social structure social learning theory provides an explanation of offending at the **meso-level**. The meso-level, in this book, refers to an explanation of behavior that occurs at the macro- and micro-levels. With this understood, we are now able to shift to the three major theories that make up this area.

Sutherland

The earliest contribution to criminological versions of social learning theory came from Edwin Sutherland. Sutherland (1939, 1947) argued that criminal behavior should be understood as a process. The process that takes place is either occurring in the moment (i.e., situational) or is coming from the history of the individual (i.e., objective). He did not value one of these understandings of **process** more than the other; rather he saw them as both being desirable. Sutherland (1939, 1947) viewed the situational process as being attractive to physical and biological scientists. He also considered those that worked in this area as having a complicated task because the situation-person interaction was very complex and difficult to grasp.

The objective form of criminal behavior was important because it created an environment that allowed criminal behavior to occur. For instance, an individual may steal from a store when no one is around, but the same individual may not steal from a store when someone else is present. One way to view this is that the situation is not exclusive of the individual. To clarify, the importance of the situation is defined by the individual that is involved. That is, the variation of a "crime-committing" situation cannot be divorced from prior life experiences of the criminal. This means that the individual sees a situation as defined by inclinations, abilities, and skills that have been acquired. For Sutherland (1939, 1947), this type of explanation was largely historical. To arrive at the historical explanation of criminal behavior, Sutherland (1939, 1947) provided the nine following propositions of differential association theory as his view of the crime committing process:

1. *Criminal behavior is learned.* The initial perspective is that criminal behavior is not inherited. This also means that the person has to be trained in criminal behavior. Sutherland (1939, 1947) argued that the individual that is not already trained in crime does not invent criminal behavior, just as the individual that has not had training in mechanical engineering does not make mechanical inventions.

2. *Criminal behavior is learned in interaction with other persons in a process of communications.* For Sutherland (1939, 1947), communication was largely verbal, but he did not discount the view that communication occurred non-verbally through gestures.

3. *The principal part of the learning of criminal behavior occurs within intimate personal groups.* This means that individuals that are close in proximity to one another play an important role in communicating criminal behavior. Conversely, this means that communicative tools that are distant from an individual (e.g., movies or newspapers) are not an important part of the beginning criminal behavior.

4. *When criminal behavior is learned, the learning includes (a) techniques of committing the crime, which are sometimes very complicated, sometimes very simple; and (b) the specific direction of motives, drives, rationalizations, and attitudes.*

5. *The specific direction of motives and drives is learned from definitions of the legal codes as favorable and unfavorable.* In many societies, the individual is surrounded by others who argue that the rules should be followed, but in other societies the individual is surrounded by those that do not observe the rules. For Sutherland (1939, 1947), in American society, the definitions for criminal behavior are almost always mixed, creating an environment for culture conflict with respect to the legal codes.

6. *A person becomes criminal because of an excess of definitions favorable to violation of law over definitions unfavorable to violation of law.* For Sutherland, this was the key to differential association. This view places an emphasis on the criminal and non-criminal forces serving counteracting agents. To clarify, an individual becomes criminal when they are surrounded by criminal patterns and isolated from non-criminal patterns. In other words, the individual tends to assimilate to his or her environment until forces from another environment creates a conflict. An important perspective to note is that Sutherland (1939, 1947) gives more credence to forces that are criminal or non-criminal. Forces that promote neutrality are not important for swaying behavior criminally or non-criminally, but they serve as a mechanism for occupying time.

7. **Differential associations** *may vary in frequency, duration, priority, and intensity.* This means that the associations that create criminal behavior and non-criminal behavior vary. Frequency and duration are rather self-explanatory. Priority refers to lawful and unlawful behavior that begins in childhood and may persist throughout life. The issue with priority is that it is selective. Some behaviors from childhood are continued throughout life, but others are not. Intensity refers to the prestige of the associations or source of criminal or non-criminal behavior and emotional reactions related to these associations.

8. *The process of learning criminal behavior by association with criminal and anticriminal patterns involves all of the mechanisms that are involved in any other learning.* This suggests that learning criminal behavior is similar in process to other behaviors (e.g., reading). Further, this view takes the emphasis away from learning through imitation. In other words, criminal behavior is not learned through imitation but by association with others that are criminal.

9. *While criminal behavior is an expression of general needs and values, it is not explained by those general needs and values, since non-criminal behavior is an expression of the same needs and values.*

These propositions are not as self-explanatory as they may seem. Keeping with ideas around interaction, Sutherland cogently argued that the acquisition of criminal knowledge began with the idea of communicating with others. It is in this part of the learning nexus that the individual has a safe environment with willing teacher(s) (e.g., close friends, relatives, family, or peer acquaintances) to acquire the knowledge that is necessary for offending. In this environment and from these teachers, Sutherland claimed that an individual has to learn the physical techniques for an offense. For instance, an individual has to physically learn how to become a bully. The environment and the teachers do not just provide the physical know-how to perform offenses; they also provide the psychological ability to ease the conscious to perform the offenses. For instance, in the interaction, peers are able to persuade an individual to adjust his or her values or attitudes towards a behavior or the law. In other words, differential association is the amount of interaction that an individual has with others and the variance of these interactions. This is an emphasis that the amount of interaction is insufficient for offending behavior. The perception of importance and weight given to others (e.g., best male friend or best female friend) are the important facets of the theory. To complete the theory, Sutherland argued that learning to offend was like learning any other form of behavior. Importantly, Sutherland believed that his theory did have scope limits. He did not believe that his theory could explain all offending all of the time, but the theory was able to explain most offending behavior.

The development of differential association was pivotal to criminological theory. The development of this theory provided the foundation for a number of extensions to the theory. For instance, Sutherland argued that a **macro-level** version of the theory was possible. In his theory of **differential social organization**, Sutherland argued that areas of cities were able to provide fertile grounds for widespread differential associations to occur. He provided that high crime areas may be characterized by some group organization. This would account for why some areas had more crime than others. Social learning theory is a further development of Sutherland's theory.

Burgess and Akers

Akers's (1998) version of social learning theory was one of the most important advances in criminology. Akers and colleagues (1966, 1998) combined many concepts from previous theories and research and provided a number of testable propositions. Burgess and Akers's (1966) journal article gave birth to criminology's version of social learning. They named their theory differential social reinforcement theory, to pay homage to the fusion of differential association and reinforcement theory. Naming their theory this way also kept the confusion low between their theory and Bandura's (1969) theory. In later journal articles and books, Akers (1977, 1985) referred to the theory as social learning theory. He also clarified his positions and addressed criticisms of the theory.

Burgess and Akers (1966) worked to better develop a social learning theory. To do this, they asserted that Sutherland did not fully explain the social learning components for offending. Burgess and Akers (1966) explained the social learning mechanisms, and their explanation is a full reformulation of Sutherland's theory. The reformulation retained all of the propositions of differential association but combined and restated them in the context of operant conditioning. Akers (1977, 1985, 1998) provided additional information about the social learning concepts with empirical tests in the context of offending.

Akers's version of social learning theory did not compete with differential association theory. Akers (1985) argued that social learning theory subsumed differential association (i.e., retaining all of its original processes), but it was broader because differential reinforcement and imitation had been added. Adding these concepts to the theory provided additional mechanisms for behavior acquisition, continuation, and cessation. Because of this, Akers (1985, 1998) argued that positive empirical research results were positive for social learning theory. The caveat was that social learning theory provided a richer explanation of behavior.

Burgess and Akers's (1966) effort identified the social learning components necessary to better understand offending. They began by retaining the original ideas of differential association and definitions. This allowed Burgess and Akers (1966) to retain the focus on interaction and communication. The central propositions from Burgess and Akers (1966) were as follows:

1. Criminal behavior is learned according to the principles of operant conditioning.

2. Criminal behavior is learned both in non-social situations that are reinforcing or discriminative and through social interaction in which the behavior of other persons is reinforcing or discriminative for criminal behavior.

3. The principal part of learning criminal behavior occurs in those groups which comprise the individual's major source of reinforcements.

4. The learning of criminal behavior, including specific techniques, attitudes, and avoidance procedures, is a function of the effective and available reinforcers and existing reinforcement contingencies.

5. The specific class of behaviors that are learned and their frequency of occurrence are a function of the reinforcers, which are effective and available, and the rules or norms by which these reinforcers are applied.

6. Criminal behavior is a function of norms that are discriminative for criminal behavior, the learning of which takes place when such behavior is more highly reinforced than non-criminal behavior.

7. The strength of criminal behavior is a direct function of the amount, frequency, and probability of its reinforcement.

These propositions gave Burgess and Akers (1966) the foundation to make some clarifications in a behavioral context. In addition, they cogently added operant behavior to the theory. Adding this component allowed them to explain why some individuals continued their behavior (i.e., rewards) or ceased their behavior (i.e., punishment). Bringing this component to the theory allowed them to add other components, including respondent conditioning or reflex behavior; discriminative behavior or cues (i.e., internal or external) for behavior; and schedules for reinforcement, or the rate, ratio, or timing of rewards or punishments. These are not the only components added, but they are the primary ones.

Akers

In later developments, Akers (1998) argued that "learning" was not solely related to new behaviors. Social learning theory was developed in a way that would allow for explanations of new behaviors, but also the maintenance of previously learned behaviors. Another way of thinking about this was that social learning theory was able to explain the motives that either brought an individual to, or kept them away from, offending. Akers (1998) argued:

> The basic assumption of social learning theory is that the same learning process in a context of social structure, interaction, and situation, produces both conforming and deviant behavior. The difference lies in the direction . . . [of] balance of influences on behavior.
>
> The probability that persons will engage in criminal and deviant behavior is increased and the probability of their conforming to the norm is decreased when they differentially associate with others who commit criminal behavior and espouse

definitions favorable to it, are relatively more exposed in-person or symbolically to salient criminal/deviant models, define it as desirable or justified in a situation discriminative for the behavior, and have received in the past and anticipate in the current or future situation relatively greater reward than punishment for the behavior (Akers, 1998, p. 50).

Akers (1998) argued that the theory relies on four main concepts: differential association, definitions, differential reinforcement, and imitation.

Differential association is the interaction with others in a primary group who engage in and support certain types of behavior in direct association as well as with identifications toward secondary and more distant reference groups. While differential association theory primarily focuses on peer associations, the influences of other groups such as family members, neighbors, religious institutions, school teachers, the law, and authority figures also plays a role (Sellers & Akers, 2006). **Definitions** are the attitudes, values, orientations, rationalizations, definitions of situations, and other moral and evaluative attitudes that help an individual decide whether an act is right or wrong or appropriate or not (Akers, 2008). **Differential reinforcement** relates to the anticipation of rewards and punishments for specific acts based on past, present, and future occurrences. The majority of these rewards are social; however, the concept of differential reinforcement allows for the influence of both nonsocial physiological and physical stimuli (Akers, 2008). Finally, **imitation** is engaging in a behavior after observing similar behavior in others. In peer groups, this behavior can be both prosocial and deviant and occur during the initial acquisition and performance of novel behaviors as well as during the time established behaviors cease or are being maintained (Akers, 2008).

When just examining this version of social learning theory, researchers have provided support. The above concepts are the primary sets of variables that contribute to an individual's learning history. These factors influence an individual's reaction when the opportunity to commit a crime arises. Learned definitions, imitation of criminal or deviant models, and the anticipation of reinforcement produce an individual's initial deviant or criminal act. Facilitative factors of these variables occur in subsequent deviant acts. Social and non-social reinforcers and punishers affect how frequently (if at all) future criminal acts will occur. An individual's past learning history as well as specific, situational reinforcement contingencies dictate whether or not a person will commit a deviant act when the situation presents itself. It is important to note that past learning history produces habitual and behavioral tendencies that are relatively stable but can change over time as an individual's personal and social situations—and what they learn from these situations—change (Akers, 1998). This model of social learning is applicable cross culturally and in differing structural associations with crime (Akers & Jensen, 2003).

Social learning theory has been studied extensively for many decades (see Akers, 2008). In examining social learning theory alone, as well as in comparison with other theories, the majority of research has shown varying levels of support (Akers, 2008). Differences can occur depending on the social learning variable(s) studied, the type of deviance studied, how the variable(s) is measured, or by the type of sample, but overall the theory has largely been supported by empirical evidence (Akers, 2008).

This theoretical premise has substantial empirical support. Pratt, Cullen, Sellers, Winfree, Madensen, Daigle, Fearn, and Gau (2010) performed a meta-analysis of more than 100 studies of social learning theory. A meta-analysis is a study of studies to determine the size and magnitude of effects between variables. In this case, the difference is between the social learning variables and offending and substance use. Their results show that differential association and definitions have strong links with offending, and that differential reinforcement and imitation have moderate links with offending and substance use. Given Akers's (1999) comments that support for any one piece of social learning theory may be seen as support for the overall theory, the results that Pratt et al. (2010) presented may be seen as support for the social learning theory in its entirety.

In 1998, Akers presented an extension of the original social learning theory. The extension attempts to provide important insight into how the social structure of society has an influence on social learning and how this leads to criminal and deviant behavior. Akers (1998) is clear that four dimensions of social structure (i.e., differential social organization, differential location in the social structure, theoretically defined structural variables, and differential social location) are necessary to provide insight into this view from the macro- (structural) and meso- (individual) levels.

Differential social organization refers to the structural correlates of crime in the community or society (i.e., macro-level) (Akers 1998). These are structural correlates that would reflect parts of society, including but not limited to population density, age composition, and other measures that would be central to social structure. According to Akers (1998), differential location in the social structure suggests that demographic factors influence social learning (meso-level). In particular, demographic measures such as age, race, sex, and marital status will provide insight into social learning. Akers (1998) argued that theoretically defined structural variables, including anomie, social disorganization, or group conflict are just a few measures that can influence the social learning process (meso-level). Further, Akers (1998) suggested that differential social location is the individual's membership in and relationship to primary and secondary reference groups (meso-level).

Akers (1998) argued that these components placed an emphasis on the context in which learning takes place. For instance, differential social organization and differential location of a person provide a more immediate context for the learning process to take place and may increase or decrease the likelihood of crime. The more proximal issues rest with differential location. This occurs because the differential location is where an individual spends the majority of his or her time. Thus, the location of the individual provides the more immediate context that places limits on the exposure to other parts of the social learning process.

This version of Akers's (1998) theory has support in the empirical literature. Lanza-Kaduce, Capece, and Alden (2006) used data from college students to examine the central components of the theory examining the link with alcohol use, following the Akers's claim that the theory should substantially mediate the effect of social structure measures (e.g., belonging to a Greek organization) and alcohol use. Their results found support for this view. Whaley, Smith, and Hayes-Smith (2011) examined this theoretical premise using data from over 85,000 students in 202 school districts. Specifically, they examined whether social learning would substantially mediate the effect of gender, age, and class on substance use. Their results were supportive of Akers's (1998) contention that this is the case. Others (Capece & Lanza-Kaduce, 2013; Orcutt & Schwabe, 2012; Morris & Higgins, 2010; Schaefer, Vito, Marcum, Higgins, & Ricketts, 2014) found similar results that support the theory. The support does not mean that other hypotheses should not be tested, but that enough support is present to suggest the plausibility of the theory.

CASE STUDY 6.1
TECH BOYZ HEIST

Parents in North Carolina turned their teenagers over to police recently after they recognized them in burglary footage featured on the local evening news.

The teenage boys, ages 14 and 16, allegedly broke into Tech Boyz, a local electronics store, in Fayetteville on Dec. 29 around 3:30 a.m. along with three other people. The group took laptops and cell phones and damaged the store, officer Antoine Kincade told USA TODAY Network.

Explain the role of the parents in this situation.

 Policy Implications

Social learning theory has a number of policy implications that could reduce instances of crime. Key propositions of the theory are relevant for criminal justice policy. These propositions have been the foundation for rehabilitation, prevention, and behavior modification programs that take place in correctional institutions and therapeutic contexts (Akers & Jensen, 2006). Beyond these forms of programs, the empirical validity of the theory has served as a basis of evidence for a number of other programs. These programs include role modeling, peer norming, and pro-social skills development. These programs occur at the juvenile and adult levels. In essence, social learning theory provides an evidence-based foundation for rehabilitation. The key to rehabilitation is to modify an individual's "definitions" of law-abiding behavior through the environmental change of positive social networks.

Summary

As a whole, social learning theory outlines how individuals learn to commit crime. By assuming that individuals are rational and not any different than non-criminals, individuals are social blanks and learn everything. The learning takes place in a number of ways. Central to learning is an individual's associations, which includes peers and family. Within these associations, an individual learns criminal and non-criminal behavior. In some instances, the learning of these behaviors will continue when they are reinforced.

Discussion Questions

1. Explain the role of reinforcement in learning.
2. Discuss the role of Sutherland in the development of social learning theory in criminology.
3. Compare and contrast the role of peers and other institutions (e.g., schools or churches) in the context of differential association from Akers's (1998) perspective.

REFERENCES

Akers, R. L. (1977). *Deviant behavior: A social learning approach*. Belmont, CA: Wadsworth.
Akers, R. L. (1985). *Deviant behavior: A social learning approach*. Belmont, CA: Wadsworth.
Akers, R. L. (1998). *Social learning and social structure: A general theory of crime and deviance*. Boston, MA: Northeastern University Press.
Akers, R. L. (2008). Self-control, social learning, and positivistic theory of crime. In Erich Goode (Ed.), *Out of control: Assessing the general theory of crime* (pp. 1-55). Stanford, CA: Stanford University Press.

Akers, R. L., & Jensen, G. F. Eds. (2003). *Social learning theory and the explanation of crime: A guide for the new century*, v. 11. New Brunswick, NJ: Transaction Publishers.

Akers, R. L., & Jensen, G. F. (2006). The empirical status of social learning of crime and deviance: The past, present, and future. In F. T. Cullen, J. P. Wright, & K. R. Blevins (Eds.), *Taking stock: The status of criminological theory, advances in criminological theory*, v. 15, 37-76. New Brunswick, NJ: Transaction.

Bandura, A. (1969). *Principles of behavior modification*. New York, NY: Holt, Reinhart, & Winston.

Burgess, R. L., & Akers, R. L. (1966). A differential association-reinforcement theory of criminal behavior. *Social Problems, 14*, 128-147.

Capece, M., & Lanza-Kaduce, L. (2013). Binge drinking among college students: A partial test of Akers' social structure-social learning theory. *American Journal of Criminal Justice, 38*, 503-519.

Lanza-Kaduce, L., Capece, M., & Alden H. (2006). Liquor is quicker. *Criminal Justice Policy Review, 17*, 127-143.

Lilly, R. J., Cullen, F. T., & Ball, R. A. (2002). *Criminological theory: Context and consequences*. Thousand Oaks, CA: Sage.

Morris, R., & Higgins, G. E. (2010). Criminological theory in the digital age: The case of social learning theory and digital piracy. *Journal of Criminal Justice, 38*, 470-480.

Orcutt, J. D., & Schwabe, A. M. (2012). Gender, race/ethnicity, and deviant drinking: A longitudinal application of social structure and social learning theory. *Sociological Spectrum, 32*, 20-36.

Pratt, T. C., Cullen, F. T., Sellers, C. S., Winfree Jr., L. T., Madensen, T. D., Daigle, L. E., Fearn, N. E., and Gau, J. M. (2010). The empirical status of social learning theory: A meta-analysis. *Justice Quarterly*, 765-802.

Schaefer, B. P., Vito, A. G., Marcum, C. D., Higgins, G. E., & Ricketts, M. L. (2015). Heroin use among adolescents: A multi-theoretical examination. *Deviant Behavior, 36*, 101-112.

Sellers, Christine S., and Ronald L. Akers (2006). Social learning theory: Correcting misconceptions. In Henry Stuart and Mark M. Lanier (Eds.), *The essential criminology reader*, 89-99. Boulder, CO: Westview Press.

Sellin, T. (1938). *Culture conflict and crime*. New York, NY: Social Science Research Council.

Shaw, C. R., & McKay, H. D. (1942) *Juvenile delinquency and urban areas: A study of delinquents in relation to differential characteristics of local communities in American cities*. Chicago, IL: University of Chicago Press.

Sutherland, E. H. (1942). *Criminology*. Philadelphia, PA: J. B. Lippincott.

Tarde, G. (1902). *Gabriel Tarde's laws of imitation*. E. Parsons (Trans.). New York, NY: Henry Holt.

Warr, M. (2002). *Companions in crime: The social aspects of criminal conduct*. Cambridge, United Kingdom: Cambridge University Press.

Whaley, R. B., Smith, J. M., & Hayes-Smith, R. (2011). Teenage drug and alcohol use: Comparing individual and contextual effects. *Deviant Behavior, 32*, 818-845.

Williams, F. P., & McShane, M. (2010). *Criminological theory*. Upper Saddle River, NJ: Prentice Hall.

Control Theories

CHAPTER OUTLINE

Introduction

Assumptions of Control Theories

Progression of Control Theories
Reiss's Theory of Personal and Social Control
Nye
Reckless
Sykes and Matza
Hirschi

Contemporary Control Theories

Gottfredson and Hirschi
Case Study 7.1: Land Surveyor Fined $3,000 for Verbally Abusing ICA Officer
Tittle

Policy Implications

Summary

Discussion Questions

References

Key Words and Concepts

Attachment	Control Balance Desirability	Personal Control
Belief	Drift	Pushes and Pulls
Bonding	Internalized Control	Rational Beings
Crime	Involvement	Self-Control
Commitment	Neutralization	Social Control
Contingencies	Parental Management	Socialization

Introduction

Control theories began to have mass appeal when the popularity of labeling and conflict theories waned. The idea of control referred to any perspective that discussed human behavior. Most control theories attributed crime and delinquency to the usual sociological variables (i.e., family, education, peers).

Control theories varied in the way that they explained criminal behavior, but all attempted to answer one basic question: Why don't people commit crime? The crux of this question was that deviant and criminal behavior was expected. Hirschi (1969) argued that the key explanation for control theories was why people obey the rules. At the root of Hirschi's (1969) view was Hobbes's belief that individuals were inherently evil. The aim of control theories was to explain the concepts that kept people from committing crime.

Because this view was often met with resistance, control theorists began to emphasize the idea of **socialization**. This meant that unsocialized individuals would act on their desires without the presence of other individuals. The most consistent way to exercise control was through the process of socialization. In the process of socialization, right and wrong was taught using informal and formal means through family and schools. Control theories placed particular emphasis on the quality of socialization. This chapter outlines the assumptions and development of control theories, then moves to the different theories that make up this perspective, and finally discusses the policy implications of control theories.

Assumptions of Control Theories

Control theorists made a number of assumptions when developing these theories. As mentioned above, the theorists began with the idea that the central question of interest was not why do people commit crime, but why *don't* people commit crime. Focusing on why people commit crime was tantamount to discovering the stimulus or motivation for criminal behavior. Recognizing that the majority of society does not commit crime, control theorists were interested in the restraining qualities of individuals; thus, control theorists were entrenched in why individuals do not commit crime.

Another assumption that control theorists made was that individuals were **rational beings**. This means that individuals were able to weigh the possible pleasure of an act against the possible pain. When individuals perceived the potential pleasure of an act to outweigh the potential pain, he or she would be more likely to perform the act. Control theories were designed to determine how individuals recognized the potential pain of an action. The pain of the action would be consequence of the action and a potential constraint. This view of control theories was consistent with the classical school of thought.

Progression of Control Theories

Control theories have a long history in criminology. These theories include those written by Reiss, Nye, Reckless, Sykes, and Matza, and they provide the foundation for contemporary control theories. We will examine each of these theories.

Reiss's Theory of Personal and Social Control

As part of his doctoral dissertation, Reiss developed personal and social controls. In this theory, he defined **personal control** as the individual's ability to refrain from acting on and obtaining desires that were in conflict with the norms and rules of the community. Reiss (1951) defined **social control** as the ability of social groups or institutions to make norms or rules effective. Reiss (1951) wrote:

> Delinquency results when there is a relative absence of internalized norms and rules governing behavior in conformity with the norms of the social system to which legal penalties are attached, a breakdown in previously established control, and/or a relative absence of or conflict in social rules or techniques for enforcing such behavior in the social groups or institutions of which the person is a member [p. 196].

This view had a control theory emphasis but was influenced by social disorganization.

Reiss (1951) argued that conformity was a product of acceptance of or submission to the rules. This view was similar to Durkheim's perspective of regulation. At this point, Reiss (1951) began to further define personal control. Personal control had Freudian roots. Reiss (1951) wrote that a mature ego could help with conformity to meet non-delinquent group expectations, but personal controls maintained enough flexibility for rational controls over behavior to permit conscious guidance of action.

Control and conformity were defined to be held in two areas. First, in the individual, control and conformity were about the submission to and acceptance of rules. Second, in the context of the group, control and conformity were based in the institution.

Reiss (1951) was not silent on the roles of control and peer association. He was not concerned about peer association itself; rather, he was concerned about the process that took place before the development of peer associations. He focused on the underlying processes that (1) occur prior to any conflicting cultural transmission, and (2) are necessary before any subsequent processes. This emphasized the role of control and conformity prior to peer association as being first and necessary. Overall, peer associations, in Reiss's (1951) eyes, were a function of the failure of personal and social control.

An important issue that must be considered was the reason why Reiss was relevant to control theories. His intention was to develop an instrument that would predict delinquency. It should be emphasized that Reiss was not trying to explain the causes of delinquency. Reiss's (1951) prediction instrument was to figure out the antecedents of delinquency. The primary antecedent was the lack of submission to social controls.

Reiss (1951) went on to define primary groups. Primary groups were the basic institution for the development of personal controls and the exercise of social control. Reiss (1951) wrote, "delinquency and delinquent recidivism may be viewed as a consequence of the failure of primary groups to provide the child with appropriate non-delinquent roles and to exercise social control over the child so these roles are accepted or submitted to in accordance with needs" (p. 198). Schools, neighborhoods, and family were identified as primary groups.

The family served as a central role in the acceptance of norms. However, the decline of the family would lead to a decline in social controls. This would occur because of the needs of family members not being met. Not meeting the needs of family members would result in some sort of remediation. Reiss (1951) argued that the proper remediation was purchasing material goods and services.

Nye

Nye (1958) developed a theoretical premise that was designed to focus on explaining conformity rather than non-conformity. His view was that a number of factors were operating that did not allow conformity. When conformity was not present, crime and delinquency were possible. Nye's (1958) premise was focused on adolescents' need of family structure. The family was designed to be the most important socializing factor for social control. With this premise, Nye (1958) proposed that family could provide a number of different controls. He suggested that these types of controls could be developed by social institutions, but they would be less powerful than the family.

Nye's four types of social control were: direct controls, internalized control, indirect control, and control through alternative means of need satisfaction. Nye (1958) argued that direct controls were imposed by external factors that included parents, teachers, or police. **Internalized control** occurred when the individual regulated his or her own behavior. Indirect control was the extent of influence and identification integrating the individual with authority figures in general and parents in particular. This form of control served to keep the individual in line with regulation when direct or internalized control was minimal (Lilly, Cullen, & Ball, 2002). Nye (1958) suggested that control through alternative means of need satisfaction would provide the means for satisfaction, but the pursuit of this satisfaction would keep the individual in line and controlled.

Nye (1958) argued that these types of control were all important. He argued that in certain situations different forms of control would matter more than others. Nye (1958) also argued that these types of control were mutually reinforcing for future situations in which control would be needed. This would be of particular interest in the context of acceptance and submission. The relationship with family members would be strong enough to provide the impetus for acceptance and submission to control. In other words, it was up to the family to prepare the individual to accept and submit to norms. This would allow the individual to successfully integrate into society. Finally, integration and regulation would reinforce one another, and this would result in the reduction of non-conforming behavior.

Reckless

Reckless, along with Dinitz, developed containment theory. The theoretical premise was largely attributed to Reckless. The central premise behind the theory was that two forms of control were able to explain delinquency: internal (i.e., inner) and external (i.e., outer). Reckless argued that containment theory was able to account for conformity and criminal behavior, but he did not make bold claims that his theory could account for all types of criminal behavior. Specifically, his theory did not explain behavior from inner pushes. These behaviors came from psychological or mental health problems. His theory, also, did not account for behaviors that were expected from subcultures (e.g., organized crime or culture conflict). While these behaviors were not explained in the theory, the theory does explain a number of other behaviors.

Two forms of containment were presented in the theory. Inner containment was central to the self. The "self" included a number of concepts: self-control, self-concept, ego strength, superego, high frustration tolerance, high goal orientation, high sense of responsibility, and the ability to find suitable alternatives for satisfaction. Outer containment was viewed as the external environment. The environment consisted of family and school reinforcement of social norms and values, discipline, and monitoring.

The key to Reckless's theory was inner containment. The self-concept was present in individuals and was developed when the individuals were young. The self-concept provided the positive or negative evaluation that served as an insulator between the self and social influences. Reckless argued that there were a number of **"pushes"** or **"pulls"** toward delinquent and criminal behavior.

The success of the "pushes" or "pulls" depended on the strength of the inner and outer containments. When the self-concept was bad, outer controls would have little effect on the individual and delinquency would be more likely. When the self-concept was good, the individual would be strong enough to resist the temptations of crime and delinquency. From this discussion, internal controls were deemed to be the stronger parts of the self and central to his theory.

Sykes and Matza

Sykes and Matza (1957) were responding to Cohen's version of the subcultural theory of deviance. The critique of Cohen's theory was the idea that lower class gang members were bound to the dominant value system of the society. Sykes and Matza (1957) argued that individuals became free to commit crime and delinquency through techniques of **neutralization**. The techniques of neutralization allowed the individual to temporarily become free of his or her commitments to society's values. This created the freedom and environment to become criminal or delinquent. Sykes and Matza (1957) argued that there were five techniques of neutralization:

1. denial of responsibility (i.e., acts are forces beyond the control of the delinquent);
2. denial of injury (i.e., acts do not really cause harm);
3. denial of the victim (i.e., given the circumstances, acts were not really wrong);
4. condemnation of the condemners (i.e., the motives and behaviors of those who disapprove of the acts were suspicious); and
5. appeal to higher loyalties (i.e., societies rules have to take a "back seat" to the demands of loyalty to important others or groups).

Matza (1964) developed neutralization theory. In his development, he discussed the ideas of bond to moral order and **drift.** The issue was the strengthening or weakening of the bond between the individual and the values of the dominant culture. Under this conception, neutralizations were the mechanisms that made the individual available for delinquency. Once the individual neutralized the behavior, he or she moved into a state of drift that made delinquency permissible.

Action in the theory was not solely about neutralization. Action was based on the individual's will to do something. The will to do something was predicated on two features: (1) preparation (i.e., repetition of old behavior), and (2) desperation (i.e., a state that precipitates new behavior). These two conditions bring the individual out of a state of drift and allow the behavior to take place. The performance of delinquent or conforming behavior depends on the situation and form of the neutralization.

Hirschi

One of the most popular control theories came from Travis Hirschi (1969). Hirschi's main premise intended to provide an understanding of social bonds. He used the idea of social bonds to make assertions not about committing delinquency or conformity, but about how morality played a role in criminal and delinquent behavior. Specifically, internalized norms, conscience, and desire for approval were important components of his view. Hirschi (1969) argued that when an individual's bonds were worn or broken they were more likely to be "free" to commit crime or delinquency. Key to Hirschi's (1969) view, motivation was rejected, and he asserted that individuals were self-interested and would behave in a manner that provided the greatest benefit. Behavioral restraints were provided by society, and when the restraints were loosened, self-interested behavior would emerge.

This may suggest that rational choice was at the root of Hirschi's (1969) version of control theory but, actually, social disorganization was the root of the theory. This was clear: The notion of weakened controls came from social disorganization. Hirschi was not silent on the roots of his theory; he discussed how he had to hide the underlying pieces that came from social disorganization (because social disorganization was not popular at the time). While these were the roots of the theory, Hirschi (1969) did take exception to the concept of deviance and criminal behavior that came from social disorganization. In social disorganization, deviance and some criminal behavior were viewed as relative. Hirschi (1969) did not agree with this sentiment and cogently argued that deviance and criminal behavior were governed by conventional society.

Hirschi (1969) used four concepts to underlie his version of social bonds: attachment, involvement, commitment, and belief. **Attachment** was where the individual developed strong connections and ties with significant others (e.g., parents, friends, or role models) or institutions (e.g., schools or churches) that would inhibit behavior. The strength of the attachment would produce conformity when significant others or institutions behaved in deviant or criminal ways.

Involvement referred to the amount of time or energy that was available to perform conforming or non-conforming activities. Hirschi (1969) argued that individuals who spent more time performing conforming activities would have less time to perform non-conforming activities. This would mean that participation in prosocial clubs, recreational activities, and other extracurricular activities would increase conformity.

Commitment referred to an individual's level of share in conventional society. The share in conventional society could be along the lines of reputation or education. At this point, the individual with greater commitment would have more to lose if they performed a non-conventional behavior. The threat of losing a good reputation may preclude some in business from unethical or non-conventional behavior.

The final social bond was **belief.** Belief referred to a moral obligation to follow the rules because of an internalized form of respect and obligation to the rules. Key to belief was the idea that the individual had respect for the society's value system. Generally, the more an individual agreed with behaving morally, the more likely he or she would do so.

The four bonds were critical to conforming behavior. Central to social **bonding** theory was the notion that when one of the four bonds were worn or broken, the individual would feel "free" to commit crime or deviance. One issue for criminologists to examine was how much one bond had to be weakened to arrive at deviant or criminal behavior. Further, Hirschi (1969) intended for the social bonds to interact with each other to produce the varying effects. He did not go too far with this assertion; it was left as an empirical question.

Hirschi's (1969) presentation of control theory and social bonds had groundbreaking tendencies. Specifically, Hirschi (1969) made use of a self-report survey to collect data and empirically examine the theory. He felt that this was necessary because other forms of data were not good representations of the social control approach. This was important given that, even with roots in social disorganization, the focus was not on society, but on the individual and his or her connection to society.

 ## Contemporary Control Theories

Gottfredson and Hirschi

The development of control theories in criminology seemed to slow and stop from 1969 to the early 1990s. One of the most important developments in criminology during the 1990s was Gottfredson and Hirschi's general theory of crime. Dismayed with the trend and shift toward longitudinal data and an emphasis on the age and crime, Gottfredson and Hirschi (1990) wrote their theory as an advance to control theories. They began their theory by emphasizing the role of rationality in behavior. Specifically, they argued that individuals would weigh the potential pleasure of an action against the potential pain of an action. When the individual perceived that the potential pleasure of an action outweighed the potential pain, he or she was more likely to perform the behavior.

Gottfredson and Hirschi (1990) argued that individuals would be more likely to perform two types of behavior: **crime and deviance.** Disgruntled with the inability of the law to provide satisfactory explanations of why individuals commit **crime,** they redefined the concept of crime to lay the foundation for better explanations. Specifically, they referred to crime as acts of force or fraud that the individual would pursue in their interests. They explained that crime has a number of characteristics. Crime was risky, thrilling, and provided immediate gratification. Gottfredson and

Hirschi (1990) went on to say that deviant acts hold the same characteristics. They argued that individuals would be attracted to crime and deviance when they had low levels of **self-control**.

Gottfredson and Hirschi (1990) also argued that individuals with low levels of **self-control** would evaluate crime and deviance as pleasurable rather than painful. This evaluation would take place because of the characteristics of low self-control. Individuals with low self-control were characterized as being impulsive, insensitive, risk taking, physical rather than mental, short-sighted, and nonverbal. Those that ranked high in these characteristics would not be able to foresee the long-term consequences of their actions, which was Gottfredson and Hirschi's (1990) formal definition of low self-control. Gottfredson and Hirschi (1990) argued:

> The dimensions (i.e., characteristics) of self-control are . . . factors affecting calculation of the consequences of one's acts. The impulsive or short-sighted person fails to consider the negative or painful consequences of his acts; the insensitive person has fewer negative consequences to consider; the less intelligent person also has fewer consequences to consider (he has less to lose) [1990, p. 95].

The individual with low self-control was a product of poor or ineffective parenting practices. Gottfredson and Hirschi (1990) argued that parenting and other institutions (e.g., schools) had the best opportunities for developing self-control in an individual; however, they emphasized the role of parenting. Gottfredson and Hirschi (1990) argued that parents had to perform four tasks (i.e., **parental management**) consistently and effectively for acceptable levels of self-control: form an emotional bond with the child; monitor the child to gather behavioral information; analyze the behavioral information; and perform non-corporal discipline when the behavior was deviant. These tasks were to be performed on a consistent and effective basis before the child reached the age of eight. After the age of eight, the child's level of self-control was to remain relatively stable.

This is a simple presentation of Gottfredson and Hirschi's (1990) theory. The theorists also explain other parts of life that may account for variation in offending. Within their theory, they take into account biological assumptions of crime, the role of peers and schools, differences in male and female offending, and differences between races and ethnicities in offending.

Gottfredson and Hirschi's (1990) theory has implications for explaining the utility in gender differences in criminal behavior. The issue with general theories is that they do not always take the needs of different genders into account. A debate exists over whether Gottfredson and Hirschi's theory adequately considers gender. Regardless of the debate, Gottfredson and Hirschi (1990) contend that the same variables can account for criminality for males and females.

When considering gender, Gottfredson and Hirschi (1990) believed that females were less likely to commit crime and deviance because they had higher levels of self-control than males. The variation in self-control for males and females comes from the socialization that takes place to instill levels of self-control. Specifically, parents are more vigilant in parenting their females than males. This means that parents are more likely to monitor, gather more behavioral information, analyze the information for crime or deviance, and to discipline the behavior of females more than males. Parents are also more likely to perform these tasks more consistently. Overall, Gottfredson and Hirschi (1990) argue that the gender differences in criminal and deviant behavior come from the perspective that parents do a better job with their female children, instilling a higher level of self-control in them, thus reducing criminal and deviant behavior among females.

Gottfredson and Hirschi (1990) also discussed racial and ethnic differences in self-control. Their perspective on racial and ethnic differences in criminal and deviant behavior is similar to their views on gender differences. Specifically, the differences in criminal and deviant behavior between race and ethnicity may be traced back to parental management practices. Careful to not implicate any specific race or ethnicity, Gottfredson and Hirschi (1990) argued that minority group members were less likely to properly or consistently apply the parental management practices. To clarify, minority groups were less likely to monitor a child's behavior, making them less likely to recognize criminal and deviant behavior in a child. Minority groups were also more likely to use corporal punishment. These differences would result in self-control level differences across race and ethnicity. Their position is as follows:

> There are differences among racial and ethnic groups . . . in levels of direct supervision by family and there is a delinquency component to the racial differences in delinquency rates, but as with gender, differences in self-control probably outweigh differences in supervision accounting for racial or ethnic variations [Gottfredson & Hirschi, 1990].

Gottfredson and Hirschi (1990) argued that socialization for proper levels of self-control did not just come from parents, although they were the primary source. They argued that different institutions had a role in developing self-control. Specifically, Gottfredson and Hirschi (1990) argued that the school had an opportunity to assist in the development of self-control.

> We do not restrict the meaning of "familial institution" to the traditional family unit composed of the natural father and mother. The socialization function does not, in our view, require such an institution. It does, however, require responsible adults committed to the training and welfare of the child.

This was their recognition that other institutions outside of the family may have input in a child's level of self-control. For them, the school served as a socializing institution because it provided discipline that restricted the pursuit of self-interest.

In other words, schools provided an environment that enabled teachers to serve as "responsible adults" that could help instill proper levels of self-control.

Schools were advantageous in developing self-control for a number of reasons. First, schools put teachers into a position where they could monitor a child's behavior. Second, teachers were able to recognize a child's misbehavior. Third, teachers were able to impose discipline to maintain order in the educational environment. In other words, teachers were able to provide the parental management tasks in the school environment that parents cannot perform when their child is away at school. To that end, Gottfredson and Hirschi (1990) argued:

> Most people are sufficiently socialized by familial institutions to avoid involvement in criminal acts. Those not socialized sufficiently by the family may eventually learn self-control through the operation of other sanctioning systems or institutions. The institution is given principal responsibility for this task in modern society.

At this point, the discussion has centered on the socializing parts of self-control, and little has focused on the consequences of self-control. For Gottfredson and Hirschi (1990), peer-group association is a consequence of self-control rather than a socializing force. While they acknowledge that peer-group association has a link with crime and deviance, they have important views concerning group participation and crime participation.

For Gottfredson and Hirschi (1990), peer-group participation is a manifestation of an individual's self-control level. For instance, those with higher levels of self-control tend to make good friends and are likely to have a number of them. Those that have lower levels of self-control are less likely to make good or many friends; rather, their friendships occur by accident with others that have low levels of self-control. In other words, those with low self-control are likely to find and befriend one another because no one else wants to be around them. This is a reasonable assertion when considering individuals with low self-control. They tend to be untrustworthy, selfish, and thoughtless, but they may also be "fun" because they are risk takers, adventuresome, and reckless. For Gottfredson and Hirschi (1990) this type of peer-group participation will create groups with low self-control.

Pratt and Cullen (2002) presented a meta-analysis of more than 20 studies examining self-control theory, and their results provided support. Specifically, their results suggested that low self-control had a moderate link with offending. They went on to argue that self-control theory was an important advance to criminology. Hay and Forrest (2006) used a national probability sample to show that self-control levels remained relatively stable over the life course. Higgins (2002) used a sample of college students to show that parental management does have a link with deviance through self-control (as Gottfredson and Hirschi predicted).

Higgins and Tewksbury (2006) showed that the link between self-control and delinquency through opportunity differed for males and females (as Gottfredson and Hirschi predicted). Kirchner and Higgins (2014) showed that the link between parental management and delinquency through self-control differed (as Gottfredson and Hirschi predicted). Turner, Piquero, and Pratt (2005) showed that school does influence self-control levels (as Gottfredson and Hirschi predicted). Chapple's (2005) study showed that individuals with lower levels of self-control experienced higher levels of peer rejection.

The empirical testing and advances of self-control theory did not escape the eyes of Gottfredson (2006) and Hirschi (2004). In separate book chapters, they argued that the theory should be revised. The chief reason for the suggested revision was the reliance on the Grasmick, Tittle, Bursik, and Arneklev (1993) scale. This scale was developed from a number of personality measures that came from the California Personality Inventory. Using this scale moved the theory away from its original intent: to be an advance in control theories. The reliance on the personality inventory shifted the testing away from why people do not commit crime to why people do commit crime. The former was a critical question for control theories, but the later was a question that other motivational theories of crime (e.g., social learning theory) were designed to answer. While taking the results of the studies that used the Grasmick et al. (1993) scale as support for the theory, Hirschi (2004) argued that the theory should be revised to address and answer the proper question. He began by reducing the focus on those with control issues, so the emphasis would be on seeing any consequences rather than only the long-term consequences. This allowed Hirschi (2004) to argue that those who can see any consequences of their actions had high levels of self-control. Further, he argued that those with high levels of self-control would have strong social bonds, and that social bonds would then be indicators of self-control.

This version of the theory had been examined in the literature and was shown to be valid. For instance, Hirschi (2004) used data from the Richmond Youth Survey and nine items that capture a variety of social bonds (e.g., attachment, commitment, and belief). He showed that this conceptualization of self-control has a negative link with delinquency. In addition, Piquero and Bouffard (2007) used data from college students to examine the reconceptualization of self-control. Their perspective was to examine more of Hirschi's views for the rational choice perspective than the social bonding tradition. To do this, they had students write a list of "bad" things that may occur from a given situation, and the students were asked to present the percentage of the likelihood that these "bad things" would occur. When combined, Piquero and Bouffard argued that this was a greater indication of inhibitions. In comparison, the "bad things" measure had a stronger link with scenarios of drunk driving and sexual aggression than the original Grasmick et al. scale. Higgins, Wolfe, and Marcum (2008) used data from college students to examine this view.

They used measures of bonding, the "bad things" measure, and the original Grasmick et al. scale in their study. Their results indicated that all three measures were influential in understanding the likelihood of illegally downloading digital media (i.e., digital piracy). Overall, the research indicates that self-control theory has empirical support, no matter the version.

CASE STUDY 7.1
LAND SURVEYOR FINED $3,000 FOR VERBALLY ABUSING ICA OFFICER

SINGAPORE—A land surveyor was fined $3,000 on Wednesday for using abusive and insulting language with an immigration and checkpoints officer. Malaysian Lee Eng Soon, 40, admitted shouting a vulgar word and "idiot" at Corporal Farmi Al Faqeh, 24, at the arrival car booth of Woodlands checkpoint on May 14 this year. Investigation showed that Lee, who is a Singapore permanent resident, was driving in from Malaysia with his family at about 7.26 a.m. that day to send his two children to school when his daughter's passport could not be scanned due to a system error. As the children were late for school, Lee's wife told Cpl. Farmi to speed up. Cpl. Farmi said he was trying his best, but he still could not scan the daughter's passport after several attempts. Lee became increasingly impatient and shouted at the victim to hurry up, accusing him of purposely wasting his time. When the victim replied that the delay was due to a system error, Lee shouted the four-letter word and "idiot." Asked why he used the vulgarity, Lee refused to respond and proceeded to utter the word "pui" at the victim several times. Two officers who overheard Lee scolding the victim intervened. Lee was not arrested but was directed to report to Jurong Police headquarters later that day. Lee's lawyer M. Kalidass said it was a one-off loss of self-control by his client and urged the court to take into account Lee's good character. Deputy Public Prosecutor Tay Jingxi said Lee's plea of guilt had to be balanced against his completely unwarranted behavior as well as public interest in protecting public servants from verbal abuse and maintaining order at border checkpoints. Lee could have been fined up to $5,000 and/or jailed for up to one year.

See more at: http://www.straitstimes.com/news/singapore/courts-crime/story/land-surveyor-fined-3000-verbally-abusing-ica-officer-20141217#sthash.IJWccWbd.dpuf

Can you explain these actions through low self-control?

Tittle

In his general theory of deviance, Tittle (1995) argues that individuals (no matter their age, sex, or race) are fundamentally concerned with balancing control in their lives. He further asserts that individuals may use deviant behavior to correct actual or perceived control imbalances that occur in their lives. Control imbalances can take place in two ways: a control deficit (the individual is experiencing more control than they are expressing) and a control surplus (the individual is expressing more control than they are experiencing). The control imbalances are relative to an individual's inclination to performing certain forms of deviance.

Because the control ratio is the indicator of control for an individual, it is hypothesized to have a link to the likelihood of deviance in specific ways, depending upon the type of imbalance. For instance, an individual that experiences a control deficit is likely to engage in forms of repressive deviance, such as predation (e.g., theft, rape, homicide, assault, and fraud) and defiance (e.g., contempt or hostility for social norms, groups, or an individual). Individuals with control surpluses are likely to engage in forms of deviance that are consistent with exploitive (e.g., coercion and manipulation of others), plunderous (e.g., pursuing self-interested endeavors without regard for others), and decadent acts (e.g., impulsive acts or thriving for excessive gains).

The control balance process may be reliant on conditions or **contingencies**. A contingency is a property (i.e., aspect of the individual) or an entity (e.g., social relationship, organizational structure, or physical environment) that influences the control balancing process. That is, risks, sensation-seeking, pleasure, and low self-control are viewed as types of concepts that are possible contingencies. Overall, because some of the empirical research has indicated problems with the link between the control ratio and deviance, contingencies may be an important part of the process that could alleviate issues with the control ratio.

Overall when considering the empirical studies on control balance theory (CBT), findings are mixed. With the first examination of the CBT, Wood and Dunaway (1997/1998) examined the link between the control ratio and sex offenses, using 125 self-reported responses from convicted sex offenders. Their findings indicated that the perception of lack of control in their lives resulted in offenders turning to crime for the sensation of power and control; thus, their findings support CBT. Piquero and Hickman's (1999) study provided a measurement strategy for CBT. Using scenarios as the dependent variables, they found that a control surplus explained both predation and defiance. This was counter to Tittle's (1995) predictions. Hickman, Piquero, Lawton, and Greene (2001) extended the reach of CBT by examining the link between the control ratio and police officer deviance. Again, their results did not support the theory because the control ratio explained multiple forms of deviance that the theory did not predict. Piquero and Hickman (2002) examined the role of rational choice as a contingency within CBT. Using data from college students they showed that CBT had problems and that the contingency argument did not necessarily hold as predicted. Others also found problems with the control ratio and contingency argument (Curry & Piquero, 2003; Higgins & Lauterbach, 2004; Higgins, Lauterbach, & Tewksbury, 2005; Nobles & Fox, 2013). These studies used important control measures that included morals, peers, and low self-control. That is, the vignette studies tended to not find support for the behavior of the control ratio using college student samples; rather, opposite findings were present using non-college student samples. Further, when support was found using college student samples, a causal logic was imposed. Although consistent with CBT, this seems to reveal methodological problems (e.g., temporal ordering) in the collection of the data. Thus, the mixed findings suggest at least two problems with CBT: (1) the behavior of the control ratio, and (2) the generality of the theory to find consistent results no matter the sample. Therefore, attention may need to be given to the revised version of CBT.

Heeding the results of theoretical and empirical research, Tittle (2004) offers a revised version of CBT. The newer version of CBT focuses on refining the definition of deviance, while retaining the other portions of the theory. That is, Tittle (2004) argues that deviance should be considered as a single continuum rather than six discrete categories. To be clear, Tittle (2004) sees the continuum as:

> ... deviance with points on the continuum differentiated with respect to what will be called their **control balance desirability**. By definition, control balance desirability will refer to the quality possessed in different degrees by various potential acts. In empirical terms, it is a composite variable composed of two indicators: 1) the likely long-range effectiveness of the deviant act in question for altering the imbalance; and 2) the extent to which a given form of misbehavior requires a perpetrator to be directly and personally involved with a victim or an object that is affected by the deviance [p. 405].

From this perspective, the control ratio will not have a specified link with any particular form of deviance. The control ratio will have a link with control balance desirability (CBD). This view merges the specific forms of deviance and focuses them on a continuum, and the placement on the continuum occurs in relation to the individual's responses to long-term control and his or her perceived detection of acts. Tittle (2004) argues that the control ratio and contingencies (e.g., low self-control) will help with the understanding of deviance without having a predicted direction between control surpluses and control deficits with specific forms of deviance.

Just as Tittle's (1995) presentation of the theory had methodological implications, so does the revision. Specifically, Tittle (1995) argues that the control ratio will have a link with the CBD no matter if there is a dominant control surplus or a dominant control deficit. Because the control ratio captures both the control surplus and the control deficit, there is little reason to use the nonlinear approach that separates the two in individual segments as proscribed in Tittle's (1995) original theory. Therefore, a linear approach will be fruitful in understanding the relationship between the control ratio and the CBD.

If Tittle's (2004) view is correct, then the revision will have helped the theory overcome an important conceptual hurdle. Further, if this view is correct using college students—given that the theory has had the most trouble explaining the deviance of college students—the generality of the theory may be improved. In addition, no study has examined our view on the linear link between the control ratio and the CBD.

Policy Implications

The policy implications for this theoretical perspective do not require specialized understanding. In other words, the relative policies are rather common sense, which may explain the popularity of the theoretical premise. For instance, programs that keep children in conventional activities (e.g., social clubs, little league baseball, and 4-H clubs) tend to help socialize children to conventional values, and their involvement in these activities reduces their opportunity to engage in criminal or deviant activities.

Summary

In summary, control theories are based on the premise of understanding why people do not commit crime. Assuming that individuals are rational beings and that most are not criminal, control theories provide concepts and propositions to understand the majority of society. Working with historical and contemporary views on self-regulation and bonds, control theorists provide a tapestry of concepts for understanding that offending may occur because of a lack of restraint. These theories, with the exception of Tittle's CBT, place an emphasis on the development of self-restraint (i.e., self-control) learned from the parental unit. Gottfredson and Hirschi (1990), in particular, argue that two-parent families provide a foundation that allows the necessary training and tutelage to occur in order to develop the proper levels of self-control. For instance, an individual that has been exposed to the proper self-control training will not likely binge drink when he or she is a college student.

Discussion Questions

1. What are the characteristics of Hirschi's social bonding theory? Explain how an individual may become deviant using Hirschi's social bonding theory.
2. Explain the basics of self-control theory.
3. Explain the role of contingencies in control balance theory.

REFERENCES

Chapple, C. L. (2005). Self-control, peer relations, and delinquency. *Justice Quarterly, 22*, 89-106.

Curry, T. R., & Piquero, A. R. (2003). Control ratios and defiant acts of deviance: Assessing additive and conditional effects with constraints and impulsivity. *Sociological Perspectives, 46*, 397-415.

Gottfredson, Michael R. 2008. The empirical status of control theory in criminology. Pp. 77-101 In Francis T. Cullen, John P. Wright, and Kristie R. Blevins (Eds.), *Taking stock: The status of criminological theory: Vol. 15, Advances in criminological theory*, 77-101. New Brunswick, NJ: Transaction Press.

Gottfredson, Michael, and Travis Hirschi. 1990. *A general theory of crime*. Palo Alto, CA: Stanford University Press.

Grasmick, Harold G., Charles R. Tittle, Robert J. Bursik, and Bruce J. Ameklev. 1993. Testing the core empirical implications of Gottfredson and Hirschi's general theory of crime. *Journal of Research in Crime and Delinquency, 30*, 5-29.

Hay, C., & Forrest, W. (2006). The development of self-control examining self-control theory's stability thesis. *Criminology, 44*, 739-774.

Hickman, M., Piquero, A. R., Lawton, B. A., and Greene, J. R. (2001). Applying Tittle's control balance theory to police deviance. *Policing, 24*, 479-519.

Higgins, G. E. (2002). General theory of crime and deviance: A structural equation modeling approach. *Journal of Crime and Justice, 25*, 71-95.

Higgins, G. E., & Lauterbach, C. (2004). Control balance theory and exploitation: An examination of contingencies. *Criminal Justice Studies: A Critical Journal of Crime, Law, and Society, 17, (3)*, 291-310.

Higgins, G. E., Lauterbach, C., & Tewksbury, R. (2005). Control balance theory and predation: An examination of contingencies. *Sociological Focus, 38, (4)*, 241-260.

Higgins, G. E., & Tewksbury, R. (2006). Sex and self-control theory: The measures and causal model may be different. *Youth & Society, 37*, 479-503.

Higgins, G. E., Wolfe, S. E., & Marcum, C. D. (2008). Digital piracy: An examination of multiple conceptualizations and operationalizations of self-control. *Deviant Behavior, 29*, 440-460.

Hirschi, T. (1969). *Causes of delinquency*. Berkely, CA: University of California Press.

Kirchner, E. E., & Higgins, G. E. (2014). Self-control and racial disparities in delinquency: A structural equation modeling approach. *American Journal of Criminal Justice, 39*, 436-449.

Matza, D. (1964). *Delinquency and drift*. New York, NY: John Wiley.

Nobles, M. R., & Fox, K. A. (2013). Assessing stalking behaviors in control balance theory framework. *Criminal Justice and Behavior, 40*, 737-762.

Nye, I. F. (1958). *Family relationships and delinquent behavior*. New York, NY: John Wiley.

Piquero, A. R., & Bouffard, J. (2007). Something old, something new: A preliminary investigation of Hirschi's redefined self-control. *Justice Quarterly, 24*, 1-27.

Piquero, A. R., & Hickman, M. (1999). An empirical test of Tittle's control balance theory. *Criminology, 37*, 319-342.

Piquero, A. R., & Hickman, M. (2002). The rational choice implications of control balance theory. In Alex R. Piquero and Stephen G. Tibbetts (Eds.), *Rational choice and criminal behavior: Recent research and future challenges*, 85-107. New York, NY: Routledge.

Pratt, Travis C., and Francis T. Cullen. 2000. The empirical status of Gottfredson and Hirschi's general theory of crime: A Meta-Analysis. *Criminology, 38,* 931-964.

Reckless, W. (1940). *Criminal behavior.* New York, NY: McGraw-Hill.

Reiss, a. J. Jr. (1951). Delinquency as the failure of personal and social controls. *American Sociological Review, 16,* 196-207.

Sykes, G., & Matza, D. (1957). Techniques of neutralization: A theory of delinquency. *American Sociological Review, 22,* 664-670.

Tittle, C. R. (1995) *Control balance: Toward a general theory of deviance.* Boulder, CO: Westview.

Tittle, C. R. (2004) Refining control balance theory. *Theoretical Criminology, 8,* 395-428.

Turner, M. G., Piquero, A. R., & Pratt, T. C. (2005). The school context as a source of self- Control. *Journal of Criminal Justice, 33,* 327-339.

Wood, P. B., and Dunaway, R. G. (1997/1998). An application of control balance theory to incarcerated sex offenders. *Journal of Oklahoma Criminal Justice Research Consortium, 4,* 1-12.

CHAPTER 8

Labeling Theories

CHAPTER OUTLINE

Introduction

Progression of Labeling Theory
Tannenbaum
Becker
Case Study 8.1: Impact of Labeling on Juveniles
Lemert
Braithwaite
Case Study 8.2: Disintegrative Shaming?

Empirical Research

Policy Implications

Summary

Discussion Questions

References

Key Words and Concepts

Communitarianism	Falsely Accused	Reparation
Conforming Acts	Independent Variable	Restitution
Decarceration	Interdependency	Restorative Justice
Decriminalization	Labels	Secondary Deviance
Dependent Variable	Labeling Theory	Secret Deviant
Differential Social Control	Looking-Glass Self	Self as a Social Construct
Disintegrative Shaming	Meanings	Shaming
Diversion	Primary Deviance	Social Visibility
Dramatization of Evil	Pure Deviant	Symbolic Interactionism
Faith-Based Programs	Reintegrative Shaming	Tag

Introduction

The contemporary version of labeling theory was derived from the sociological concept of **symbolic interactionism**, which states that a person's identity is a result of cognitive processes, attitudes, and beliefs in the context of society's perception of what is appropriate and normal. An individual's interactions with peers and their reactions to him or her create a perception of self. In other words, a person's belief that he or she is not popular, fashionable, socially acceptable, and so on is a result of what others around him or her say and do. Symbolic interactionism enforces the notion of **meanings** of words and actions during these social interactions. Verbal and nonverbal communication, gestures, and attitudes reflect these meanings. So if an individual's peers find his or her clothing to be unfashionable and ugly, they may verbally comment, laugh at the person, or make disapproving faces to reflect the meaning of rejection.

The origins of symbolic interactionism can be traced as far back as the writings of Charles Horton Cooley's (1902) **looking-glass self**. Cooley believed that our self-concepts are a reflection of what others believe we are as people. For example, if parents stress to their daughter she is pretty but not very smart, she will internalize these concepts as her identity. This assertion supports George Herbert Mead's (1934) concept of **self as a social construct**, which is composed of the "I" and "Me." The internalization of the beliefs of others forms your "Me," or social construct. Goffman (1959) believed we could manipulate our "Me" by presenting ourselves in a certain light to others. Our true selves could be hidden in a "back stage." Mead further asserted that our responses to society's perception of the "Me" form our "I," which is never stable or completely controllable.

In summary, the conception of one's self is a result of **labels** given to us through interactions with society, and criminological **labeling theory** proposes that this labeling shapes criminal and delinquent behavior. Applying stigmatizing labels, such as criminal, felon, and child molester influences performance of criminal behavior. Furthermore, these labels can take two forms: (1) the **dependent variable** when explaining why certain behaviors are called wrong or criminal and (2) the **independent variable** when explaining how placing labels on individuals can foster further criminal behavior.

In this chapter, we present the basic premises of the classical quest for understanding criminal behavior. We outline the historical context from which those premises originate. Next, we provide illustrative examples and contemporary studies of the labeling perspective of criminology and evaluate these findings and assumptions. Finally, we suggest policy implications that may be fruitful in understanding this particular premise.

Progression of Labeling Theory

Tannenbaum

Labeling theory as a criminological theory is traced back to Frank Tannenbaum's (1938) work focusing on the delinquency of a juvenile. Tannenbaum explained that initially, juveniles who participate in mild forms of delinquency (e.g., being loud, playing pranks on neighbors, skipping class) may be seen simply as young people getting into mischief and having fun. ("Boys will be boys.") However, as the behaviors continue, communities push for punishment of the youth and control of the behavior. Behavior that originally looked suspicious changes into behavior that is definitely evil, and the young person is implied to be evil. In addition to the juvenile's personality, his or her friends and hang-out places become evil in the eyes of the community. Tannenbaum (1938) indicated that as this process progresses, the young person begins to internalize these accusations, accepts a label of delinquent, and displays increasingly defiant behavior toward authority figures.

Tannenbaum (1938) stated that a label, or **tag**, is attached to a child when caught in delinquent behavior. This tag identifies the child as a deviant and he or she adjusts his or her self-image to follow this tag. In turn, the reaction of society is based on the tag and not the child. For instance, our juvenile justice system sees a child convicted of vandalism as a delinquent (a broad categorization), rather than a foster child from a broken home with two drug-addicted parents and a history of abuse (a specific identification). **Dramatization of evil**, or the implication that a deviant individual was not a product of the person's lack of adjustment to society but rather the adjustment to a certain group, is the concept Tannenbaum coined when a person acts criminally as expected by his or her social group. The social group then proceeds to segregate and isolate the individual because of his or her behavior.

Becker

Although Tannenbaum's contribution made great headway in the introduction of labeling theory to criminological theory, it was not until Howard Becker's (1963) book, *The Outsiders,* that this theory received prominent attention. Becker believed that deviance was based on the perception of various social groups of what was right and wrong. Furthermore, the deviance required some sort of negative reaction in order to be considered deviance and labeled as such. The law is reflection of this reaction: If an action is considered deviant and wrong, laws will be passed prosecuting and punishing this act. This is important as advocates of labeling theory stress the importance of the reaction to the label and not the actual engagement in the criminal act (Becker, 1963). Williams and McShane (2010) give an excellent example of this phenomenon by discussing the effect of Hurricane Katrina on the crime rate. Many evacuees, some ex-offenders, settled in Houston, and law enforcement took aggressive steps to maintain control over this group. Any criminal activity, whether perpetrated by these former New Orleans residents or other individuals, was labeled as "Katrina-related," blaming the natural disaster for Houston's crime problem.

Labeling theory as an explanation of crime can be divided into two steps: (1) explanation of how and why individuals get labeled; and (2) the effect of the label on future deviant behavior (Gove, 1975; Orcutt, 1973). Becker (1963) asserted that "social groups create deviance by making the rules whose infraction constitutes deviance, and by applying those rules to particular people and labeling them as outsiders [p. 9]." Creating deviance involves developing rules and laws deeming behaviors as deviant. Also, the circumstances of the behavior, the reaction of society to the behavior, and the characteristics of the offender are added into the conceptualization of a deviant behavior. It is important to note that it is the reaction to the deviance that is crucial, not the actual behavior or even whether or not the behavior actually occurred. If people believe deviance occurred and act accordingly, it creates a deviant (or outsider, as termed by Becker).

Becker (1963) determined four typologies of deviant behavior based on whether the behavior performed was actually deviant or conforming and whether the reaction to the behavior was considered deviant or conforming. **Falsely accused** behaviors are those that either do not occur or are actually conforming to societal standards but receive a reaction as if a behavior was deviant. **Pure deviant** behavior includes behaviors that are actually deviant and are perceived as deviant, such as rape or murder. **Conforming acts** are appropriate behaviors not considered deviant, such as paying taxes or going the speed limit. Lastly, **secret deviant** behavior is actually deviant but is not perceived as such. It is possible that these behaviors are legally deviant, but society may not act as if they are illegal. For example, many individuals do not consider college students under the age of 21 who drink alcohol as deviants, even though the behavior is illegal.

CASE STUDY 8.1
IMPACT OF LABELING ON JUVENILES

In December 2014, the Pennsylvania Supreme Court ruled that a 2012 law that labeled juveniles as sex offenders and forced them to register as such under Megan's Law was unconstitutional. The Court stated that requiring juveniles to register assumed they would reoffend. A representative from the

Juvenile Law Center in Philadelphia stated this restriction was unnecessary, as only two percent of juvenile sex offenders reoffend and the label placed on them from registration made it very difficult to obtain employment or stay in school. Do you agree with the ruling?

Lemert

According to labeling theory, violations of the law are considered to be unplanned and inconsistent. In other words, deviants are not calculating criminals who strategize and preplan these behaviors. On the other hand, these acts of **primary deviance** are impulsive, infrequent, and unorganized. According to Edwin Lemert (1951), this is the most critical of events as it leads toward stable patterns of offending, otherwise known as a criminal career. The stigmatizing label that is applied is a societal reaction and, without it, the continued deviance would more than likely continue to be sporadic rather than constant (Gove, 1980).

In order for the label to affect an individual, it must be internalized and, according to Lemert, this is a process of eight steps:

1. Primary deviance;
2. Penalties applied by society for the primary deviant action;
3. Further primary deviant acts;
4. More severe penalties and reactions by society;
5. Further deviant behavior, possibly as a result of resentment from the negative reactions of society;
6. Ultimate severe penalties by society as a result of intolerance for the continued behavior;
7. Solidification of the deviant conduct as a result of the stigmatization; and
8. Acceptance of the label of deviant.

This process is that of **secondary deviance**, a deviant reaction as a result of a label. Essentially, it is a back and forth of behavior and reaction that eventually ends in an identity.

Lemert (1951) stated that in order for a deviant behavior to receive a reaction from the community, it must have **social visibility.** Behaviors that are more covert, such as sexual deviation, will receive less reaction because they have low visibility and the public is not generally aware of such happenings. In addition, members of a group not predominantly living in a community will have higher social visibility and be watched more closely. For instance, a Hispanic family moving into a predominantly white neighborhood will perk the curiosity of the residents in regard to their behaviors as they are new and a minority.

In addition, Lemert stated that an organized community will place certain emphasis on the severity of labels applied to different behaviors. If several members of a community had been killed because of DUI, individuals arrested for DUI would receive harsher stigmatization and punishment. Conversely, motor vehicle theft may be a rare occurrence and not an issue for residents.

Braithwaite

Critics of labeling theory have argued that it is not the label of delinquent or criminal that causes a person's continued criminal behavior. Smith and Paternoster (1990) performed a complex study on "deviance-amplification" of labeling theory in juvenile court cases and found that the relationship between appearance in court (and label of delinquent) and future delinquency is the high risk of recidivism these juveniles already have before referral to court. Those juveniles who avoid court referral (and a label) are already at a lower risk to reoffend. In summary, the label does not cause the delinquency but, rather, it is a result of all the circumstances in that juvenile's life.

Based on this critique and similar studies, theorists asserted that a revision of labeling theory would make it more valid. Rather than looking at the label as a precursor to deviant behavior, some revisions placed focus on how the labeling process occurred (Goode, 1975; Hawkins & Tiedeman, 1975). Others placed importance of the label as a method of social control (Grimes & Turk, 1978). However, one of the more contemporary revisions to influence the treatment of offenders in the criminal justice system is that of **reintegrative shaming**.

Braithwaite defined **shaming** as social disapproval with the purpose of causing remorse and awareness of the inappropriate behavior. According to Braithwaite, shaming can be implemented in a positive or negative fashion. **Disintegrative shaming,** or stigmatization, places all emphasis on shaming and punishment of the wrongdoer, with no afterthought of reintegrating an offender back into society. The label applied has the purpose of isolation. However, the reintegrative shaming method intends to reintegrate the offender back into society by allowing the individual to express remorse and request forgiveness. The offender can in turn obtain social approval.

Pulling from theories such as social learning, strain, social bonding, and social disorganization, Braithwaite asserted that labeling has indirect effects on criminality. Stigmatizing an individual with a label causes participation in delinquent groups and influences individuals to take advantage of illegitimate opportunities. However, individuals who display **interdependency** with attachments and commitments to conventional values and activities will be more receptive to reintegrative shaming. This is especially true with persons who come from strong communities who are tied to each other, otherwise known as **communitarianism.** These communities contain individuals who are independent but also dependent on each other.

CASE STUDY 8.2
DISINTEGRATIVE SHAMING?

Sheriff Joe Arpaio has been sheriff of Maricopa County, Arizona since 1993. Arpaio is well known for his punitive and often controversial treatment of inmates. In August 1993, he opened "Tent City," a canvas-covered compound outdoors that houses 2,000 of the county's inmates. In addition, Arpaio has all materials used by the inmates (e.g., towels, boxer shorts, socks) dyed pink for inventory control as well as for the calming effect he claims it has on the inmates. The only inmate materials not in pink are the black and white striped uniforms they wear. Critics of Arpaio have stated the pink underwear and other materials are demeaning to male inmates and an insult to their masculinity. Do you feel this is a form of disintegrative shaming or simply a good management tool?

Empirical Research

The support from the academic community for labeling theory was strong in the 1960s but drastically changed in the 1980s as it began to receive severe criticism of its validity and usefulness (Gove, 1980; Hirschi, 1980; Tittle, 1980). Critics argued that the focus on self-concept was too narrow and research designs using labeling theory were poorly designed. However, since the 1990s there has been a revitalization of the theory and a new revision of its potential. Matsueda (1992; 2001) developed the symbolic interaction component to explain primary and secondary deviance. He agreed that labeling originates from not only official agents, such as the police and corrections system, but also unofficial agents like parents, teachers, and peers. The self is formed based on the perceptions of others who are important in an individual's life, and all of these agents play this role of significance. Furthermore, Heimer and Matsueda (1994) stated that self-perception is a result of learned definitions of criminal behavior and the reactions to this behavior. Termed **differential social control**, this can result in appropriate behavior (a conventional direction) or delinquent behavior (a criminal direction). These contributions by Matsueda were also used to explain gender differences in criminality (Heimer, 1996; Matsueda, 1992) and over the life course (Matsueda & Heimer, 1997).

More recently, Lopes et al. (2012) examined tests of labeling theory over the past few decades and asserted that contributions have been made in a number of contexts. In regard to the effect of labeling on education, the theory asserts that stigmatization from interaction with law enforcement can have a negative effect on a juvenile's experiences in school. Teachers and administrators may treat the juvenile differently based on his or her label as a "troublemaker," such as suspending or transferring these students to get rid of the problem (Bowditch, 1993). Furthermore, Bernburg (2002) found that when schools are notified of formal labeling events, such as an arrest or adjudication, there is a higher likelihood that male students will drop out of school completely. Multiple studies have confirmed that a stigmatizing label has a negative effect on educational success (Bernburg, 2002; Bernburg & Krohn, 2003; Hjalmarsson, 2008; Lopes et al., 2012; Sweeton, 2006).

Labeling can also have negative effects on employment. Obtaining or maintaining employment can be difficult with the label of offender or felon (Irwin, 2005; Kurlychek, Brame & Bushway, 2007). Research has shown that employers were less likely to hire individuals with a criminal history and incarceration record (Boshier & Johnson, 1974; Pager, 2003). Bernburg and Krohn (2003) and Davies and Tanner (2003) found that keeping a stable job was extremely difficult with a formal record with the criminal justice system. Hypothetically, employers are willing to hire ex-offenders convicted of drug crimes (Pager & Quillian, 2005); however, they are more likely to call back applicants without a criminal history (Uggen, Vuolo, Ruhland, Whitham, & Lageson, 2012).

The first two factors affected by the stigmatizing effects of labels—education and employment—will in turn influence a person's financial stability. Dependents are especially affected by parental decisions and financial stability. Sampson and Laub (1993) found that childhood delinquency is predicted by welfare reliance for young adults and individuals in their late 20s. This affect can be cyclical as reliance on welfare influences interaction with police, just as individuals with previous police interaction rely on welfare as they are unable to obtain or maintain employment (Bernburg, 2002). Furthermore, a successful transition into adulthood and adult responsibilities is a result of financial stability, which for most individuals involves gainful employment (Settersten, Furstenberg, & Rumbaut, 2005; Uggen, 2000).

Policy Implications

According to Kraska (2004), labeling theory would suggest that limiting the negative reaction by society to criminal behavior would reduce crime, decrease moral panics, and hold the media more accountable for their reporting. The criminal justice system should make efforts to redirect some of the pressure and punishment put on offenders for their offenses. Einstadter and Henry (2006) believed a multipronged corrections stance focusing on four strategies would be most successful in managing offenders in the criminal justice system.

Decriminalization, or the legalization of some acts, would reduce the overload of the court docket as well as the overcrowding in the corrections system. Labeling theorists assert that the decriminalization of behaviors that are deemed morally wrong, but logically have no victim and are voluntarily engaged in, should not be a criminal offense. Public intoxication, prostitution between adults, drug use, and status offenses (those behaviors illegal to individuals of a certain age) would fall into the category of crimes against morality. Furthermore, some groups advocate for the decriminalization and taxing the sale of marijuana or sex (i.e., prostitution) to improve the economy, much like we tax gasoline and cigarettes.

Diversion is the redirection of offenders through less punitive forms of treatment and institutions rather than processing them in the criminal justice system. For example, drug and domestic violence courts were formed to specifically deal with these types of offenders through specialized and individualized treatment plans. Rather than immediately incarcerating them and lessening their chances for successful reintegration, these courts provide intensive supervision to their clients as well as provide them with tools for success. Labeling theories advocate for diversion as it lessens the impact of society's reaction to certain crimes and attempts to prevent further recidivism (secondary deviance).

Obviously, as incarceration is one of the most stigmatizing forms of punishment, the appropriate noninterventionist route is **decarceration**. A shorter sentence of incarceration allows an offender to return to normal life more quickly, and removes the individual from a breeding ground of criminality. Over 30 years ago, Cohen (1979) suggested a plan to diminish the extensive control of the corrections system that would still be applicable today for decarceration. He pressed for a moratorium on the building of prisons. Rather than continuing to build facilities to fill with offenders, we should deal with them in alternative ways. Early release and reintegration programs for nonviolent offenders, as well as excarceration for drug users and sellers, would drastically decrease the overcrowding issue in facilities.

Lastly, Einstadter and Henry (2006) suggested a combination of **reparation** and **restitution** to restore the harmony between the action committed by the offender and the loss suffered by the victim. Offenses against property (e.g., theft) could be satisfied by monetary compensation while crimes against the community (e.g., vandalism) could be corrected by a community service plan. However, one of the more popular forms of restoration of the offender and victim relationship is based on the labeling theory application of shaming.

The application of Braithwaite's (1995) argument of reintegrative shaming as a supportive factor in developing the community has led to the modern-day usage of **restorative justice**. Restorative justice programs focus on not only the needs of the victim, but also those of the offender and the involved community. Rather than strictly punishing an offender, these programs stress the importance of taking responsibility for actions and redeeming oneself to the community so that the offender, in turn, can successfully reintegrate back into society. Comparable to the parent-child relationship, if a boy apologizes to his mother for taking his sister's toy, she tells him she forgives him and brings him back into the family unit without further repercussion or punishment for that act. These types of programs gained early support in Australia and New Zealand and have become part of many justice systems in the United States (Bazemore & Schiff, 2001; Braithwaite, 2002; Van Ness & Strong, 2006).

Although reintegrative shaming is not critical to the implementation of a restorative justice program, use of the theory does predict a reduction in crime. Components of relevant programs involve the following steps:

1. Approaching the offender with his or her crime in a respectful way;
2. Avoiding stigmatization of being a "bad" person by also allowing loved ones to explain the good traits of the individual; and
3. Ensuring a commitment to reintegration through restoration of relationships, repair of damage, and issuing apologies in a sincere fashion (Braithwaite, 2006).

Specific examples of restorative justice programs include community service cleanups, victim–offender mediation, and restorative conferencing between offenders, victims (if they are alive), and family members of both parties (Bazemore & Schiff, 2001; Braithwaite, 2002; Van Ness and Strong, 2006). Schools in Oakland, California; Portland, Oregon; and Chicago, Illinois are implementing restorative justice circles in the classroom to bring students together to make meaningful reparations rather than building resentment. Many of the students have difficult lives outside the school walls and are allowed to discuss life situations and feelings. Rather than using tools of expulsion or suspension, these schools try to keep students on the right track to graduation rather than getting sending them into a permanent life of crime (Brown, 2013).

One of the more recent, and controversial, examples seen in the media in the United States involved a shocking murder in Florida. On March 28, 2010, Conor McBride walked into the Tallahassee Police Department and told police officers he had just shot his fiancée, Ann Grosmaire, in the head. Both individuals only 19 years old, the couple had been fighting for the past few days over trivial matters when McBride snapped and shot Grosmaire, who later died in the hospital. Neither had been in serious trouble with the criminal justice system and they were pursuing degrees at the local community college. After Grosmaire passed away, both of her parents reached out to McBride and his family, and eventually the prosecutor on the case, expressing that they had forgiven McBride for his crime and did not want him to waste his entire life in prison. Rather than charging McBride with first-degree murder, which can result in a death penalty sentence, the Grosmaires pressed for an alternative charge of manslaughter.

Finally, after persistent contact with the prosecutor, all parties agreed to a restorative justice conference. Both families were present, as well as McBride, and a representative for the community. All were allowed to speak, but the Grosmaires were allowed to silence any party by holding up a picture of Ann. The conference was extremely candid and all parties spoke extensively of their experiences and involvement. In the end, the prosecutor offered McBride a 20-year sentence plus five years of probation and he agreed. Furthermore, a condition of his probation requires him to speak at teen-dating violence seminars. The Grosmaires are satisfied with the process and believe that justice was served (Tullis, 2013).

The Grosmaires insisted their willingness to forgive was based on their Christian faith and its message to forgive. **Faith-based programs** are based on this concept and are utilized in the prison system. Often sponsored by different Christian denominations or run by inmate groups, these self-help programs focus on religiosity and rehabilitation for the offender. They provide counseling, Bible study, worship services, and reformation services for prisoners based on a faith in God. These programs teach forgiveness, reconciliation, and growth. Groups such as Prison Fellowship Ministries and Kairos Prison Ministries have been extremely successful in these institutions and find a way for inmates to channel their negative energy in a positive outlet (Van Ness & Strong, 2006; Johnson, 2011).

In regards to outcome, restorative justice programs aim to reduce recidivism with rehabilitation a natural result of the lack of criminal activity. However, critics of the programs challenge its effectiveness. A meta-analysis of 35 programs showed inconsistent evidence that restorative justice programs reduced recidivism (Latimer, Dowden, and Muse, 2005). For example, Tyler et al. (2007) found that the Australian Reintegrative Shaming Experiments (RISE) did not affect recidivism, but Rodriguez (2005; 2007) asserted that young offenders who completed these programs had less criminal activity afterward. Latimer et al. (2005) believed that most of the evaluations of these programs did not focus on crime reduction but rather satisfaction of the participants with the process.

Summary

The basic assertions of labeling theory present a logical connection between how others perceive us and our reaction to that perception. Specifically, it focuses on the label given to us by the criminal justice system for our deviant behaviors and how that affects our future behaviors. Support for labeling theory as an explanation of crime has varied in waves. During its origination and into the 1960s, academics supported its assertions, but heavy criticisms limited its credible use in the 1980s.

However, in the early 21st century, it has reemerged as a viable option for explaining criminality.

One of the best uses of the theory is the development of programs and policies that address positive methods of surviving a negative label. For instance, prison education and vocation programs provide offenders with the skills to positively reintegrate back into the community after incarceration. Further, faith-based programs give offenders a positive spiritual outlet to use as a method of handling stress in a positive outlet rather than criminally. Even if recidivism behaviors of the offenders do not diminish immediately, it gives them tools to better themselves after the application of the label rather than to continue to live as permanent offenders.

Discussion Questions

1. Explain how a label placed on you affected your behavior. Does this give support to labeling theory?
2. Labeling theory has received a lot of criticism, including that it only attempts to explain juvenile crime. Do you agree with this assertion, and why?

REFERENCES

Bazemore, G., & Schiff, M. (Eds.). (2001). *Restorative and community justice: Repairing harm and transforming communities.* Cincinnati, OH: Anderson Publishing Co.

Becker, H. (1963). *Outsiders: Studies in the sociology of deviance* (21st ed., pp. 1-215). New York: Free Press.

Bernburg, J.G. (2002). Anomie, social change, and crime: A theoretical examination of institutional-anomie theory. *British Journal of Criminology. 42,* 729–42.

Bernburg, J. G., & Krohn, M. D. (2003). Labeling, life chances, and adult crime: The direct and indirect effects of official intervention in adolescence on crime in early adulthood. *Criminology, 41*(4), 1287-1318.

Boshier, R. & Johnson, D. (1974). Does conviction affect employment opportunities? *British Journal of Criminology. 14,* 264-268.

Bowdich, C. (1993). Getting rid of troublemakers: High school disciplinary procedures and the production of dropouts. *Social Problems, 40,* 493-507.

Braithwaite (1989). *Crime, shame, and reintegration.* New York: Cambridge.

Braithwaite, J. (1995). Reintegrative shaming, republicanism and policy, in H. Barlow (ed.), *Criminology and public policy: Putting theory to work,* Boulder: Westview Press.

Braithwaite, J. (2002). *Restorative justice and responsive regulation.* New York: Oxford Univ. Press.

Braithwaite, John (2006). Accountability and responsibility through restorative justice, in Michael W. Dowdle (ed.), *Public accountability, designs, dilemmas, and experiences. Cambridge,* UK: Cambridge University Press.

Brown, P. (2013, April 3). Opening up, students transform a vicious circle. *New York Times.* Retrieved July 23, 2013, from: http://www.nytimes.com/2013/04/04/education/restorative-justice-programs-take-root-in-schools.html?pagewanted = all

Cohen, S. (1979). The punitive city: Notes on the dispersal of social control. *Contemporary Crises, 3:* 339-363.

Cooley, C. (1902). *Human nature and the social order.* New York: C. Scribner's Sons.

Davies, S. & Tanner, J. (2003). The long arm of the law: A test of labeling theory. *Sociological Quarterly, 44*(3), 385-404.

Einstadter, W. J., & Henry, S. (2006). *Criminological theory: An analysis of its underlying assumptions.* Boulder, CO: Rowman and Littlefield.

Furstenberg, F. F., Rumbaut, R. G., & Settersten, R. A. (2005). *On the frontier of adulthood: Emerging themes and new directions.* (pp. 3-25). Chicago: The University of Chicago Press.

Goffman, E. (1959). *The presentation of self in everyday life* (1st ed., pp. 1-259). Anchor.

Goode, E. (1975). On behalf of labeling theory. *Social Problems, 22*(5), 570-583.

Gove, R. (1975). *Labeling of deviance: Evaluating a perspective.* Hoboken: John Wiley & Sons Inc.

Gove, R. (1980). *Labeling of deviance: Evaluating a perspective* (2nd ed., pp.1-428). Sage Publications Inc.

Grimes, R.M. & Turk, A.T. (1978). *Labeling in context: Conflict, power, and self-definition* (pp. 1-20). Sage Publications Inc.

Hawkins, R. & Tiedeman, G. (1975). *The creation of deviance: Interpersonal and organizational determinants.* Columbus: C.E. Merrill Publishing Company.

Heimer, K., & Matsueda, R.L. (1994). Role-taking, role commitment, and delinquency: A theory of differential social control. *American Sociological Review, 59,* 365-390.

Heimer, C.A., (1996). *Gender differences in the distribution of responsibility* (pp. 241-273). Boulder, CO: Westview Press.

Hjalmarsson, R. (2012) Can executions have a short-term deterrence effect on non-felony homicides? *Criminology & Public Policy. 11*(3): 565-571.

Hirschi, T. (1980). *Labelling theory and juvenile delinquency: An assessment of the evidence* (2nd ed., pp. 271-302). New York: Wiley.

Irwin, J. (2005). *The warehouse prison: Disposal of the new dangerous class.* Los Angeles: Roxbury.

Johnson, B. R. (2011). *More God, less crime: Why religion matters and how it could matter more.* Conshohocken, PA: Templeton Press.

Kraska, P. B. (2004). *Theorizing criminal justice: Eight essential orientations.* Prospect Heights, IL: Waveland Press.

Kurlychek, M., Bushway,S., & Brame R. (2007). Enduring risk? Old criminal records and predictions of future criminal involvement. *Crime & Delinquency, 53*(1), 64-83.

Latimer, J., Dowden, C., & Muise, D. (2005). The effectiveness of restorative justice practices: A meta-analysis. *Prison Journal, 85,* 127-145.

Lemert, E. (1951). *Social pathology: A systematic approach to the theory of sociopathic behavior.* New York: McGraw-Hill.

Lopes, G., Krohn, M. D., Lizotte, A. J., Schmidt, N. M., Vasquez, B. E., & Bernburg, J. G. (2012). Labeling and cumulative disadvantage: The impact of formal police intervention on life chances and crime during emerging adulthood. *Crime & Delinquency, 58*(3), 456-488.

Matsueda, R.L. (1992). Reflected appraisal, parental labeling, and delinquency: Specifying a symbolic interactionist theory. *American Journal of Sociology. 97(6),* 1577-1611.

Matsueda, R.L. (2001). Labeling theory: Historical roots, implications, and recent developments. In R. Paternoster and R. Bachman (Eds.), *Explaining criminals and crime,* 223-241. Los Angeles: Roxbury Press.

Matsueda, R. L. & Heimer, K. (1997). *A symbolic interactionist theory of role transitions, role commitments, and delinquency.* New Brunswick: Transaction Publishers.

Mead, G. (1934). *Mind, self, and society.* Chicago: University of Chicago Press.

Orcutt, J. (1973). Societal reaction and the response to deviation in small groups. *Social Forces. 52,* 259-267.

Pager, D. (2003). The mark of a criminal record. *American Journal of Sociology, 108,* 937-975.

Pager, D. & Quillian, L. (2005). Walking the talk: What employers say versus what they do. *American Sociological Review. 70,* 355-80.

Rodriguez, N. (2007). Restorative justice at work: Examining the impact of restorative justice resolutions on juvenile recidivism. *Crime & Delinquency, 53*, 355-379.

Sampson, R.J. & Laub, J.H. (1993). *Crime in the making: Pathways and turning points through life.* Cambridge, Mass.: Harvard University Press.

Smith, A. & Paternoster, R. (1990). Formal processing and future delinquency: Deviance amplification as selection artifact. *Law and Society Review 24*, 1109-1131.

Sweeten, G. (2006). Who will graduate? Disruption of high school education by arrest and court involvement. *Justice Quarterly*, 23, 462–480.

Tannenbaum, F. (1938). *Crime and the community.* New York and London: Columbia University Press.

Tittle, C. (1980). *Labeling and crime: An empirical evaluation* (2nd ed., pp. 241-263) New York: Wiley.

Tullis, P. (2013, January 4). Can forgiveness play a role in criminal justice? *New York Times*. Retrieved July 23, 2013, from http://www.nytimes.com/2013/01/06/magazine/can-forgiveness-play-a-role-in-criminal-justice.html?pagewanted = all

Tyler, T. R., Sherman, L., Strang, H., Barnes, G. C. & Woods, D. (2007). Reintegrative shaming, procedural justice, and recidivism: The engagement of offenders' psychological mechanism in the Canberra RISE drinking-and-driving experiment. *Law and Society Review, 41*, 553-585.

Uggen, C. (2000). Work as a turning point in the life course of criminals: A duration model of age, employment, and recidivism. *American Sociological Review*, 65, 529–546.

Uggen C., Vuolo M., Ruhland E., Whitham H., Lageson S. (2012). *An experimental audit of the effects of low-level criminal records on employment.* Unpublished manuscript.

Van Ness, D.W., Strong, K.H. (2006) *Restoring justice: an introduction to restorative justice* (3rd ed). London: LexisNexis/Anderson Publishing.

Williams, F., & McShane, M. (2010). *Criminology theory: Selected classic readings.* (2nd ed., pp. 1-350). Elsevier.

Conflict and Critical Theories

CHAPTER OUTLINE

Introduction

Conflict Criminology

Development of Conflict Theories
Pluralist Conflict
Vold
Turk
Quinney
Blalock
Case Study 9.1: Racial Profiling

Radical Conflict Perspective

Critical Criminology

Notable Critical Criminologists
Young
Ferrell
Pepinsky and Quinney

Policy Implications

Summary

Discussion Questions

References

Key Words and Concepts

Conflict Theory
Constitutive Criminology
Cultural Criminology
Critical Realism
Critical Theory
Hegemony

Interest Groups
Law
Left Idealist
Left Realism
Peacemaking Criminology
Resources

Restorative Justice
Postmodern
Power
Radical Theory
Replacement
    Discourse

Introduction

At the time of its emergence, Marxist theory was viewed as an extremist view of criminology that provided an explanation of criminal behavior developed from conflict theory. Despite being a separate category of theoretical thought, the term Marxist theory was used interchangeably with **conflict theory, radical theory, and critical theory**. Rather than assuming that Marxist theory is the umbrella explanation for those theoretical explanations, some contemporary literature categorizes various viewpoints under the label of radical or critical criminology. Radical criminology focuses on the struggles against state control and powerful entities controlling what is viewed as normal and acceptable behavior (De Giorgi, 2014). In other words, it is an examination of different forms of oppression against the poor and weaker classes. For example, Takagi (1974) investigated police violence against black men as a control of "surplus labor." Feminist theory was also one of the early components of radical criminology, exploring the plague of rape victimization on the female society (Schwendinger & Schwendinger, 1974). Further, early studies discussed how male oppression and patriarchal roles fueled violence against women (see Chapter 11).

It is important to note the time period in which radical or critical criminology was reborn into the criminological field. In the 1960s and 1970s, during the Vietnam War, Women's Liberation, and Civil Rights Movement, there was a strong push for social justice. The dominant view by criminologists at this time was that crime was a result of macro-level forces, such as economic and political groups, rather than individual motivators (Agnew & Cullen, 2003; Lanier & Henry, 1998). As a result, there was a push for policies that promoted lessening governmental control and more rehabilitative measures for those in the criminal justice system.

Conflict Criminology

The development of conflict theories occurred at approximately the same time as labeling theory. Both labeling and conflict theories foundationally used politics to examine the nature of the law. When both labeling and conflict theories were in development, labeling theory seemed to attract more attention. The attention came because labeling theory was less radical to conservative criminologists than conflict theories. This trend persisted until the 1970s, when conflict theories began to emerge as an important set of viewpoints.

Conflict theories have one main assumption: Society was best viewed as consistent conflict rather than being under a consensus. Because of this view, a number of conflict theories were possible. The number of conflict theories and their different foci allowed them to be placed on a continuum. At one end of the continuum, pluralist versions of conflict theory arose that assumed that groups of varying sizes and temporary power would struggle to see their interests maintained in any number of issues. On the other end of the continuum, class-conflict versions of conflict theory suggested that there were two classes that struggled to dominate society.

No matter the position on the continuum, conflict theorists viewed consensus as an abnormality that would give way to conflict yet again. Consensus was viewed as a drain on resources that would be nearly impossible to sustain. Conflict was inevitable because it was less costly. The theorists in this perspective viewed power as a tool to keep up the illusion of consensus, which would be the main problem that conflict theorists study. An important perspective for conflict theorists was that individuals were not interesting, so they did not concern themselves with individual behavior. Conflict theorists focused on making the laws rather than enforcing the laws.

Development of Conflict Theories

Labeling theory provided an avenue for the development of conflict theories. Labeling theorists began asking questions about symbolic interactionism, but a number of social events took place that pushed some to begin to ask questions about social and legal structures. For instance, in the 1950s and 1960s, many Americans began to become disenfranchised with society. The civil rights movement paved the way for other groups to seek equality in social opportunities. The tenor of this period in American history was one of questioning or rejection of middle-class values. Some suggestions were being made to decriminalize "victimless" crimes. Other events fueled the questions about society or government, such as the Watergate scandal, which casted major doubt on morality and integrity. In this scandal, the U.S. president was implicated in a number of crimes. This led criminologists to begin to theorize about society as a whole.

Conflict theories had not been very popular. This does not mean that conflict theories were not present in the sociological or criminological literature. Sociologically, conflict theories were evident during the early 20th century. For instance, Bonger's (1916) conflict theory was an integration of psychoanalytic theory and Marxist thought. In the mid-20th century, others were writing about conflict theory (Coser, 1956 & Dahrendorf, 1958, 1959). During the 1960s, with American society in flux, conflict theories began to flourish. The development of conflict theories during this period was fueled by the radicalization of academia. Academics breathed new air into Marx's theory with applications to crime and legal structures.

Conflict theories were not developed in a way that used the same concepts, but they did have a common theme: the notion that conflict is natural to society. The multitude of concepts used in conflict theory implies that a number of theories were present in the conflict theory literature. Be that as it may, these theories can be grouped in one of two ways: pluralist or critical-radical.

Pluralist Conflict

These theories used **power** as the key concept. They also viewed power as a tool that could be used to exercise control over particular situations, events, or social issues. Social issues came from problems in everyday life. Noticing these problems was not simple. Lobbying for social issues by **interest groups** or some other entity (i.e., business group or political group) led to a number of decisions. The decisions were of interest to some groups, and the decisions would spark a reaction. The reaction would be to exert additional influence to continue to have their issues heard and noticed. The amount of influence that each group would have would be contingent on the amount of a group's resources. Power was the equivalent of having resources.

This process is present today. In the legislative process, special interest groups will consistently lobby members of the United States Congress. To gain their attention, these interest groups may provide campaign financing or campaign advertisements to get their issues noticed by Congress. The issues that have the largest amount of support or have special interest with the largest amount of resources will get their issues heard or noticed.

The idea that power was equal to **resources** implied that those with resources were more likely to be powerful. This implication indicated that class was an important issue. Those higher up in social class would be more likely to influence decisions than those that were in a lower social class. The influence would allow them to impose their values and morals onto others. Conflict theorist believed that this was why there was a dominant middle class. This view gave way to the perspective that society's laws were wrapped in middle-class values. Because conflict theorists were questioning power and its connections to laws, they were really questioning middle-class values.

Conflict theorists saw the **law** as a resource. The law could be used as a benefit to any group that felt it represented their values. These groups could use agents of law enforcement to uphold the values of the dominant group that provided a corollary keeping those in power who already had power. This meant that those that were outside the dominant group were subjected to the power of law enforcement agents. Here, a connection between conflict and labeling theories can be made. Specifically, those that are subjected to law enforcement were stigmatized because of their opposition or existence outside the dominant group. Conflict theorist assumed that laws were created and modified to enrich the official reactions to the less powerful.

Conflict theorists thought more about the connection between power and the creation of the law. Law was used to make the behaviors of other groups illegal. The dominant group was not subjected to this type of legal action. One way of thinking about this was that behavior by others not in the dominant group was viewed as wrong, and subjected to legal attention; thus, the behavior of those in the dominant group was viewed as prosocial. The law was not just used to criminalize the behavior of those not in the dominant group. Conflict theorists believed that the law was used as a weapon to reduce the opportunity for those not in the dominant group to become powerful. A number of conflict theorists (Vold, Turk, Quinny, and Blalock) used these assumptions to provide conflict views of criminal behavior.

Vold

Vold (1958) presented a sociological conflict theory. His theory emphasized the group nature of society and competing interests. The central premise was that groups came into conflict when their interests would overlap and collide. During the conflict, the members of the groups would become closer and tightly knit. Vold (1958) argued that groups were always being watchful for their interests. When their interests were being threatened, the groups were ready to defend them. This created an environment of constant struggle for the group. The election process provided an example of this process (i.e., Republican vs. Democrat).

This perspective had been applied to crime and criminal law. Vold and Bernard (1986) argued that the process of lawmaking, law breaking, and law enforcement were products of special interests. The special interests represented groups that desired the control of law enforcement. Vold (1958) observed that minority groups would be particularly vulnerable to lawmaking. Minority groups did have direct access to the legislative process; thus, their behavior would be seen as outside of the behavior of the dominant group. In other words, minority group behaviors would be seen as criminal, and the dominant group would consistently legislate the behavior of minority groups as criminal.

Turk

Turk (1964) developed a conflict theory that attempted to explain the connection between social order and powerful groups. In his conflict theory, power groups were attempting to control society. These groups used criminal law to do so. Criminal law seemed to follow the values of the power groups. This led Turk to suggest that the important mechanism for study was criminal law. Specifically, Turk argued that the link between criminal law and the notion of criminal status should be examined. One way of thinking about this was to be concerned about the conditions under which an individual would be considered a criminal in an authority-subject relationship. Criminal status was usually given to the less sophisticated individuals because they were more likely to have their interactions with law enforcement be seen as conflict.

Turk (1969, 1976) used the authority-subject relationship to further develop his theory. He saw that society needed to be controlled. The control came in two forms: coercion and legal images. Coercion was seen as a delicate method of control. Turk felt that the more a population was forced to obey the law, the more difficult it would be to control the society. This would require a delicate balance between consensus and coercion.

Legal images were also important to Turk's perspective. Turk wrote that the law itself could be something that was more important than people. Turk proffered two types of law: the legal statutes that provided a list of illegal behaviors with punishments and the process of moving people through the legal system. A legal process that favors the powerful will provide subtle control over the powerless. Turk (1976) also developed the idea of control of living time. This idea suggested that after a period of coercion, society would adjust itself to a new set of rules. As time passes, those that were part of the pre-coercion period would die off, and the remaining people who only knew the new society would remain. There would be fewer comparisons between the old and new societies. Eventually, little questioning about the rules would occur.

Turks' theory provided a number of propositions. First, as coercion increased, higher crime rates were to be expected. Second, the greater the power of the controlling group, the higher the crime rate among the powerless group. Third, when the less powerful were organized, the rate of conflict with the powerful group would be higher.

Quinney

Quinney (1970) viewed humans as rational beings. While humans were rational, they were subjected to an unequal distribution of power that would result in conflict. The conflict took place between competing groups of society that were trying to advance their position. Relying on Vold's ideas of a group, Quinney suggested that the group did not have to be organized. Those with an interest and power to shape legislation did so through legislators and judges to formulate definitions of crime that controlled those with whom they were in conflict. The conflict did not always have to be a political struggle, but the conflict could be an act of resistance. Criminalization was done with the view toward maintaining the current balance of power, or it was done to increase the powerful group's position.

The definitions of crime were not only pieces of legislation, they were also part the public's view of crime. The public became educated about crime through the media. To develop his ideas on social reality, Quinney (1970) argued some ideas of crime were present because of the representations of crime in the media. This is where the perception of criminal as villain was personified.

Quinney (1970) argued that criminal definitions were applied by the authorized agents of those segments of society having power. The application of the criminal definitions was contingent on the perception of threat that came from the powerless group. When the powerless group committed visible crimes that seemed to threaten the standing of the powerful, criminal processing would increase. Quinney (1970) argued that the social reality of crime was designed to protect the interests of one group over another group's interest.

Blalock

Another theoretical perspective that falls under pluralism is Blalock's (1967) version of racial threat. Rather than follow the previous conflict theories that suggest group conflict occurring through wealth and class, Blalock (1967) argued that the conflict was due to racial differences in society. He suggested that whites were in the political and economic majority. When other racial or ethnic groups attempted to challenge this majority—whether real or imagined— they would be met with opposition. The opposition would come in the form of legislation or law enforcement. The major challenge to the majority was the growth of the minority populations, which would eventually lead to increased political power and opposition. The majority would respond in a number of ways. First, it would restrict access to the political process, as has been done by felon disenfranchisement. Second, the majority would increase symbolic forms of segregation. Third, the majority would create a threat-oriented ideological system. Overall, Blalock argued that discrimination would increase when the power-threat increased. Hawkins (1987) argued that the challenges to the majority did not have to be real challenges and proffered that the challenges had to only be perceptions.

CASE STUDY 9.1
RACIAL PROFILING

Rev. Theron Williams, who pastors a church with 3,000 members, remembers taking his Corvette convertible out several years ago in Indianapolis and being pulled over not once, not twice, but three times within an hour. Separate officers checked whether the car was stolen, cautioned him on his speed, and asked if he'd done some midday drinking. Exasperated after the third stop, he went home without a ticket, convinced his only crime had been driving a sports car while black.

Explain these actions using Blalock's theory.

Radical Conflict Perspective

The radical conflict perspective was even more disparate than the pluralist perspective. While they differ, the radical theories have a common thread. The thread of interest is Marxist theory. Marx had very little to say about crime and criminals. The radical criminologists that had applied this theory to crime and criminals adapted the general model for their explanations. For Marx, conflict was about resources and historical inequality. Marx believed that resources were scarce and that this created conflict; and the inequality would create conflict between those that have power and those that do not have power. Marx named these two power groups. The proletariat was known as the working class, and the bourgeoisie was a group of nonworking owners of wealth.

Applying this theory, Marx argued that conflict between the proletariat and the bourgeoisie was due to ownership of production. The proletariat was the means of production, but the bourgeoisie owned the means of production. The bourgeoisie tended to exploit the proletariat causing a struggle to develop. Group position was used to shape the image of society. The bourgeoisie designed a method to suggest that capitalism was in the interest of the proletariat. As the proletariat became aware of their actual group position, they would band together with others in the proletariat and create overt conflict. The conflict would result in an attempted overthrow of the ruling class.

At the center of the applications of Marxist theory to criminology was the use of class and class struggle. This was evident in three positions by Marxist criminologists. The first position was that the law was the tool of the ruling class. The ruling class values were used to develop the law that would continue their views toward property and the distribution of wealth. The ruling class was not necessarily held to the same standard as the rest of the working class. This was a view that was presented by other conflict theorists. However, Marxist criminologists saw law breaking as more of a violation of human rights.

The second position was that all crime was due to the struggle in class position. The struggle in class position increased the necessity for competition and individualism. This would lead to conflict between and within the classes to accumulate wealth and property. In other words, the attempts to make their way in the world would show itself in criminal behavior. Therefore, criminal behavior was a product of capitalism.

The third position was that there was a link between the mode of production and criminal behavior. The main issue was that there was a surplus of labor. The surplus of labor provided a guarantee that wages would be low, but when the labor surplus was too low, this would cause a substantial amount of problems. These problems ranged from theft to drug use. With these problems, as long as the group that was producing them was quiet or invisible, the ruling class would not expend very much energy on them; but when they became active, they would pose a threat to the ruling class where controlling its members was important.

Critical Criminology

Henry and Milovanovic (1991; 1996) asserted that the term critical criminology still lacked clarity, so they suggested using the term **constitutive criminology.** Constitutive criminology could include a variety of themes, including critical and other **postmodern** perspectives, as well as peacemaking, feminism, or race theories. Postmodern theorists concerned themselves with discrediting **hegemony** (or all-encompassing influence) and pushed for the agenda favoring underprivileged individuals (Schwartz & Friedrichs, 1994). Henry and Milovanovic (1991) stated that although constitutive criminology is not aggressively oppositional, it does reject mainstream criminology. They suggested that the way crime and power are related should be redefined, as power is often distributed unequally and in turn causes harm to the powerless. According to them, the law selects only some of the harmful relations and determines them to be a crime.

Constitutive criminologists assert that there are two types of crime: crimes of reduction and crimes of repression. Crimes of reduction are those that offend an individual based on a loss, such as a hate crime that causes a person shame. A crime of repression occurs when a person is blocked or restricted from a goal based on a characteristic, such as sexism (Henry & Milovanovic, 2003). Obviously, these categories do not consider the physical repercussions of a crime, or even financial or property loss. Instead, they consider the psychological consequences of criminal behavior and push for a system that is more considerate of the well-being of those involved. For this chapter, we will examine three forms of critical (or constitutive) criminology: left realism, cultural criminology, and peacemaking criminology. While these theories are not necessarily supported with extensive empirical studies, they do pose a different way to view current theoretical thought.

 ## Notable Critical Criminologists

Young

The concept of **left realism** emerged from the works of British criminologists focusing on radical criminology in the 1970s. Developed by Jock Young (1987), these were extreme positions that individuals had taken regarding crime, as well as a reaction to increasing criminal victimization in Britain and the rise to power of political conservatives. In the 1980s, both Britain and the United States had conservative governments that supported tough-on-crime policies for crime control. Left realists called for the return of traditional liberal as well as radical approaches to managing crime. In addition, their views were a reaction to those of the **left idealists**, who overlooked the pain suffered by the victims of crime. According to Lowman (1992), left idealists believed criminals to be revolutionaries who were determined but blameless, and punishment was unnecessary for their behaviors.

Left realists also criticized left idealists for their beliefs that crime is fiction created by the dominant authority figures (the ruling class) and that the criminal justice system simply oppresses individuals with no crime control. Instead, left realists lessened their critiques of law enforcement and instead advocated for rehabilitative policies, such as victim services, community service, community policing, and shorter prison sentences (Gibbons, 1994; Curran & Renzetti, 2001). While left realists believe they are making innovative recommendations in regard to policy recommendations, their views are not that different from mainstream liberal agendas that promote crime prevention and less punitive policies.

A more recent derivation of left realism is **critical realism**, which acknowledges that there are objective dimensions of crime that are not adjustable simply through verbal discussion (Matthew, 2010). In other words, changes in defining crime and in the criminal justice system policies require more effort than instantaneous decision making. However, despite the versions, these views of realism are not theoretical explanations of crime or testable assertions; instead, they are simply philosophical and political statements about how a criminal justice system should operate.

Ferrell

One of Young's colleagues, American Jeff Ferrell, developed **cultural criminology**. Cultural criminology focuses on the importance of using cultural dynamics to develop meanings of crime and crime control (Ferrell et al., 2008). Culture is not a stable concept, but is comprised of traditions, values, and norms that are carried about by societal members and change based on how they are constructed by the offenders. In other words, crime is defined based on those who experience the event and the emotions associated with it, as well as the range of symbolic meanings and words used to explain crime (Ferrell, 2010). Cultural criminologists see crime as a part of everyday expression, and crime control is an attempt to suppress that expression. Rather than being a black and white concept and legal definition of a behavior, it is a constructed phenomenon determined by society and the media. The media contorts criminal events to create a story that will sell to the public based on what is culturally interesting.

Cultural criminology is seen as critical criminology as Ferrell and colleagues strongly criticize orthodox criminology. They support earlier sociological and subcultural approaches, such as the ethnographic studies of the 1920s and 1930s of the Chicago school. Further, there is support for the concept of symbolic interactionism, social disorganization, labeling, and conflict theories. Cultural criminologists are extremely critical of theorists that use complex statistical analyses from quantitative data that removes human emotions, perceptions, and human agency from the study. Theories such as rational choice theory or routine activities theory are disregarded by cultural criminologists as they portray crime as a cold, calculating act that is a simple choice. These theories are supportive of harsh, punitive punishments that do not consider treatment of the offender (Ferrell et al., 2008).

Pepinsky and Quinney

Peacemaking criminology found its roots thousands of years ago in early Eastern philosophies and religions that focused on a peaceful way of life (Pepinsky & Quinney, 1991). For instance, Buddhists and Taoists taught mindfulness and connectedness with self. Upon their emergence into America, the Quakers (a Christian group) are credited with breaking from Britain's violent reign of terror and implementing a peaceful and meditative method of punishment and solitude for offenders (Hamm, 2003). Further, the Quakers led the first social rights movements for women's suffrage, black civil rights, and protection of Native American rights.

As time progressed and we were forced into a social justice movement during the 1960s and 1970s, young scholars such as Harold Pepinsky and Richard Quinney, as well as social activists like Martin Luther King, Jr., promoted the use of peacemaking to criminal justice issues. Meditation, rehabilitation, and incarceration alternatives were better options compared to punitive measures (Quinney & Wildman, 1991). Pepinsky and Quinney (1991) asserted that the relationship between offenders and the other stakeholders in the criminal justice system is one full of aggression and violence (war-like). As an alternative, they suggest peacemaking techniques to better not only the relationship between all individuals involved, but also to decrease the need for punitive (and expensive) measures in the criminal justice system. Programs such as conflict resolution and mediation are calm, peaceful methods of bringing people together and fostering forgiveness rather than anger.

Quinney's prior theoretical viewpoints involved conflict and Marxist concepts, but peacemaking criminology derives from Christian and Buddhist beliefs. He specifically believed that crime was a form of suffering for all involved: When suffering ends, crime ends. Further, rather than deriving ideas of justice from science and media propaganda, justice should be visualized through spirituality and faith (Braswell, McCarthy, & McCarthy, 2002).

Policy Implications

Mainstream theories argue for various types of policies and practices to deter and diminish crime. However, radical theorists argued that these suggestions do more than attempt to control crime; instead, they increase governmental control on its citizens. Working with police, courts, and corrections (controlling agencies of the criminal justice system) to reduce crime places unnecessary increased control on individuals in a society. For instance, the War on Drugs has caused drastic over-crowding in our prison system (Johns, 1992), and undercover police work has caused a "maximum-security society," putting all of us under constant scrutiny (Weiss, 1987).

Rather than promoting measures of social control to decrease crime, postmo-dernists encourage the use of **replacement discourse.** Rather than sensationalize criminal activity, criminologists and practitioners are encouraged to communicate correct and positive interpretations of crime. Instead of promoting punishment, replacement discourse advocates for alternative solutions that change an offender (e.g., drug and alcohol therapy, self-help groups, and anger management). Replace-ment discourse advocates especially promote programs categorized as **restorative justice**, which focus on reintegrating the offender back into society through com-munication and forgiveness. Restorative justice advocates see crime as a violation of the offender, victim, and society, and they believe that it is the responsibility of the community to help the offender understand his or her responsibility in the event and how to correct it. Together, the victim and community should determine the appropriate punishment for the offender, and once justice is served, forgiveness is received (Braswell et al., 2002).

Much like the other two critical theories discussed in this chapter, peacemaking criminology is not a theory that attempts to explain criminal behavior or can be empirical tested (Fuller & Wozniak, 2006). Instead, it offers suggestions of how to live a non-violent and accepting existence through peaceful religious values. For example, Christianity focuses on forgiveness, reintegration, and kindness, rather than obtaining power and wealth. Contemporary policy evolutions of these concepts for the criminal would include prison ministries, community policing, and gun control measures. Further, opposition of capital punishment and war of any form would be supported by peacemaking criminologists (Fuller & Woziniak, 2006). Friedrichs (1996) asserted that programs such as problem-oriented policing and victim–offender mediation can be effective and are worth further resourcing.

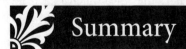 # Summary

The conflict perspective changed the nature of criminological theorizing. Most criminologists acknowledge the presence of conflict in American society. However, criminologists have not been in consensus about the extent that conflict has on crime. Conflict theories were shown to be diverse, but they did show some common threads. The first thread was that conflict was natural in society. The second thread was that resources were scarce and the possession of these resources conveyed power over others. The third thread was that competition for these resources always existed. The fourth thread was that the use of competition, law, and law enforcement allowed those with resources to maintain their position in society. When a group maintains power long enough, this may result in a class system that includes a ruling and a working class.

Critics would argue that the three critical criminological theories presented were not actually theories at all, but rather suggestions of how to better live one's life. These concepts are not empirically tested like the other theories mentioned in this book and often seem idealistic to many. However, it is possible that these thought patterns and suggestions for a less punitive criminal justice system could evolve into a testable theory. Although not original ideas, these are ideas that have been pushed aside for years for use of mandatory sentencing, capital punishment, and other retributive measures of controlling crime. The future of these theories is yet to be seen.

Discussion Questions

1. Discuss how the law is used today in our criminal justice system to support who is currently in power in the White House. How will our criminal justice system change when someone new takes the presidential office?
2. Explain the differences between racial conflict in the 1960s and today. Do you believe racial conflict affects our criminal justice system today?

REFERENCES

Blalock, H. M. Jr. (1967). *Toward a theory of minority-group relations*. New York, NY: John Wiley.

Bonger, W. (1916). *Criminality and economic conditions*. Boston, MA: Little Brown.

Braswell, M., McCarthy, B., & McCarthy, B. (Eds.). (2002). *Justice, crime and ethics* (4th ed.). Cincinnati: Anderson.

Coser, L. (1956). *The functions of social conflict*. New York, NY: MacMillian.

Curran, D. & Renzetti, C. (2001). *Theories of crime* (2nd ed.). Boston: Allyn & Bacon.

Dahrendorf, R. (1958). Out of utopia: Toward a reconstruction of sociological analysis. *American Journal of Sociology, 67*, 115-127.

Dahrendorf, R. (1959). *Class and class conflict in an industrial society*. London: Routledge & Keagan Paul.

Di Giorgi, A. (2014). Reform or revolution: Thoughts on liberal and radical criminologies. *Social Justice, 40(1/2)*, 24-31.

Ferrell, J. (2010). Cultural criminology: The loose cannon. In E. McLaughlin and T. Newburn (Eds.), *The Sage Handbook of Criminological Theory* (pp. 303-318). Los Angeles: Sage.

Ferrell, J., Hayward, K., & Young, J. (2008). *Cultural criminology: An invitation*. London: Sage.

Friedrichs, D. (1996). Peacemaking criminology and the punitive conundrum: A new foundation for social control in the twenty-first century? In C. Sistare (Ed.), *Punishment: Social control and coercion* (pp. 27–54). New York: Peter Lang.

Fuller, J. & Wozniak, J. (2006). Peacemaking criminology: Past, present and future. In F. Cullen, J. Wright, and K. Blevins (Eds.), *Taking stock: The status of criminological theory. Advances in criminological theory*, 251-273. New Brunswick, NJ: Transaction.

Gibbons, D. (1994). *Talking about crime and criminals: Problems and issues in theory development in criminology.* Englewood Cliffs, NJ: Prentice Hall.

Hamm, T. (2003). *The Quakers in America.* New York: Columbia University Press.

Hawkins, D. F. (1987). Beyond anomalies: Rethinking the conflict perspective on race and capital punishment. *Social Forces, 65*, 719-745.

Henry, S. & Milovanovic, D. (1991). Constitutive criminology: The maturation of critical theory. *Criminology, 29*, 293-315.

Henry, S. & Milovanovic, D. (1996). *Constitutive criminology: Beyond postmodernism.* London: Sage.

Henry, S. & Milovanovic, D. (2003). Constitutive criminology. In M. Schwartz & S. Hatty (Eds.), *Controversies in critical criminology* (pp. 57-69). Cincinnati, OH: Anderson.

Johns, C. (1992). *The War on Drugs.* Westport, CT: Greenwood Press.

Lanier, M., & Henry, S. (1998). *Essential criminology.* Boulder, CO: Westview Press.

Lowman, J. (1992). Rediscovering crime. In J. Young and R. Matthews (Eds.), *Rethinking criminology: The realist debate.* London: Sage.

Matthews, R. (2010). Realist criminology revisited. In E. McLaughlin & T. Newburn (Eds.), *The sage handbook of criminological theory* (pp. 193-209). London: Sage.

Quinney, R. (1970). *The social reality of crime.* Boston, MA: Little Brown.

Quinney, R., & Pepinsky, H. (Eds.) (1991). *Criminology as peacemaking.* Bloomington: Indiana University Press.

Quinney, R., & Wildman, J. (1991). *The problem of crime: A peace and social justice perspective.* Mountain View, CA: Mayfield.

Schwartz, M. & Friedrichs, D. (1994). Postmodern thought and criminological discontent: New metaphors for understanding violence. *Criminology, 32*, 221-246.

Schwendinger, J. R., & Schwendinger, H. (1974). Rape myths: In legal, theoretical, and everyday practice. *Crime and Social Justice, 1*, 18–26.

Takagi, P. (1974). A Garrison state in "democratic" society. *Crime and Social Justice, 1*, 1-13.

Turk, A. (1964). Prospects for theories of criminal behavior. *Journal of Criminal Law, Criminology, and Police Science, 55*, 454-461.

Turk, A. (1969). *Criminality and the legal order.* Chicago, IL: Rand McNally.

Turk, A. (1976). Law as a weapon in social conflict. *Social Problems, 23*, 276-291.

Vold, G. B. (1958). *Theoretical criminology.* New York, NY: Oxford University Press.

Vold, G. B., & Bernard, T. J. (1986). *Theoretical criminology* (3rd ed.). New York, NY: Oxford University Press.

Weiss, R. (1987). From "slugging detectives" to "labor relations." In C. Shearing and P. Stenning (Eds.), *Private policing* (pp. 110-130). Beverly Hills, CA: Sage.

Young, J. (1987). The tasks facing a realist criminology. *Contemporary Crises, 11*, 337-356.

CHAPTER 10

Feminist Theory

CHAPTER OUTLINE

Introduction
Chivalry Hypothesis

Progression of Feminist Theory
Adler
Simon
Hagan
Messerschmidt
Case Study 10.1: Piper Kerman
Daly and Chesney-Lind

Empirical Research

Policy Implications
Case Study 10.2: Outward Bound

Summary

Discussion Questions

References

Key Words and Concepts

Andocentric
Chivalry Hypothesis
Economic Marginalization
   Hypothesis
Egalitarian Family
Feminism
Feminist
Gendered Pathways
   Perspective

Intimate Partner Violence
   (IPV)
Liberal Feminism
Marxist Feminism
Masculinity
Masculinity
   Hypothesis
Opportunity
   Hypothesis

Paternalism
Patriarchal
Patriarchal Family
Power Control
   Theory
Radical Feminism
Socialist
   Feminism
Structured Action

Introduction

Prior to the introduction of feminist theory in the 1970s, female behavior was generally explained by simple thoughts and motives (Klein, 1973). Early criminological theorists believed that due to their extremely emotional nature and inability to rationalize, females were only able to commit crimes of a sexual nature or drunkenness. As criminological theory progressed, females were credited with the ability to commit more serious crimes but criminology remained **andocentric**.

In the 1960s and 1970s, the civil rights movement sensitized society not only to race issues, but also to gender inequality. The women's liberation movement brought feminist issues to the forefront, especially regarding how our **patriarchal** society had allowed male rights and privileges to dominate. In this type of society, females are subordinates in personal and professional settings. Further, because of the differences in male–female power, females are also more likely to become victimized in the home by intimates, as well as outside the home by strangers.

Frances Heidensohn (1968; 1992; 2000) shook the criminological world by asserting the feminist critical view of current criminological theory. She stated that the past lack of female crime was due to social control, based on the expected role of female domestication in the home and the fear implanted in women to fear aggressive men at night. Women had expected roles to fill, which gave them less opportunity to commit crime. However, in the 1970s during the Women's Liberation Movement, female opportunities outside the home began to grow and the female crime rate followed. Those women who began to push for more social, cultural, economic, and political opportunities and equality, often referred to as **feminists**, began a revolution called **feminism** that has been the recipient of confusion and misunderstanding by those on the outside looking in.

Stereotypically, the view of feminism that emerged from this period in history is one of bra-burning women who were protesting male oppression. Criminological theory has recognized four main types of feminism: liberal, radical, Marxist, and socialist (Daly & Chesney-Lind, 1988). **Liberal feminism** views gender discrimination as a matter of equal rights between males and females. These feminists want to end discrimination through institutional changes, specifically by legal changes that would increase female opportunities (Adler, 1975; Edwards, 1990; Simon, 1975). **Radical feminists**, on the other hand, see gender inequality issues as a result of patriarchy, or male domination (Smart, 1976; 1979). This domination is a result of viewing women as sexual objects rather than equals. Radical feminists believe that changing views of the female role in society, especially in relation to family, would adjust unequal treatment of women (Simpson, 1989). Further, exposing the physical, sexual, and mental abuse of women would enlighten the need for change (Chesney-Lind & Faith, 2001). Unlike liberal feminists, radical feminists do not believe that women's liberation is the cause of the female crime rate (Klein & Kress, 1979).

The other two forms of feminism involve differences in economic roles between sexes. **Marxist feminism** acknowledges the relationships between gender relations and patriarchy, but focuses more on how classes are viewed in regard to gender. Historically, women have been seen as a subordinate class compared to men and their labor role is in the home as a domestic caregiver, while men are the financial providers. As a result, women have achieved this social role and are economically weak. Lastly, **socialist feminists** recognize the role of technology and class relations, as well as stereotypical gender roles in regard to domestic and child care, and how the two work together to cause gender inequality (Currie & Klein, 1991; Eisenstein, 1979). As a solution to overcome this inequality, socialist feminists promote construction of a nonpatriarchal, noncapitalist society (Einstadter & Henry, 2006).

While there are notable differences between these forms of feminism, Caulfield and Wonders (1994) assert that they share core beliefs that have contributed to feminist criminology. These shared principles are: gender, power, context, social process, and social change. They discussed how the first three principles work together to shape relations by the sexes through social process. Further, the latter two principles represent the desire of all feminists to understand why and how this process occurs and how to change it. Caulfield and Wonders (1994) believed that feminists do not just focus on women, but instead want to change gender relationships into a positive and equal manner.

Chivalry Hypothesis

Directly related to patriarchal societies is the concept of **paternalism**, which views women as passive and gentile creatures that need protection (Chesney-Lind, 1988; Horowitz & Pottieger, 1991). Further, women who committed crime were simply led astray by aggressive and persuasive men. This sentiment fueled investigation of the **chivalry hypothesis** application in the criminal justice system (Pollak, 1950). The chivalry hypothesis asserts that male law enforcement and court players (i.e., prosecutors and judges) treat women more leniently than men as they feel the need to protect them. For instance, women are less likely to receive traffic tickets or get arrested for offenses. Or if actually processed through the court system, women are more likely to receive lenient sentences compared to men.

Some research has indicated that the chivalry hypothesis does exist. For instance, Mallicoat (2007) found that females are less likely to be perceived as dangerous criminals. Sentencing studies have indicated that there is leniency toward adult female offenders, even taking into account offense seriousness or previous criminal record (Steffensmeier, Kramer & Streifel, 1993; Frankling & Fearn, 2008). In regard to female juveniles, research has indicated the opposite in regard to punitive treatment. Chesney-Lind (1988; 1989), Chesney-Lind and

Shelden (2004), and MacDonald and Chesney-Lind (2001) all found that female juveniles were treated more harshly than male juveniles. These females were more likely to be brought into court and incarcerated.

The next section will examine the theorists who have made a critical impact in introducing, as well as developing, feminist theoretical thought. Based on the concepts discussed above, as well as the recognition of the need to better explain criminality through specialized research, these theorists have changed the way society sees female offending. We outline the historical context that the premise originates. Next, we provide illustrative examples and contemporary studies of the feminist perspective of criminology and evaluate these findings and assumptions. Finally, we suggest policy implications that may be fruitful in understanding this particular premise.

 ## Progression of Feminist Theory

Adler

At the initiation of the feminist criminological revolution, Freda Adler (1975) wrote, "women are no longer indentured to the kitchens, baby carriages or bedrooms of America" when discussing the change in female behavior. Traditionally, boys and girls were treated very differently beginning at birth in regard to expectations for deviancy and social norms. The saying that girls, being made of "sugar and spice and everything nice," inferred that little girls are inherently good and are expected to steer away from inappropriate behavior (e.g., uncleanliness, bad manners, and sexual activity). Boys, or those beings made from "snakes and snails and puppy dog tails," are expected to participate in mischief, get dirty, and express aggressiveness. As boys and girls get older, this continued pattern of socialization creates dominant, bread-winning men and passive, nurturing women.

Scientists and scholars have consistently debated the origin of female passivity. Is it biological or sociological? Adler (1975) argues that the sexes differ in four ways: size, shape, aggression, and dominance. Size and shape are obviously biologically determined, as males tend to be larger than females. Aggressiveness can be a result of the hormone testosterone, found mostly in males. However, girls of current day are often raised to be able to protect themselves, rather than rely on a man to do it for them. Aggression leads to dominance, as those who exert the ability to protect receive the respect of the family, tribe, neighborhood, etc. Adler (1975) asserted that females who were socialized to be more aggressive and dominant were those participating in criminal behavior.

Sisters in Crime, a book written by Adler, provides some statistical evidence, but mostly includes personal stories illustrating the rise of female crime. Adler asserted that the women's liberation movement brought changes in the perception of gender roles, women in the workforce, and equality. Further, the shakeup in traditional thoughts on women and emerging opportunities to females produced a faster rate of female arrests and immersion in the criminal justice system. Adler called this the **masculinity hypothesis**, as it describes how women are attempting to equate themselves with men in every manner. Adler (1975) believed that women would begin to mirror the characteristics of men in multiple ways, including health diagnoses due to stress and participation in athletics. Further, she stated that as women are aggressively entering the business world, they too will pursue participation in aggressive and financial crimes like men.

Simon

Rita Simon (1975) presented a narrower explanation of the relationship between increased female criminality and the women's liberation movement. Simon first discussed that while female property offense rates were increasing, violent crime for females was not increasing. She believed this was a result of women flooding the workforce, and therefore obtaining more opportunities to participate in white collar and financial crimes (**opportunity hypothesis**). Additionally, she asserted that the reason the female violent crime rate was not growing was because educated and independent women entering the workforce would not find violence acceptable, especially in intimate relationships (Simon, 1975).

Hagan

The work of John Hagan and colleagues (1985; 1987) on female delinquency is based on a theoretical integration of feminist and social control. He attempted to explain the gender differences in delinquency and how they are influenced by family dynamic and role management. Hagan believed that power relationships in the workforce are mirrored by the relationship dynamic in the family. The adult who has the dominant role in the family structure will in turn be powerful and authoritative in the workplace. In a **patriarchal family**, the father is employed, placing him in a "command" position that allows him to be the authoritarian figure in the household. Further, the mother either stays at home or works in a position where she is in a subordinate ("obey" position). Conversely, in an **egalitarian family**, both parents work in either a command or obey position, or the father is not in the household (Hagan, Gillis, & Simpson, 1985; Hagan, Simpson, & Gillis, 1987).

Hagan and colleagues' (1985; 1987) **power-control theory** also explains the dynamic of control of the mother and father in regard to parenting. In both types of families described above, the mother is more like to directly supervise (instrumental control) and form bonds with the children that indirectly prevent deviant behavior (relational control). However, in patriarchal families, mothers retain the role of exerting more control over the behavior of the daughters. In other words, mothers teach their female children to be reserved individuals who know how to assume domestic roles, while fathers provide instruction on masculinity and aggressiveness. Sons are less supervised, as "boys will be boys," and are more likely to participate in risky and deviant behavior (Hagan et al., 1985; 1987). In egalitarian families, the control balance is somewhat different. Mothers are more likely to exert less control over daughters and more over sons, allowing for both genders to get involved in more risky activities. Essentially this theory asserted that families who have a father as the authoritarian figure are more likely to have a gender gap in criminality between male and female children.

Recently, Hagan and colleagues (2004) amended power-control theory as they noticed that there are less patriarchal families in contemporary Western societies and the gender role beliefs have changed. Consistent with the original version of the theory, they still assert that mothers in patriarchal families are more lenient on their sons in regard to supervision and punishments. However, in egalitarian families where the mother and father are more occupationally balanced, mothers gave instruction and guidance to their daughters on how to access opportunities available to them and succeed. This is different than the past theory, which asserted that the sons were simply given more freedoms (Hagan et al., 2004).

Messerschmidt

Other theories more broadly define power including social practices, motivations, and desires that help shape the concept of gender (Bottcher, 2001). James Messerschmidt (1986, 1993, 1997, 2004) asserted that social structure creates our perception of the definition and role of sex, race, and class, and also how people act according to those roles. In a capitalist social structure, the importance of the economy and financial success supports a white, male-dominated society. According to Messerschmidt, street crimes are a result of powerlessness felt by females and lower class, minority males. Powerful men, on the other hand, are more likely to participate in white collar and sex crimes. Furthermore, Messerschmidt (1997) acknowledges that men can be powerless in their menial jobs, but dominant at home, making the concept of masculinity and femininity a continuum. As a result, crime is a **structured action**, meaning criminality is adopted based on the definition of gender in a particular social structure.

Structured action is greatly influenced by the concept of **masculinity**, which Messerschmidt (1993) asserts has multiple levels based on social structure. In other words, being masculine is not a concrete concept and can manifest itself in various forms. A person's sex is not only judged by biological features, but gender qualities. Furthermore, being deemed masculine by society can be earned in multiple ways.

CASE STUDY 10.1
PIPER KERMAN

Piper Kerman was born in September 1969 to a wealthy family of doctors, lawyers, and educators in Boston, Massachusetts. She was raised in a high income community and attended Smith College, a prestigious school for females. In the early 1990s, Piper (a bisexual) graduated from Smith College and began a relationship with a woman who dealt heroin for a drug kingpin in West Africa. In 1993, she convinced Piper to fly to Belgium with a suitcase full of money to be delivered to a West African drug lord. Shortly after, Piper ended their relationship but still suffered the repercussions of her short stint as lawbreaker. In 1998, she was indicted for drug trafficking and money laundering. She pled guilty to the charges and served 13 months in FCI Danbury in Connecticut from 2004-2005. She turned her story into a best-selling novel, which became the award winning television series, *Orange Is the New Black*.

Kerman currently works as a communications specialist for a nonprofit agency and speaks nationwide about her experience.

Daly and Chesney-Lind

The **gendered pathways perspective**, which mirrors life course perspective in many ways, focuses on the life histories of females to understand criminality. Recognizing that females experience unique biological, psychological, and social situations, the pathways perspective asserts that female criminality is based on factors that fall into the following categories: (1) not seen with men; (2) seen with men but more often with women; or (3) seen equally with both sexes, but has distinct effect for women (Belknap & Holsinger, 2006; Chesney-Lind & Shelden, 2004; Gavazzi, Yarcheck & Chesney-Lind, 2006; Reisig, Holtfreter, & Morash, 2006). Several individuals have contributed to the development and support of the pathways perspective, but most notably are the works of Kathleen Daly and Meda Chesney-Lind.

Daly (1992, 1994) contributed to the gendered pathways perspective by discussing how experiences with issues such as abuse, addiction, poverty, and intimate relationships occur differently across female offenders. Based on the review of court records of 40 female offenders, Daly reported five pathways to felony court for women:

1. Harmed and harming women, who were labeled "problem children" based on reoccurring behavior, and suffered from abuse and mental illness;

2. Street women, who had fled abusive homes and were generally involved in prostitution to survive and feed drug habits;
3. Battered women, who had earned criminal records based on their experiences with violent intimate partners;
4. Drug-connected women, who suffered from addiction as a result of intimate or family relationships; and
5. Women falling into the "other" category, who were generally economically motivated with no history of abuse, addiction, or other negative issues.

Daly has noted that while abuse and trauma is often found in female offenders, not all women in the system have histories of abuse and not all victims of abuse become offenders. However, there are several recent studies that have indicated that abuse is a risk factor for future offending behaviors for females (Siegel & Williams, 2003; Van Voorhis, Salisbury, Wright, & Bauman, 2008).

Chesney-Lind (1997, 2000), along with studies performed with other colleagues (Chesney-Lind & Rodriguez, 1983; Chesney-Lind & Shelden, 2004), have argued that male and female pathways to criminality are very different. For women, victimization leads to mental illness (such as depression), which often leads to self-medicating drug abuse. Female juvenile runways are generally arrested more often than boys (Chesney-Lind, 2000), which can lead to placement in detention centers, prostitution, or inappropriate relationships with men to meet financial needs (Chesney-Lind & Shelden, 2004).

 ## Empirical Research

There has been varying support for feminist theoretical thought in regard to empirical findings. Research has indicated that there is lack of support for Adler's (1975) masculinity hypothesis and Simon's opportunity hypothesis (Chesney-Lind & Pasko, 2004), as there has not been a demonstration that the rise in female crime rate and the changes in female equality are related. In fact, Steffensmeier (1980) found that the female crime rate actually began to increase prior to the Women's Liberation. Furthermore, multiple studies have indicated that the narrowing of the gender crime gap is actually a result of a decrease in offending since the 1990s (Lauritsen, Heimer, & Lynch, 2009; Schwartz, Steffensmeier, Zhong, & Ackerman, 2009).

The **economic marginalization hypothesis** (Feinman, 1986; Naffine, 1987) was created as a third potential explanation of the rising female crime rate and as a challenge to the earlier estimations of Adler (1975) and Simon (1975). Rather than blaming the powerful and liberated female for a rise in their respective criminal behavior, scholars have asserted that female offenders are lower class individuals who are poor and unemployed, as well as lacking opportunities beyond criminal means to support themselves and their children (Box & Hale, 1984; Chapman, 1980). Even if employed, many female offenders are concentrated in a "pink-collar ghetto," where pay is lower and unsatisfying. Simon and Ahn-Redding (2005) asserted that as more women are posing as heads of households, economic necessity is forcing them into lives of crime. Various types of studies have supported the claims of this hypothesis (DeWees & Parker, 2003; Hunnicutt & Broidy, 2004; Reckdenwald & Parker, 2008).

Hagan and colleagues' (1985; 1987) assertions of the effect of fathers' versus mothers' authoritative control on the deviancy of children has received mixed support. While research has supported the notion that daughters tend to fall under maternal control and sons fall under paternal control (Leiber & Wacker, 1997), there has been little support that the mother is more important than the father in regard to discipline and control. There are several methodological flaws causing the lack of support. Studies vary on the type of measure used for occupational authority, with some studies using measures of social class or other indirect concepts and others using more direct models. Further, the majority of studies examine gender delinquency differences between individuals who are not actually siblings. Of those who use siblings, support has been found to support the gender gap in delinquency (Blackwell & Reed, 2003; Hadjar, Baier, Boehnke, & Hagan, 2007; Hagan, Boehnke, & Merkens, 2004). After Hagan et al.'s (2004) revision to the theory, data from a sample gathered in Berlin and Toronto indicated that mothers in a patriarchal family still control daughters more than sons, while mothers in an egalitarian family controlled sons more than daughters.

A multitude of studies have used feminist theory to examine the effect of gender roles on intimate partner violence (IPV). The emergence of feminist theory has allowed IPV to be recognized as a serious social problem (Greenblat, 1985). According to Falchikov (1996) and Sugarman and Frankel (1996), IPV is a result of cultural norms that supported acts of violence against women. Further, research has suggested that there is a relationship between tolerant views of IPV by men and male willingness to commit acts of violence against women (Marciniak, 1998). Specifically in regard to gender roles, radical feminists have asserted that IPV is a result of patriarchal views (Gelsthorpe & Morris, 1990; Messerschmidt, 1993). In other words, men who believe that men are supposed to be the dominant and authoritative leader of the household are more likely to support IPV to intimidate and control their female companion (Greenblat, 1985; Falchikov, 1996; Marciniak, 1998; Simonson & Subich, 1999). Although egalitarianism has been recognized as a deterrent of IPV, as individuals who support male-female equality at home and in the workplace are not in support of violence as a form of partner intimidation.

There are criticisms of this particular viewpoint in regard to patriarchal gender roles influencing IPV behaviors. First, societal attitudes toward women are now much more egalitarian. When feminist theory was created in the 1960s and 70s, gender role measurement devices such as the Attitudes Toward Women Scale were also developed. Critics have argued that these measurement tools are outdated and not applicable in our current socio-political climate (Glick & Fiske, 1997; McHugh & Frieze, 1997; Swim & Cohen, 1997). Newer scales have been developed and allow respondents to express gender role perceptions in a more socially acceptable form. Further, research has demonstrated that there is a clear difference between the attitudes from the original scales and today's perceptions (McHugh & Frieze, 1997; Swim & Cohen, 1997).

The second criticism of using traditional gender role attitudes to measure IPV was raised by Glick and Fiske (1997). They point out that not all traditional perceptions are necessarily negative towards women, but some involve benevolent feelings toward females such as affection or protectiveness. In other words, traditional beliefs about a woman's role include positive and negative attitudes, which justify the use of a patriarchal system. The scale developed by Glick and Fiske (1997) supported this assertion and found hostility and benevolence to be related but separate constructs.

Bradley and Khor (1993) asserted that in order to better understand gender inequality and the effect of patriarchy on IPV, it is important to understand the status of a female in regard to political, economic, and social dimensions. Political status involves a woman's access to power and representation, while economic status includes female inclusion in "institutions constructed around production, distribution, and consumption of goods and services" (p. 349). For example, Baron and Straus (1989) found that more women in power in a state equated to lower rape rates. Lastly, Bradley, and Khor (1993) assert that social status is measured by a woman's access to education, as well as to how she is viewed in regard to sex and reproduction. Several studies have tested the link between status and violence against women and revealed that when men play dominating roles in these status levels, violence can be used as a tool to control women (Walby, 1990; Yodanis, 2004). Further, fear of sexual violence (violent crime in which men are generally not vulnerable) is significantly related to women's fear of men and their inability to escape domination (Culbertson, Vik, & Kooiman, 2001; Ferraro, 1996; Killias & Clerici, 2000).

There has been consistent support for the gendered pathways perspective as an explanation for female offending over the life course. Retrospective interviews with female offenders have consistently demonstrated that female offenders have life histories marked by various forms of abuse, poverty, and addiction (Belknap, 2007; Chesney-Lind & Rodriguez, 1983; Chesney-Lind & Shelden, 2004; Daly, 1992). McClellan, Farabee, and Crouch (1997) investigated male and female inmates and found that females tended to have higher rates of victimization, abuse, and mental illness. Further, it appeared as if childhood abuse affected women more greatly in regard to experiencing depression as an adult, as well as substance abuse. Marquart, Brewer, Simon, and Morse (2001) found similar results with a sample of 500 female inmates.

Policy Implications

Studies have consistently demonstrated that female offenders experience life circumstances that are often unique to them, and therefore they have additional issues to handle while processed through the criminal justice system. Females are especially vulnerable to multiple forms of abuse, pregnancy, and single parenting, and they require medical care for physical issues unique to females. Chesney-Lind and Pasko (2004) stressed the usefulness of treatment programs over punitive measures due to these life circumstances. They felt that programs targeted at the physical and psychological needs of females would better equip them for a crime-free lifestyle rather than long prison sentences or harsh fines. While a review of evaluation studies of programming revealed that gender-specific programming is no more successful than juvenile programs targeted at both sexes, Zahn, Day, Mihalic, and Tichavsky (2009) did find that gender-specific programming produces multiple positive outcomes that can empower females, such as better outcomes with education, relationships, self-esteem, and employment.

CASE STUDY 10.2
OUTWARD BOUND

Outward Bound is a nonprofit organization that focuses on education and outdoor expeditions. Serving the nation for over 50 years, it promotes positive self-discovery. A specific outdoor expedition, Outward Bound Struggling Teens is designed to address destructive behavior in 12- to 24-year-olds by working with curriculum focusing on self-awareness, independence, and life skills. In addition, the program provides resources for families to facilitate a peaceful home, while the youth spend three days on a beautiful, outdoor adventure to gain new perspective.

Research based on the gendered pathways model has indicated that female offenders need to receive individualized treatment in order to avoid recidivism behaviors. For example, Covington (1998) asserted that programs aimed at the development of coping skills to address early victimization experiences, such as child abuse, are imperative to help women recover from addictions and manage mental illness. These co-occurring disorders lead to criminal behavior if not properly handled. Other research has supported the use of holistic correctional treatment programs to help females manage prior traumatic experiences, whether they occurred in childhood or adulthood (Bloom, Owen, & Covington, 2003; Chesney-Lind, 1997; Covington, 1998). Again, the repeated assertion is that females can better handle future life experiences if equipped with tools to positively cope with prior negative experiences.

Furthermore, according to Flavin (2004), positive family relationships are necessary for females to maintain a crime-free lifestyle. La Bodega de la Familia is a family case management program in New York City that treats both male and female probationers and parolees with addictions. Building off the human capital model, this program engages at least one family member willing to participate to help rehabilitate the offender. In other words, offenders with healthy family relationships and support are more likely to reintegrate into society rather than recidivate (Sullivan, Mino, Nelson, & Pope, 2002).

Summary

Steffensmeier and Allan (1996) stressed the importance of advancing criminological theory by using a gendered approach including the following four elements. First, the theory should explain male and female criminality, as well as how we organize gender. Second, the theory should examine differences between genders in regard to type of crime, amount of crime, and how crime is committed. Third, the theory should consider how men and women become involved in criminal behavior. Lastly, a gendered approach should consider sociological and biological differences between men and women when considering criminal behavior (Steffensmeier & Allan, 1996).

Although feminist theory is fairly new compared to other criminological thought, it has made waves in the field and has provided new insight into explaining female behavior. The separation and explanation of the feminism mindset allowed society to better recognize the issues supported by these individuals, rather than categorizing them all as man-hating, bra-burning women. Further, these theories have investigated the effect of family structure and life experiences as predictors of criminal behavior. And, if nothing else, these theories have stressed the importance of criminal justice policy development based on the necds of females and not just offenders as a whole.

Discussion Questions

1. Discuss how American society has changed in regards to its expectations of masculinity and femininity. How has this affected our outlook on female crime?
2. Provide an example of the chivalry hypothesis still in effect today in our criminal justice system. Is this fair? Why or why not?
3. Should males and females be treated exactly the same while incarcerated? Why or why not?

REFERENCES

Adler, F. (1975). *Sisters in crime: The rise of the new female criminal.* New York: McGraw-Hill.

Belknap, J. (2007). *The invisible woman: Gender, crime, and justice* (3rd ed). Belmont, CA: Thompson Wadsworth.

Belknap, J. & Holsinger, K. (2006). The gendered nature of risk factors for delinquency. *Feminist Criminology, 1,* 48-71.

Blackwell, B. & Reed, M. (2003). Power-control as a between- and within-family model: Reconsidering the unit of analysis. *Journal of Youth and Adolescence, 32,* 385-400.

Bloom, B., Owen, B., & Covington, S. (2003). *Gender responsive strategies: Research, practice, and guiding principles for women offenders.* Washington, DC: U.S. Department of Justice, National Institute of Corrections.

Bottcher, J. (2001). Social practices of gender: How gender relates to delinquency in the everyday lives of high-risk youths. *Criminology, 39,* 893-932.

Box, S. & Hale, C. (1984). Liberation/emancipation, economic marginalization, or less chivalry. *Criminology, 22,* 473-498.

Bradley, K. & Khor, D. (1993). Toward an integration of theory and research on the status of women. *Gender & Society, 7,* 347-378.

Caufield, S. & Wonders, N. (1994). Gender and justice: Feminist contributions to criminology. In. G. Barak (Ed.), *Varieties of criminology: Readings from a dynamic discipline* (pp. 213-219). Westport, CT: Praeger.

Chapman, J. (1980). *Economic realities and the female offender.* Lexington, MA: Lexington.

Chesney-Lind, M. (1988). Girls in jail. *Crime and Delinquency, 34,* 150-168.

Chesney-Lind, M. (1989). Girls' crime and woman's place: Toward a feminist model of female delinquency. *Crime and Delinquency, 35,* 5-29.

Chesney-Lind, M. (1997). *The female offender: Girls, women, and crime.* Thousand Oaks, CA: Sage.

Chesney-Lind, M. (2000). What to do about girls? Thinking about programs for young women. In M. McMahon (Ed.), *Assessment to assistance: Programs for women in community corrections* (pp. 139-170). Lanham, MD: American Correctional Association.

Chesney-Lind, M., & Faith, K. (2001). What about feminism? Engendering theory-making in criminology. In R. Paternoster and R. Bachman (Eds.), *Explaining criminals and crime* (pp. 297-302). Los Angeles: Roxbury.

Chesney-Lind, M. & Rodriguez, N. (1983). Women under lock and key. *The Prison Journal, 63,* 47-65.

Chesney-Lind, M. & Shelden, R. (2004). *Girls, delinquency, and juvenile justice* (3rd ed.). Belmont, Ca: Wadsworth/Thomson Learning.

Covington, S. (1998). The relational theory of women's psychological development: Implications for substance abuse. In S. Wilsnack & R. Wilsnack (Eds.), *Gender and alcohol: Individual and social perspectives* (pp.113-128). Gaithersburg, MD: Aspen.

Culbertson, K., Vik, P., & Kooiman, B. (2001). The impact of sexual assault, sexual assault perpetrator type, and location of sexual assault on perceived safety. *Violence Against Women, 7,* 858-875.

Currie, D. & Klein, M. (1991). Challenging privilege: Women, knowledge and feminist struggles. *Journal of Human Justice, 2,* 1-36.

Daly, K. (1992). Women's pathways to felony court: Feminist theories of lawbreaking and problems of representation. *Southern California Review of Law and Women's Studies, 2,* 11-52.

Daly, K. (1994). *Gender, crime, and punishment.* New Haven, CT: Yale University Press.

Daly, K. & Chesney-Lind, M. (1988). Feminism and criminology. *Justice Quarterly, 5,* 497-538.

Dewees, M. & Parker, K. (2003). Women, region, and types of homicide: Are there regional differences in the structural status of women and homicide offending? *Homicide Studies, 7,* 363-393.

Einstadter, W. & Henry, S. (2006). *Criminological theory: An analysis of its underlying assumptions.* Lanham, MD: Rowman & Littlefield Publishers, Inc.

Eisenstein, Z. (1979). *Capitalist patriarchy and the case for socialist feminism.* New York: Monthly Review Press.

Falchikov, N. (1996). Adolescent attitudes to abuse of women: Are wives and non-marital partners viewed differently? *Journal of Interpersonal Violence, 11(3),* 391-409.

Feinman, C. (1986). *Women in the criminal justice system.* New York: Praeger.

Ferraro, K. (1996). Women's fear of victimization: Shadow of sexual assault? *Social Forces, 75,* 667-690.

Flavin, J. (2004). Employment counseling, housing assistance . . . and Aunt Yolanda? How strengthening families' social capital can reduce recidivism. *Criminology & Public Policy, 3,* 209-216.

Franklin, C. & Fearn, N. (2008). Gender, race, and formal court decision-making outcomes: Chivalry/paternalism conflict theory or gender conflict? *Journal of Criminal Justice, 36,* 279-290.

Gavazzi, S., Yarcheck, C., & Chesney-Lind, M. (2006). Global risk indicators and the role of gender in a juvenile detention sample. *Criminal Justice and Behavior, 33,* 597-612.

Gelsthorpe L., & Morris, A. (Eds). (1990). *Feminist perspectives in criminology.* Philadelphia: Open University Press.

Greenblat, C. (1985). Don't hit your wife . . . unless . . . *Victimology, 10(1-4),* 221-241.

Hadjar, A., Baier, D., Boehnke, K., & Hagan, J. (2007). Juvenile delinquency and gender revisited: The family and power-control theory reconceived. *European Journal of Criminology, 4,* 33-58.

Hagan, J., Boehnke, K., Merkens, H. (2004). Gender differences in capitalization processes and the delinquency of siblings in Toronto and Berlin. *British Journal of Criminology, 44,* 659-676.

Hagan, J., Gillis, A., & Simpson, J. (1985). The class structure of gender and delinquency: Toward a power-control theory of common delinquent behavior. *American Journal of Sociology, 90,* 1151-1178.

Hagan, J., Simpson, J., & Gillis, A. (1987). Class in the household: A power control theory of gender and delinquency. *American Journal of Sociology, 92,* 788-816.

Horowitz, R. & Pottieger, A. (1991). Gender bias in juvenile justice handling of seriously crime involved youths. *Journal of Research in Crime and Delinquency, 28,* 75-100.

Hunnicutt, G. & Broidy, L. (2004). Liberation and economic marginalization: A reformulation and test of formerly competing models. *Journal of Research in Crime and Delinquency, 41,* 130-155.

Killias, M. & Clerici, C. (2000). Different measures of vulnerability in their relation to different dimensions of fear of crime. *British Journal of Criminology, 40,* 437-450.

Klein, D. (1973). The etiology of female crime: A review of the literature. *Issues in Criminology, 8,* 3-30.

Klein, D. & Kress, J. (1979). Any woman's blues: A critical overview of women, crime, and the criminal justice system. In F. Adler & R. Simon (Eds.), *Criminality of deviant women* (pp. 82-0). Boston: Houghton Mifflin.

Lauritsen, J., Heimer, K., & Lynch, J. (2009). Trends in the gender gap in violent offending New evidence from the National Crime Victimization Survey. *Criminology, 47,* 361-399.

MacDonald, J. & Chesney-Lind, M. (2001). Gender bias and juvenile justice revisited: A multiyear analysis. *Crime & Delinquency, 47,* 173-195.

Mallicoat, S. (2007). Gendered justice. *Feminist Criminology, 2(1),* 4-30.

Marciniak, L. (1998). Adolescent attitudes toward victim precipitation of rape. *Violence and Victims, 13(3),* 287-300.

Marquart, J., Brewer, V., Simon, P., & Morse, E. (2001). Lifestyle factors among female prisoners with histories of psychiatric treatment. *Journal of Criminal Justice, 29,* 319-328.

McClellan, D., Farabee, D., & Crouch, B. (1997). Early victimization, drug use, and criminality: A comparison of male and female prisoners. *Criminal Justice and Behavior, 24,* 455-476.

McHugh, M., & Frieze, I. (1997). The measurement of gender-role attitudes. *Psychology of Women Quarterly, 21,* 1-16.

Messerschmidt, J. (1986). *Capitalism, patriarchy, and crime: Toward a socialist feminist criminality.* Totowa, NJ: Rowman & Littlefield.

Messerschmidt, J. (1993). *Masculinities and crime: Critique and reconceptualization of theory.* Lanham, MD: Rowman & Littlefield.

Messerschmidt, J. (1997). *Crime as structured action: Gender, race, class, and crime in the making.* Thousand Oaks, CA: Sage.

Messerschmidt, J. (2004). *Flesh and blood: Adolescent gender diversity and violence.* Lanham, MD: Rowman and Littlefield.

Naffine, N. (1987). *Female crime: The construction of women in criminology.* Boston: Alen and Unwin.

Pollak, O. (1950). *The criminality of women.* Philadelphia: University of Pennsylvania Press.

Reckdenwald, A., & Parker, A. (2008). The influence of gender inequality and marginalization on types of female offending. *Homicide Studies, 12,* 208-226.

Reisig, M., Holtfreter, K., & Morash, M. (2006). Assessing recidivism risk across female pathways to crime. *Justice Quarterly, 23,* 384-405.

Schwartz, J., Steffensmeier, D., Zhong, J., & Ackerman, J. (2009). Trends in the gender gap in violence: Reevaluating NCVS and other evidence. *Criminology, 47,* 401-425.

Siegel, J. & Williams, L. (2003). The relationship between child sexual abuse and female delinquency and crime: A prospective study. *Journal of Research in Crime and Delinquency, 40,* 71-94.

Simon, R. (1975). *Women and crime.* Lexington, MA: Lexington Books.

Simon, R. & Ahn-Redding, H. (2005). *The crimes women commit* (3rd ed.). Lanham, MD: Lexington.

Simonson, K. & Subich, L. (1999). Rape perceptions as a function of gender role traditionalist and victim-perpetrator association. *Sex Roles, 44(9-10),* 599-610.

Simpson, S. (1989). Feminist theory, crime and justice. *Criminology, 27,* 605-632.

Smart, C. (1976). *Women, crime and criminology: A feminist critique.* Boston: Routledge and Kegan Paul.

Smart, C. (1979). The new female criminality: Reality or myth? *British Journal of Criminology, 19,* 50-59.

Steffensmeier, D. (1980). Sex differences in patterns of adult crime, 1965-77. *Social Forces, 58:* 1080-1109.

Steffensmeier, D., & Allan, E. (1996). Gender and crime: Toward a gendered theory of female offending. *Annual Review of Sociology, 22,* 459-487.

Steffensmeier, D., Kramer, J., & Streifel, C. (1993). Gender and imprisonment decisions. *Criminology, 31,* 411-446.

Swim, J. & Cohen, L. (1997). Overt, covert, and subtle sexism. *Psychology of Women Quarterly, 21,* 103-118.

Sugarman, D. & Frankel, S. (1996). Patriarchal ideology and wife assault: A meta-analytic review. *Journal of Family Violence, 11(1),* 13-40.

Sullivan, E., Mino, M., Nelson, K., & Pope, J. (2002). *Families as a resource in recovery from drug abuse: An evaluation of La Bodega de la Familia.* New York: Vera Institute of Justice.

Van Voorhis, P., Salisbury, E., Wright, E., & Bauman, A. (2008). *Achieving accurate pictures of risk and identifying gender responsive needs: Two new assessments for women offenders.* Washington, DC: U.S. Department of Justice, National Institute of Corrections.

Walby, S. (1990). *Theorizing patriarchy.* Oxford, UK: Basil Blackwell.

Zahn, M., Day, J., Mihalic, S., & Tichavsky, L. (2009). Determining what works for girls in the juvenile justice system: A summary of evaluation evidence. *Crime and Delinquency, 55,* 266-293.

CHAPTER 11

Integrative Theory

CHAPTER OUTLINE

Introduction

Theoretical Competition

Theoretical Integration
Elliot and Colleagues
Shaming
Krohn's Network Analysis

Life Course Perspective
Case Study 11.1: Turning My Life Around

Summary

Discussion Questions

References

Key Words and Concepts

Criminal Careers	Multiplexity	Theoretical
Density	Neuropsychological	Integration
Disintegrative shaming	Deficits	Tipping Point
End-to-End	Social Network	Trajectory
Integrative Shaming	Theoretical Competition	Transition

Introduction

The development of criminological theory had seen growth from the 1960s through the 1990s. In the mid- to late 1980s, the development of criminological theory had slowed, but the development regained speed in the late 1980s. The development of routine activity theory, or lifestyle theory, came during this time. This development continued until around 2000, when it slowed but did not end.

The development of new theories took a different form. Specifically, these new theories were the combination of other theories. While criticized by some, the development of new theories came from the theoretical competition or **theoretical integration** of older theories. Because some parts of all theories are similar and other parts are dissimilar, testing multiple theories at one time would allow criminologists to better understand which theory may provide a better explanation of crime or delinquency. Other criminologists would be able to use this information to be able piece together the relevant parts of multiple theories to better understand crime and delinquency. In this chapter, the reader will be able to understand the differences between theoretical competition and theoretical integration. We present some examples of theoretical integrations.

Theoretical Competition

Theoretical competition was an advance to criminological theory that allowed criminologists to better understand theories. The crux of **theoretical competition** was the empirical study of the theories. From the quantitative perspective (i.e., statistical study), information gathered about crime or delinquency criminologists would use indicators of multiple theories to better understand which theories would provide the best explanation.[1]

While this explanation of how to perform theoretical competition seems simple, the reality was that it was far too complex. Some criminologists believed that the theories were incompatible with one another (Akers, 1989; Hirschi, 1979). They feared that this sort of work would lead to theoretical integrations that would ultimately be meaningless. This means that the theories provided explanations of criminal behavior that were very different, and that they used different mechanisms to do so; thus, competition would not provide the understanding of interests.

---

1. We acknowledge that this is only one example. Of course, qualitative analysis can be performed to provide a rich understanding of multiple theories.

Agnew (1995) argued the opposite. He suggested that criminological theories were very similar. For instance, he suggested that social bonds and self-control theory had similar explanations for crime and delinquency as social learning theory. Further, Agnew argued that social learning theory had similar causal mechanisms for crime and delinquency as strain theory. To further complicate matters, Agnew (1995) argued that the differences between the major crime theories were so minor that the motivational components of the theories were necessary to provide different explanations. By utilizing the motivational components of the theories, criminologists would be able to complete the theories in their empirical studies and understand the differences between the theories.

Theoretical Integration

Theoretical integration referred to the deliberate attempt to combine two closely related theories. Often the basis of this information came from the theoretical competition. Hirschi (1979) was opposed to this practice because he believed that the differences between the theories were irreconcilable. That is, the differences between the theories were so vast that integration was not possible. At the same time, criminologists understood the development and use of empirical knowledge in the context of theory building. Using information that came from theoretical competitions, criminologists were fusing theories together. Since the 1970s, a number of theoretical treatments were necessary to understand crime and delinquency.

As can be seen in the empirical literature, many criminologists did not agree with Hirschi (1979). Some worked under the view that theories did not always compete with one another, but the theories would provide explanations of crime and delinquency at different levels (Short, 1998; Williams, 1984). This view opened the door for theoretical integrations, as long as the assumptions were compatible. From this perspective, if a number of theories worked at different levels, criminologists should work to determine how best to organize them to provide the desired explanations.

Theories integration had taken place in a number of ways in the empirical literature, but two predominate ways of integrating theories were present: end-to-end and fully integrated. **End-to-end** (ETE) integration involved putting theories together that accommodated different levels of explaining crime and delinquency. For instance, criminologists may integrate theories involving social disorganization and self-control theory. The view here is that social disorganization may influence how parents parent their children and this would influence the child's self-control level. Because of this influence, the child's self-control level may make the child susceptible to crime or delinquency. The ETE focus of this theoretical principle was present because it allowed for an explanation at different levels.

The other method integrating theories was to use theoretical concepts from other theories, with no regard for their assumptions, and put them together in a new way. This approach was called fully integrated theoretical integration. While we refrained from an example here of fully integrated theory, the practice has been well under way in criminology, and the rest of the chapter provides examples of this approach. It is important to note that these examples and the theories that follow were not endorsed by the authors, but were presented as a means of illustration of the two approaches.

Elliot and Colleagues

Elliot, Ageton, and Cantor (1979) developed an ETE type of theory. Their theory utilized the concepts and logic from social bonds, strain, and social learning theories. Their theory appeared to retain the concepts from each of the theories but they provided additional logic to make the theories work together for a better explanation of crime and delinquency.

Elliot and colleagues began by relying on social bonds. They used Hirschi's (1969) logic of the concepts as the foundation. Specifically, they believed that the bonds were a means of socialization. In other words, an environment was necessary to provide a better understanding of the norms, values, and rules of society. If a child was socialized properly, he or she would have strong bonds. In other words, the better the socialization, the better the child would be integrated into society.

Further, they used the idea of strain in their theory. Elliot and colleagues suggested that as a child ages he or she would be exposed to a number of experiences. This exposure may result in successful or unsuccessful experiences. The lack of success in experiences would come from stressful exposure. The lack of success or poor exposure would result in weakening the social bonds.

Elliot and colleagues were not silent in the area of social learning theory. They argued that the aging child would encounter peers. Further, his or her network of peers would grow to a point that the child would encounter peers with alternative attitudes toward crime and delinquency. Encountering these peers would result in attitude changes in the child toward criminal and delinquent behavior. Peers also served the role of reinforcers for behavior.

At this point, the presentation of their theory has been linear (i.e., one concept leads to another concept). It is instructive to remember that Elliot and colleagues argued that their theory was also interactive. In other words, the concepts were not all or nothing for behavior to occur. For instance, socialization could vary and this could impact exposure, or peer association could vary and this could impact socialization. This theory broke important ground because it showed how integrations could be performed that allowed for the better predictive power.

Shaming

Braithwaite's (1989) theory of shaming relies on integrated opportunity, subcultural, control, learning, and labeling theories. To begin, Braithwaite discusses issues pertaining to the opportunity for legitimate and illegitimate means. Crime and delinquency occurs when legitimate means are blocked. That is, illegitimate means are then learned and transmission of law breaking values occurs. However, social control can balance this process by providing cues for conforming behavior. That is, an individual may learn conforming values. Therefore, crime and delinquency are central when there is a "**tipping point**".

For Braithwaite, the tipping point is shaming. In criminology, several forms of shaming exist. However, in Braithwaite's theory, two are central. The first area of shaming is disintegrative shaming. **Disintegrative shaming** does not attempt to create or provide an environment that is conducive to allowing the offender to come back into society. That is, there are not any attempts to allow an offender to be welcomed back into society, thereby branding the offender an outcast from society. The second area of shaming is integrative. This view of shaming suggests that reconciliatory acts help separate the offender from the action. **Integrative shaming** allows the offender to be welcomed back into society and an opportunity to be forgiven for his or her transgressions.

Krohn's Network Analysis

Krohn (1986) devised a series of arguments that explain delinquency through social learning and social control theories. This theory suggests that social networks are important to the commission of criminal behavior. To be clear, a **social network** is a set of actors, individuals, or groups that are linked by some type of relationship (e.g., friendship, kinship, school, or church). Krohn (1986) stays consistent with control theory that the social networks constrain an individual's behavior. However, he then diverges from control theory by arguing that the constraints do not have to exist for conforming behavior (similar to social learning theory). That is, an individual may be constrained to crime or delinquent behavior given to parts of the social network: multiplexity and density.

Multiplexity is the number of different relationships or contexts that a social network maintains. That is, friends may attend the same school, live in the same neighborhood, and attend the same church. Krohn (1986) argued as multiplexity was high, the greater the constraints on behavior. In general, the constraint would lower multiplexity, but this is generally because the family, church, and schools made up the multiplexity (as these activities and institutions make up conventional activities). Under this view, the key is that multiplexity is able to account for who the individual is in contact with and how the individual is in contact with them.

Density is a ratio of the number of connections an individual has in a social network that is relative to the total possible number of connections that an individual could have in network. This view hypothesizes about behavior as well. On one hand, when density is high, the delinquency rate is generally lower. On the other hand, when density is low, delinquency is generally higher.

Life Course Perspective

The life course perspective of criminology has had an important impact on the study of crime. The life course perspective is a direct response to better understand the connection between age and crime. That is, an inspection of age and crime indicates that at the age of 7, some individuals begin to commit crime. However, by the age of 17, many individuals have stopped committing crime. This chapter provides an overview of the life course perspective and two theories (i.e., Sampson & Laub, 1993; Moffitt, 1993), provides the specific propositions that these theories have to understand race and crime, and then presents three articles that examine these views.

Because of the age and crime connection, many criminologists spent a substantial amount of effort studying juveniles during the ages of 7 to 17. These studies have been assisted by the development and use of self-report surveys. A self-report survey is a series of questions or statements that has been developed by a researcher and given to a research subject to complete. When the subject completes the self-report survey, the researcher is able to determine the things that may or may not have a connection to the individual's criminal behavior. The advent of the self-report survey has resulted in a substantial growth in criminology and criminal justice research and theories because a researcher could simply capture an entire group of students in a community at the local junior or high school. Therefore, the individuals that were between the ages of 7 and 17 have been adequately captured and the researcher did not have a need to carry out expensive longitudinal studies (i.e., studies over time).

The popularity of longitudinal studies began to grow. These studies were able to document that the events in one stage of life effects the events that take place in another stage of life. In the life course perspective, this view is often referred to as the different pathways that occur at different stages of life that are shaped by transitions and turning points. Caspi et al. (1990) argued that the life course was a "sequence of culturally defined age-graded roles and social transitions that are enacted over time" (p. 15). In essence, these age-graded transitions are embedded in different social institutions and can be influenced to change by different events.

The life course perspective is reliant on two major components: trajectories and transitions. A **trajectory** is a pattern or sequence of events. A **transition** is a specific event that is embedded in a trajectory. Transitions may or may not be reliant on age. Thus, the key to the life course perspective is the normative timing and the sequencing of the changes that take place in an individual's life.

CASE STUDY 11.1
TURNING MY LIFE AROUND

Famous media moguls such as Curtis Jackson III, a.k.a. 50 Cent (rapper and movie star), Dwayne Johnson (pro wrestler turned movie star), and Kevin Mitnick (infamous hacker) each possessed lengthy rap sheets, long arrest records, and multiple convictions of damaging and/or violent offenses. Now, these men are law-abiding, tax-paying citizens who lead productive lives. While originating from different backgrounds, they each made a difficult and immense change in behavior, often at the displeasure of family and friends still involved in criminality. What makes some people turn their life around and others stay with what they know?

Trajectories and transitions are by definition joined. Because they are joined they may have important implications for the individual by creating specific turning points or changes in an individual's life course (Elder, 1985). The same event may (or a transition followed by a different event may) change an individual's life trajectory. It is clear now that the childhood path of an individual then has a connection to the adulthood path of that individual. However, the trajectory may not always be long term. A short-term trajectory can redirect an individual's trajectory. Further, transitions and trajectories are influenced by social institutions (e.g., schools, marriage, and military experience).

The life course perspective can be applied to several different themes in an individual's life. This perspective has been applied to crime. For instance, many see the life course perspective as a criminal career perspective on crime; that has roots in cohort studies. In these studies, the focus is generally on the onset (i.e., the beginning of crime career), duration (i.e., how long the career lasts), frequency (i.e., lambda), and ending of the criminal career (i.e., desistance). Others have focused on developing specific theories to explain these phenomena.

For instance, Sampson and Laub (1993) utilize a control perspective that is combined with social learning theory. They proposed that individuals that have transitions that come with getting older increase social bonds. One example of this is individuals who get married or find stable employment who develop this sort of bond. From this point of view, those that are younger are more likely to offend but desist when they grow older. However, if these transitions do not occur, the individual is likely to persist in their offending. Thus, the stability of one's behavior has a relationship to the stability of the events that produce the behavior. That is, as long as the individual has stable employment, he or she is likely to refrain from criminal activity.

Terri Moffit (1993) has developed a theory to understand life course criminality. The premise of her perspective is that **neuropsychological deficits** are instrumental in the development of behavioral problems. That is, when an individual demonstrates behavioral problems as a child and begins delinquency and criminality at an early age, these issues are more likely to be life-course persistent. However, some individuals begin their criminality later in life (i.e., adolescence). These individuals do not continue their criminal behavior beyond this point in life. Moffitt refers to these individuals as adolescent limited. For Moffitt, the life-course persistent individual has shown signs of problems due to hyperactivity, low verbal ability, and impulsive personality. These individuals are rather resistant to the peer influences. However, the adolescent-limited individual is much more responsive to peer influences and is less likely to commit crime in adulthood.

These theories have enjoyed some empirical support in the criminological literature. However, less research has been conducted in the areas of race and crime. For instance, Sampson and Laub (1993) would argue that racial minorities have less stable social bonds with society. Therefore, racial minorities are likely to have higher rates of criminal activity. Whereas, Moffitt (1993) would argue that racial minorities are more likely to experience higher levels of neuropsychological deficits because they are often unable to afford quality prenatal and perinatal care for their children.

Summary

This chapter provides the basis of understanding theoretical competition and theoretical integration. Using this information allowed criminologists to develop better empirical studies, which have led to the development of important criminological theory. For instance, Elliot et al. (1979) showed how social bonding, strain, and social learning theory can be combined to better understand crime and delinquency. From a different perspective, Braithwaite's (1989) shaming focus relies on a "tipping point" to suggest influence in criminality and crime rates. That is, when individuals are disintegratively shamed, they are likely to contribute to the crime rates and criminality because they do not have ties to the community that constrain their behavior. However, when individuals are integratively shamed, they are less likely to contribute to the crime rates and criminality. Combining social control and social learning theories, Krohn (1986) argued that social networks that were not very large and did not have multiple connections were likely to produce contributions to crime rates and criminality. This perspective maintained that some individuals may commit crime at different points in their lives or maintain rather consistent and long-term **criminal careers**. The determination of these issues can be understood by determining the key turning points in an individual's life trajectories.

Discussion Questions

1. Explain how a criminal may continue his or her offending through adulthood.
2. How would you explain the similarities and differences between adolescence-limited offending and social networks in offending?

REFERENCES

Agnew, R. (1995). Testing the leading crime theories: An alternative strategy focusing on motivational processes. *Journal of Research in Crime and Delinquency, 32,* 363-398.

Akers, Ronald L. (1989). A social behaviorist's approach on integration of theories of crime and deviance. In Steven Messner, Marvin D. Krohn, and Allen Liska (Eds.), *Theoretical integration in the study of deviance and crime: Problems and prospects* (pp. 23-36). Albany, NY: SUNY Press.

Braithwaite, J. (1989). *Crime, shame and reintegration.* Cambridge, UK: Cambridge University Press.

Caspi, A., Elder, G. H., Jr., & Herbener, E. (1990). Childhood personality and prediction of life-course patterns. In L. N. Robins & M. Rutter (Eds.), *Straight and devious pathways from childhood to adult life.* New York, NY: Cambridge University Press.

Elder, G. H. (1985). Perspectives on the life course. In Elder, G. H. Jr. (Ed.), *Life course dynamics, trajectories, and transitions, 1968-1980.* Ithaca: Cornell University Press.

Elliot, D., Ageton, S., & Cantor, R. J. (1979). An integrated theoretical perspective on delinquent behavior. *Journal of Research in Crime and Delinquency, 16,* 3-27.

Hirschi, Travis (1969). Causes and Delinquency. Berkeley: University of California Press.

Hirschi, T. (1979). Separate and unequal is better. *Journal of Research in Crime and Delinquency, 16,* 34-38.

Krohn, M. D. (1986). The web of conformity: A network approach to the explanation of delinquent behavior, *Social Problems, 33,* 581-593.

Moffitt, T. E. (1993). Adolescence-limited and life-course persistent antisocial behavior: A developmental taxonomy. *Psychological Review, 100,* 674-701.

Piquero, A. R., MacDonald, J., & Parker, K. F. (2002). Race, local life circumstances, and criminal activity. *Social Science Quarterly, 83,* 654-670.

Sampson, Robert J. and John Laub (1993). *Crime in the making: Pathways and turning points through life.* Cambridge, MA: Harvard University Press.

Short, J. (1998). The level of explanation problem revisited: Presidential address, American Society of Criminology, *Criminology, 36,* 3-36.

Achievement orientation: places emphasis on valuing individuals based on what they possess or achieve. [Ch. 5]

Acts of primary deviance: acts that are impulsive, infrequent, and lacking in organization. [Ch. 8]

Anomie: a deregulated condition where people have lessened moral controls over their behavior. [Ch. 5]

Anticipated strain: an assessment of future stress. [Ch. 5]

Atavism: the reappearance of a characteristic or trait after it had been dormant or absent for many generations. [Ch. 3]

Attachment: occurs when the individual develops strong connections and ties with significant others (e.g., parents, friends, or role models) or institutions (e.g., schools or churches) that inhibit behavior. [Ch. 7]

Autonomy: freedom from authority, or independence. [Ch. 5]

Behavioral coping strategies: adaptation methods that maximize positive outcomes and minimize negative outcomes, either legitimately or illegitimately; can also involve vengeful behavior, or taking revenge on a person or entity. [Ch. 5]

Belief: the moral obligation to follow the rules because of an internalized form of respect and obligation to the rules. [Ch. 7]

Belonging: acceptance into a group and the feeling of involvement. [Ch. 5]

Blank slate: individual(s) who need to be taught everything. [Ch. 6]

Born criminal: a criminal who is atavistic, responsible for the most serious offenses, and likely to recidivate. [Ch. 3]

Celerity: the rate that punishment is administered after the commission of a crime. [Ch. 2]

Certain punishment: punishment that can be guaranteed to occur after the commission of a crime. [Ch. 2]

Chivalry hypothesis: asserts that male law enforcement and court players (i.e., prosecutors and judges) treat women more leniently than men, because men feel the need to protect women. [Ch. 10]

Classical conditioning: behavior that continues when it is rewarded. [Ch. 6]

Classical School: area of criminology focused on penal and judicial reform. [Ch. 2]

Cognitive coping strategies: methods of dealing with strain by minimizing the associated stress. [Ch. 5]

Collective efficacy: the perceived ability of residents in a geographic area to enforce social control. [Ch. 4]

Commitment: an individual's level of share in conventional society, along the lines of reputation or education. [Ch. 7]

Communitarianism: the notion that persons who come from strong communities are tied to each other. [Ch. 8]

Concentric zone theory: theory that states that as a city expands, every inner ring will invade the ring surrounding it, activating a process of invasion and domination; explained by Park. [Ch. 4]

Conditional free will: an acknowledgement of the factors that impede or guide decision making. [Ch. 3]

Conflict subculture: a label affiliated with violent, aggressive gangs. [Ch. 5]

Conforming acts: appropriate behaviors not considered deviant, such as paying taxes or going the speed limit. [Ch. 8]

Conformity: occurs when an individual accepts societal rules and reaches goals through legitimate means; one of Merton's adaptations. [Ch. 5]

Confrontation with negative/noxious stimuli: can include abuse by a significant other or parent, or bullying at school. [Ch. 5]

Constitutive criminology: can include a variety of themes, including critical and other postmodern perspectives, as well as peacemaking, feminism, or race theories. [Ch. 9]

Contingencies: interactions or conditions. [Ch. 7]

Control balance desirability: the quality possessed in different degrees by various potential acts. [Ch. 7]

Cost-benefit analysis: analysis affected by an individual's preferences, estimations of criminal opportunity and the consequences, and attitudes toward criminal behavior. [Ch. 2]

Crime: act of force or fraud that an individual pursues in his or her interest; more specifically: (1) in law, a violation of criminal laws of the state and government; (2) in the political realm, going against the interest of those in power; (3) in sociology, an antisocial act that is an offense against human relationships; and (4) in psychology, a problem behavior that makes living in society difficult for its norm-abiding inhabitants. [Chs. 1, 7]

Crime prevention through environmental design (CPTED): advocates for altering the physical construction of a community to deter criminal behavior. [Ch. 2]

Criminal actor: the type of person that would likely commit crime. Determined from information derived from rigorous methods providing careful observation. [Ch. 3]

Criminals by passion: people who commit crimes to relieve social injustice. [Ch. 3]

Criminal careers: a belief that some individuals may commit crime at different points in their lives or maintain consistent and long-term criminal behavior. [Ch. 11]

Criminal subculture: youth gangs organized to commit income-producing crimes; corresponds with Merton's innovation adaptation. [Ch. 5]

Criminaloid: type of occasional criminal who is weak in nature and swayed by others. [Ch. 3]

Critical realism: theory that acknowledges that there are objective dimensions of crime that are not adjustable simply through verbal discussion. [Ch. 9]

Cultural criminology: focuses on the importance of using cultural dynamics to develop meanings of crime and crime control. [Ch. 9]

Decarceration: sentencing approach where shorter sentences of incarceration allow offenders to return to normal life more quickly, removing them from a breeding ground of criminality (a prison). [Ch. 8]

Decriminalization: the legalization of some acts with the goal of controlling the overload of the court docket as well as the overcrowding in the corrections system. [Ch. 8]

Defensible space: architecture developed to reduce criminal behavior. [Ch. 2]

Delinquent subculture: delinquent culture within a culture. [Ch. 5]

Density: ratio of the number of connections an individual has in a social network that is relative to the total possible number of connections that an individual could have in network. [Ch. 11]

Dependent variable: used when explaining why certain behaviors are called wrong or criminal. [Ch. 8]

Deregulation: normlessness. [Ch. 5]

Demonology: belief that criminal behavior is a result of demon possession or witchcraft rather than a matter of rational decision making. [Ch. 2]

Determinism: theory that actions and reactions are already predetermined by a higher and/or otherworldly power and not a matter of choice by the individual. [Ch. 2]

Deterrence: weighing the punishments of a crime. [Ch. 2]

Development: describes an individual progressing through a number of mental, moral, and sexual stages of life. [Ch. 3]

Differential association: the interaction with others in a primary group who engage in and support certain types of behavior in direct association as well as with identifications toward secondary and more distant reference groups. [Ch. 6]

Differential social control: the belief that self-perception is a result of learned definitions of criminal behavior and the reactions to this behavior. [Ch. 8]

Differential social organization: when areas of cities are able to provide fertile grounds for widespread differential associations to occur. [Ch. 6]

Direct file: the prosecutor's discretion to file a juvenile case in juvenile or adult court. [Ch. 2]

Disintegrative shaming: places all emphasis on shaming and punishment of the wrongdoer; does not allow for afterthought of reintegrating an offender back into society; also known as stigmatization. [Ch. 8]

Disjuncture between expectation and reality: occurs when reality does not match expectations. [Ch. 5]

Disjuncture between fair outcomes and actual outcomes: occurs when a person feels as if the reward received is not comparable to the actual effort put forth. [Ch. 5]

Diversion: the redirection of offenders through less punitive forms of treatment and institutions rather than processing them in the criminal justice system. [Ch. 8]

Dramatization of evil: the implication that an individual who was deviant was not a product of the person's lack of adjustment to society, but rather the adjustment to a certain group; this is the concept Tannenbaum coined for when a person acts criminally as a result of the expectation of his or her social group. [Ch. 8]

Drift theory: Matza's theory that introduced will as a contributing factor of commit deviance; close relative of the original classical school assertions. [Ch. 2]

Due process model of justice: rational system of justice that has clearly defined principles and is systematic in delivering justice. [Ch. 2]

Ectomorphs: people with thin frail bodies; in Sheldon's theory, believed to have sensitive personalities. [Ch. 3]

Egalitarian family: occurs when parents work in either a command or obey position, or the father is not in the household. [Ch. 10]

Ego: the portion of the mind that contained reality. [Ch. 3]

Emotional coping strategies: one of the adaptations that individuals can perform as a result of strain, described by Agnew; can be legitimate, such as mediation of counseling, or illegitimate, such as abusing drugs or alcohol. [Ch. 5]

Empirical falsification: allows consideration of evidence that disproves a theory. [Ch. 1]

Empirical validity: supported by evidence; determines whether the support is weak or strong. [Ch. 1]

End-to-end (ETE) integration: involves putting theories together to accommodate different levels of explanation for crime and delinquency. [Ch. 11]

Endogenous community dynamics: dynamics such as social control, social capital, and collective efficacy that have been used in social disorganization models to better examine crime. [Ch. 4]

Endomorphs: people of medium height with round, soft bodies, and thick necks; in Sheldon's theory, an extroverted person who is motivated by his or her "gut." [Ch. 3]

Epileptoid: type of occasional criminal; suffering from epilepsy. [Ch. 3]

Eros: the life instinct. [Ch. 3]

Excitement: the quest for risk, danger, and thrills. [Ch. 5]

Failure to achieve positively valued goals: the inability to achieve a desired goal. [Ch. 5]

Faith-based programs: programs based on the willingness to forgive; utilized in the prison system. [Ch. 8]

Falsely accused behaviors: behaviors that either do not occur or are actually conforming to societal standards, but receive a reaction as if a behavior is deviant. [Ch. 8]

Fatalism: the focus on luck or fate. [Ch. 5]

Felicity (or hedonistic) calculus: the weighing of the pleasures and pains of an act to make a determination of how to proceed. [Ch. 2]

Feminism: promotes equality for women. [Ch. 10]

Feminists: advocates for equality for women, including more social, cultural, economic, and political opportunities. [Ch. 10]

Fetishism of money: attributes stockpiling money as the end all of success, even above possessions or power resulting from the money. [Ch. 5]

Focal concerns: way of life for juveniles characterized by issues that demand constant attention and have a large degree of emotional involvement; influenced by cultural forces in the neighborhood and the manner the juvenile perceives these forces and their meaning. [Ch. 5]

Free will: occurs when individuals make a choice to violate the law; when exercising free will, an individual calculates the risk of pain compared to the potential benefit of pleasure that would be accomplished from performing the act. [Ch. 2]

Gendered pathways perspective: methodology that focuses on the life histories of females to understand criminality; mirrors life course perspective in many ways. [Ch. 10]

Gene: the basic biological unit of heredity; has been shown to have an important link with chromosomes. [Ch. 3]

General deterrence: occurs when the state's punishment for a crime serves as an example to everyone in the general population who has not yet committed a crime. [Ch. 2]

General theory: attempts to explain crime, or at least the majority of it, in an overarching explanation. [Ch. 1]

Guardianship: the ability of persons and objects to prevent a crime from occurring. [Ch. 2]

Habitual criminal: career criminals. [Ch. 3]

Hedonistic: motivated by self-interest. [Ch. 2]

Hegemony: all-encompassing influence. [Ch. 9]

Hot spots: small geographic areas identified by law enforcement as a high-crime area in a community or city. [Ch. 2]

Imitation: engaging in a behavior after observing similar behavior in others. [Ch. 6]

Independent variable: used when explaining how placing labels on individuals can foster further criminal behavior. [Ch. 8]

Individualism: creates competitiveness between individuals to succeed rather than to work together. [Ch. 5]

Informal deterrence: the anticipated or actual social consequences of crime that prevent occurrence; shown to have more of an effect compared to arrest or actual legal penalties. [Ch. 2]

Innovation: occurs when individuals still strive for the socially acceptable goals, but do not use legitimate means to obtain them; the second adaptation described by Merton. [Ch. 5]

Insane criminals: criminals who are mentally ill. [Ch. 3]

Integrated theory: takes concepts from various sources and merges them together to provide a better explanation of crime. [Ch. 1]

Interdependency: belief that individuals who demonstrate attachments and commitments to conventional values and activities will be more receptive to reintegrative shaming. [Ch. 8]

Interest groups: an outside entity (e.g., business group or political group) that influences decisions. [Ch. 9]

Internalized control: occurs when individuals regulate their own behavior; describes the extent of influence and identification integrating the individual with authority figures in general and parents in particular. [Ch. 7]

Involvement: the amount of time or energy available to perform conforming or non-conforming activities. [Ch. 7]

Just deserts: occurs when potential offenders are aware of the punishment that will present itself for committing a crime. [Ch. 2]

Justified punishments: consequences that should fit the crime and cruel and unusual forms of treatment to offenders should be abolished. [Ch. 2]

Labeling theory: proposes that labeling shapes criminal and delinquent behavior. [Ch. 8]

Learning environment: allows a person to learn and perform skills that are either conforming or deviant. [Ch. 5]

Left realism: theory that called for the return of traditional liberal, as well as radical, approaches to managing crime; emerged from the works of British criminologists focusing on radical criminology in the 1970s. [Ch. 9]

Liberal feminism: views gender discrimination as a matter of equal rights between males and females. [Ch. 10]

Likelihood: the probability of an event occurring. [Ch. 1]

Logically consistent: when the concepts work with each other. [Ch. 1]

Low self-control: refers to the inability of an individual to foresee the long-term consequences of actions. [Ch. 7]

Macro-level theory: attempts to explain the behaviors of groups or societies in a broader spectrum. [Ch. 1]

Mandatory minimum sentencing laws: laws that require a specific amount of time for the violation of state and federal laws. [Ch. 2]

Marxist feminism: acknowledges the relationships between gender relations and patriarchy, but focuses more on how classes are viewed in regard to gender. [Ch. 10]

Masculinity: qualities traditionally associated with a man; a social construction that is not a concrete concept and can manifest itself in various forms. [Ch. 10]

Masculinity hypothesis: describes how women are attempting to equate themselves with men in every manner. [Ch. 10]

Meanings: present in verbal and nonverbal communication, gestures, and attitudes; symbolic interactionism enforces the notion of meanings of words and actions during these social interactions. [Ch. 8]

Mechanical society: early stage of society's evolution; simple form of society. [Ch. 5]

Meso-level: an explanation of behavior that occurs at the macro and micro levels. [Ch. 6]

Mesomorphs: muscular and strong people with wide shoulders and thin waists; in Sheldon's theory, insensitive to others. [Ch. 3]

Micro-level theory: focuses on the behavior of individuals. [Ch. 1]

Middle-class expectations: society's standards of expected behavior; not only imposed by society, but also teachers. [Ch. 5]

Motivated offender: a person who is willing to commit a crime when opportunities are presented. [Ch. 2]

Multiplexity: the number of different relationships or contexts that a social network maintains. [Ch. 11]

National Crime Victimization Survey: collects data from 42,000 households randomly chosen in the United States and includes individuals within those households that are twelve years of age or older. [Ch. 1]

National Incident Based Reporting System: requires all agencies to report their crime statistics annually and to give a brief summary of each act or arrest as well as provide information about the victim and the offender. [Ch. 1]

Negative reinforcement: the removal or avoidance of an unpleasant experience of a behavior. [Ch. 6]

Neoclassical school: asserted that the following factors affected decision making: (1) character of a person; (2) dynamics of the character development; and (3) rational choices made when presented with opportunities for criminal activity. [Ch. 2]

Neuropsychological deficits: linked to brain structure; instrumental in the development of behavioral problems. [Ch. 11]

Neurotransmitters: molecules that travel between neurons and the central nervous system; provide the link between monoamine oxidase (MOA) and childhood maltreatment in the context of four outcomes: conduct disorder, violence, antisocial behavior, and criminal conviction for a violent offense. [Ch. 3]

Neutralization: techniques that free individuals to commit crime and delinquency. [Ch. 7]

Objective approaches: use official criminal justice statistics to measure the severity and certainty of certain punishments as a deterrent. [Ch. 2]

Objective strain: universal stressors. [Ch. 5]

Occasional criminal: those who break the law because of environmental or societal circumstances; divided into four subtypes: *criminaloid*; *epileptoid*; *habitual criminal*; and *psuedo-criminal*. [Ch. 3]

One-sex peer unit: type of gang where the majority of male youth members come from single parent homes (generally females), and they desire the membership and tutelage of other boys. [Ch. 5]

Operant conditioning: behavior that is controlled through manipulation. [Ch. 6]

Opportunity hypothesis: refers to women flooding the workforce, and therefore obtaining more opportunities to participate in white collar and financial crimes. [Ch. 10]

Organic society: complex forms of society. [Ch. 5]

Parental management: demonstrating self-control while performing parenting tasks—attachment, monitoring, analyzing behavior for deviance, and application of non-corporal punishment. [Ch. 7]

Parsimonious theory: a theory that includes as few concepts as possible to explain the largest amount of crime. [Ch. 1]

Paternalism: views women as passive and gentile creatures that need protection. [Ch. 10]

Patriarchal society: a society that focuses on male rights and privileges to dominate. [Ch. 10]

Patriarchal family: a family where the father is employed, placing him in a "command" position that allows him to be the authoritarian figure in the household. [Ch. 10]

Peacemaking criminology: focused on a peaceful way of life; roots come from early Eastern philosophies and religions. [Ch. 9]

Perceptual measure of deterrence: used to investigate individuals' subjective perceptions of criminal punishments. [Ch. 2]

Personal control: the individual's ability to refrain from acting on and obtaining desires that were in conflict with the norms and rules of the community. [Ch. 7]

Policy implications: input that provides information to develop punishments, treatments, and programs to benefit the criminal justice system. [Ch. 1]

Positive reinforcement: the presentation of a reward for an expected behavior. [Ch. 6]

Positivism: the application of the scientific method study biological characteristics of crime. [Ch. 3]

Postmodern theories: concerned with discrediting hegemony (or all-encompassing influence) and push for the agenda favoring underprivileged individuals. [Ch. 9]

Power: a tool used to exercise control over particular situations, events, or social issues. [Ch. 9]

Power-control theory: explains the dynamic of control of the mother and father in regard to parenting. [Ch. 10]

Probabilistic concept of causality: shows, for example, that the presence of X indicates that Y is more likely to occur. [Ch. 1]

Psuedo-criminal: people who commit crime by accident. [Ch. 3]

Pure deviant behavior: includes behaviors that are actually deviant and are perceived as deviant, such as rape or murder. [Ch. 8]

Racial heterogeneity: racial diversity measured by percent of blacks in a neighborhood. [Ch. 4]

Rational beings: individuals who are able to weigh the possible pleasure of an act against the possible pain of an act. [Ch. 7]

Radical feminists: those who see gender inequality issues as a result of patriarchy, or male domination. [Ch. 10]

Rational choice theory: a more contemporary version of classical criminology. [Ch. 2]

Rebellion: response where individuals completely reject the means and ends of a system and attempt to violently overthrow it; one of Merton's adaptations. [Ch. 5]

Reaction formation: occurs when individuals repress their thoughts and desires; reaction formation of a new delinquent subculture stresses the importance of aggression and contempt for academic achievement. [Chs. 3, 5]

Removal of positively valued stimuli: the loss of someone or something of great worth. [Ch. 5]

Reparation and restitution: restoring the harmony between the action committed by the offender and the loss suffered by the victim. [Ch. 8]

Replacement discourse: method of communication for criminologists and practitioners where they are encouraged to provide correct and positive interpretations of crime; counterbalance to sensationalized criminal activity. [Ch. 9]

Residential mobility: examines the number of residents who have resided in the same dwelling for the past five years. [Ch. 4]

Resources: beneficial source or supply; possession of resources makes one more likely to be powerful. [Ch. 9]

Restorative justice: focuses on reintegrating the offender back into society through communication and forgiveness. [Chs. 8, 9]

Restorative justice programs: focus on not only the needs of the victim, but also that of the offender and the involved community.

Retreatism: response involving an escapist response to life; applies to societal dropouts such as addicts, alcoholics, or vagrants; one of Merton's adaptations. [Ch. 5]

Retreatist subculture: subculture where individuals focus on drug and alcohol use and have given up both legitimate and illegitimate goals and means, much like Merton's adaptation; the third and final type of juvenile delinquent subculture. [Ch. 5]

Ritualism: occurs when individuals do not adhere to societal norms, but still use legitimate means to live life; one of Merton's adaptations. [Ch. 5]

Role model: a person whose behavior is considered an example to others. [Ch. 6]

Routine Activities Theory: an expansion of lifestyle/exposure theory, which proposes that a variance in victimization risk is related to differences in lifestyle choices; Cohen and Felson asserted that the regularity with which events occur (rhythm), the number of events that occur per unit of time (tempo), and the duration and recurrence of the events (timing) improves the explanation of how and why criminal activity is performed. [Ch. 2]

Scope: the range of criminality explained by the concepts of a theory. [Ch. 1]

Secondary deviance: a deviant reaction as a result of a label. [Ch. 8]

Secret deviant behaviors: behaviors not perceived as deviant but are actually deviant. [Ch. 8]

Self as a social construct: composed of the "I" and "Me"; the internalization of the beliefs of others forms your "Me," or social construct; our own responses to society's perception of the "Me" forms our "I," which is never stable or completely controllable. [Ch. 8]

Self-concept: part of the self, developed when young; positive or negative evaluations of the self-concept serve as an insulator between the self and social influences. [Ch. 7]

Self-report: used in a survey, when subjects are asked to describe their own victimization, as well as offending behaviors. [Ch. 1]

Sentencing guidelines: uniform sentencing policies implemented by the federal government and multiple states. [Ch. 2]

Serial monogamy: occurs when women have multiple short-term relationships with men; when children are present in the home, this behavior does not allow youth to develop a bond with a father figure; an influence of lower class juvenile behavior. [Ch. 5]

Shaming: social disapproval with the purpose of causing remorse and awareness of inappropriate behavior. [Ch. 8]

Severity: harshness; in determining punishment, severity is based on the proportionality concept (i.e., it must fit the crime). [Ch. 2]

Smartness: having the ability persuade in order to manipulate others, as well as to obtain material goods and status. [Ch. 5]

Social capital: the relationships among people who live and work together that allow a society to operate efficiently. [Ch. 4]

Social contract: occurs when individuals agree to give up the right to enforce their own forms of justice against others to the government, and in turn receive protection and other benefits. [Ch. 2]

Social control: the ability of social groups or institutions to make norms or rules effective. [Ch. 7]

Social disorganization theory: a criminological theory based on the historical happenings involving the unsuccessful merging of immigrant culture in urban areas. [Ch. 4]

Social ecology: the study of the behavior and relationships of individuals in a specific environment. [Ch. 4]

Social network: a set of actors, individuals, or groups that are linked by some type of relationship (e.g., friendship, kinship, school, or church). [Ch. 11]

Social visibility: a deviant behavior that can be seen in a community. [Ch. 8]

Socialist feminists: feminists focused on the role of technology and class relations, as well as stereotypical gender roles in regard to domestic and child care, and how the two work together to cause gender inequality. [Ch. 10]

Socioeconomic status (SES): social standing, or class, of an individual or group; can be either a single variable, a scale of economic variables, or a combination of income level and unemployment rates. [Ch. 4]

Soft determinism: according to Matza, type of determinism that lies on the continuum between free will and hard determinism. [Ch. 2]

Specific deterrence: deterrence predicated on the belief that convicted and punished offenders will refrain from repeating crimes if they are aware of the punishment; focuses on those individuals who have already participated in criminal behavior at least once. [Ch. 2]

Status: ranking, or pecking order, of group membership. [Ch. 5]

Strain: the discrepancies between culturally defined goals and the structured means available to achieve these goals; results in stress. [Ch. 5]

Structured action: criminality that is adopted based on the definition of gender in a particular social structure. [Ch. 10]

Subjective strain: something that is stressful to a particular person. [Ch. 5]

Superego: according to Freud, contains an individual's socialization that resulted in control of the individual's morality; the superego is a reflection and summarization of an individual's experiences and it provides self-criticism and a source of guilt. [Ch. 3]

Symbolic interactionist perspective: states that a person's identity is a result of cognitive processes, attitudes, and beliefs in the context of society's perception of what is appropriate and normal; suggests that individuals use how others are treating them as the basis for their views of themselves. [Chs. 6, 8]

Tag: label. [Ch. 8]

Target hardening: makes targets less appealing for victimization by tightening security. [Ch. 2]

Target suitability: based on a person's availability as a victim, as well as his or her attractiveness to the offender. [Ch. 2]

Tautology: needless repetition; involves circular reasoning and can never be fully explained. [Ch. 1]

Testability: refers to whether a theory can be supported by evidence. [Ch. 1]

Thanatos: the death instinct. [Ch. 3]

Theoretical competition: the empirical study of more than one theory at a time. [Ch. 11]

Theoretical integration: the deliberate attempt to combine two closely related theories. [Ch. 11]

Theory: a set of propositions that describe relationships between variables, often in a causal manner. [Ch. 1]

Three strikes laws: requirement of harsh penalties, often 25 years to life sentences, for commission of three felonies in a state. [Ch. 2]

Toughness: the demonstration of physical power, courage, and machismo. [Ch. 5]

Trajectory: a pattern or sequence of events. [Ch. 11]

Transition: a specific event that is embedded in a *trajectory*. [Ch. 11]

Trouble: a commitment to breaking the law and being a problem for other people; it is a dominant feature for the lower class, and can refer to getting into trouble or staying out of trouble. [Ch. 5]

Uniform Crime Report (UCR): a statistical summary of crime reported from local agencies to the FBI. [Ch. 1]

Universalism: develops the expectation that all members of society are striving for the same goals. [Ch. 5]

Utilitarianism: concerned with the "collective human rights of society," rather than protecting certain social interest groups. [Ch. 2]

Vicarious strain: witnessing another person's experiences with strain. [Ch. 5]

Zone of transition: an area of continuous change due to the moving in and out of immigrants. [Ch. 4]

abnormal behavior, 39
   abnormalities, 31
   abnormality, 39, 131
Abraham et al., 59, 60, 61
achievement orientation, 63, 73
Adler, Freda, 143, 144, 146-147, 150,
     155, 156
adoption studies, 27, 35, 47
Age of Enlightenment, 7, 9
aggregate (macro) level, 54
Agnew, Robert, 63, 71-72, 74, 76, 78,
     79, 161, 167
   Agnew & Cullen, 130
aggression, 43, 47, 52, 68, 75, 77, 79,
     108, 139, 146
Akers, Ronald, 2, 6, 81, 82, 83, 87, 90,
     91-95, 160, 167
   Akers & Jensen, 92, 95, 96
   Akers & Sellers, 3, 6, 14, 15, 23, 76,
     92, 96
Al Faqeh, Farmi, 109
alcohol, 5, 19, 29, 53, 67, 69, 71, 72, 74,
     76, 77, 79, 94, 96, 118, 140,
     155
   Alcoholics Anonymous, 76
Allport, Gordon, 43, 46
American Dream, 50, 65, 73, 79, 80
AmeriCorps, 76
andocentric, 143, 144
anomie, 63, 64-65, 73, 75, 77, 78, 79,
     80, 93, 126
   institutional anomie theory, 73,
     75, 79
anthropological, 32
antisocial behavior, 37, 46, 47, 66, 167
Apel & Nagin, 14
Aquinas, Thomas, 8-9
Arizona, 121
Arnold et al., 19, 23
Arpaio, Joe, 121
assault, 4, 25, 26, 36, 87, 110, 156, 157
attachment, 97, 103, 108, 120
attention deficit disorder (ADD),
     37-38, 47

Attitudes Toward Women Scale, 152
Australia, 124
   Australian Reintegrative Shaming
     Experiments (RISE), 125
authority-subject relationship, 133-134
autonomy, 63, 69, 74, 75, 77, 79
avatism, 31

Bandura, 81, 85, 90, 96
Banks & Dabbs, 38, 46
Baptiste della Porte, 28
Barker v. Wingo, 13, 23
Barnes & Teeters, 8, 23
Baron and Straus, 152
Bazemore & Schiff, 124, 126
Beaver et al., 36, 46
Beccaria, Caesare, 9-13, 19, 23, 24, 25
Becker, Howard, 115, 117-118, 126
Bedau, 14, 23
behavioral coping strategies, 63, 72
behavioral genetics, 35, 47
Beirne, 11, 19, 24
Belgium, 149
belief, 9, 22, 31, 52, 69, 70, 73, 97, 98,
     103, 104, 108, 116, 138, 139,
     145, 148, 152
Belknap, 152, 155
   Belknap & Holsinger, 149, 155
belonging, 63, 70
Bennett, Holloway, & Farrington,
     59, 61
Bentham, Jeremy, 11, 19, 24
Berlin, 151, 156
Bernburg, 122, 126
   Bernburg & Krohn, 122, 126
biological theorists, 29, 33, 35
   biological explanations, 29, 30, 39
   biological perspective of
     criminology, 28, 46
   biological theories, 28, 29, 33, 35,
     39, 40, 45
biosocial criminology, 27, 34, 35-36,
     45-46
   biosocial criminologist, 33, 37, 38

Bjerregaard and Cochran, 75, 79
Blackwell & Reed, 151, 155
Blalock, 129, 133, 135, 141
blank slate, 81, 85
blocked goals, 67, 74
Bloom, Owen & Covington, 154, 155
Boggess & Hipp, 56, 61
Bonger, 131, 141
born criminal, 27, 31
Boshier & Johnson, 122, 126
Boston, 76, 149
Bottcher, 148, 155
Bouffard and Muftic, 56, 61
bourgeoisie, 136
Box & Hale, 151, 155
boys will be boys, 117, 148
Bradley and Khor, 152, 155
Braga, 22
   Braga & Bond, 24
Braithwaite, John, 115, 120, 123, 124,
     126, 163, 166, 167
Bratton, William, 58
   Braswell et al., 140
   Braswell, McCarthy, & McCarthy,
     139, 141
   Bratton & Knobler, 58, 61
Brezina, 74, 79
Britain, 137, 139
Broidy, 74, 79, 151, 156
broken windows theory, 49, 57-58,
     61, 62
Brunson, 58, 61
Buddhist, 139
bully, 89
   bullying, 72
Burgess, Ernest W, 51, 52, 61
   Burgess & Akers, 81, 82, 90-91
Bursik, Robert, 54, 55, 56, 61
   Bursik & Grasmic, 25, 54
Bynum & Thompson, 77, 79

California, 15, 26, 124
   California Personality Inventory,
     108

Cao & Maume, 19, 24
Capece & Lanza-Kaduce, 94, 96
capital punishment, 7, 11, 19-20, 24, 25, 26, 140, 141, 142
career criminals, 20, 31, 44
Caspi and colleagues, 37
    Caspi et al., 43, 46, 164, 167
Caulfield and Wonders, 145, 155
celerity, 7, 10, 14, 25
Central propositions from Burgess and Akers, 90-91
certain, 6, 7, 10-12, 14, 18, 19, 43, 53, 65, 66, 73, 85, 86, 92, 101, 110, 116, 117, 120, 123
    certainty, 11, 14-15, 23
Chamlin and Cochran, 75, 79
Chapman, 151, 155
Chapple, 108, 113
Charles Horton Cooley, 116, 127
Chen, 74, 79
Chesney-Lind, Meda, 145, 149, 150, 154, 155
    Chesney-Lind & Faith, 144, 155
    Chesney-Lind & Rodriguez, 150, 152, 155
    Chesney-Lind and Pasko, 150, 153
    Chesney-Lind and Shelden, 149, 150, 152, 155
Chicago, 50, 51, 52, 53, 57, 62, 82, 83-84, 124
    Chicago Area Project (CAP), 57, 90, 91
    Chicago School, 50, 83-84, 122, 123, 138
    University of Chicago, 50, 51, 83
childhood, 37, 41, 42, 89, 122, 152, 154, 165, 167
chivalry hypothesis, 143, 145-146, 155, 156
Christian, 8, 125, 139, 140
chromosomes, 37, 39
    chromosome theory, 37
chronic criminal offenders, 35
Civil Rights Movements, 130, 131, 144
Clarke and Cornish, 16, 21, 24
class position, 136
class struggle, 136
classical conditioning, 81, 84
classical criminology, 10, 16, 22, 37
    Classical criminologists, 9, 22
Classical School, 7, 9, 16, 19, 20, 21, 22, 23, 30, 99
    classical theorist, 11, 19, 22, 32

Clear, 21, 24
coercion, 110, 134, 141
cognitive coping strategies, 63, 72
    cognitive features, 35
    cognitive theory, 27, 44
    cognitive-behavior therapies (CBT), 77
Cohen, Albert, 63, 67-68, 70, 74, 78, 79, 102, 123, 127
    Cohen & Cantor, 18, 19, 24
    Cohen & Felson, 17, 18, 25, 24
    Cohen-Cole et al., 20, 24
    Cohen-Kettenis, 47
collective efficacy, 49, 55, 57, 61, 62
Colorado, 86
Commitment, 68, 97, 102, 103, 108, 120, 124, 127
communitarianism, 115, 120
community policing programs, 2, 58, 59, 138, 140
concentric zone theory, 49, 51, 52, 53
conditional free will, 27, 37
conditioning, 43, 85, 91
conflict subculture, 63, 71
conflict theory, 129, 130, 131-133, 156
    conflict theories, 98, 129, 130-132, 135, 138, 140
conformity, 63, 66, 99-101, 103, 167
    conforming, 52, 65, 70, 91, 102, 103, 104, 118, 163
confrontation with negative/noxious stimuli, 63, 72
Connecticut, 20, 149
Conscious and unconscious components, 41
constitutive criminology, 129, 137, 142
    constitutive criminologist, 137
containment theory, 101-102
contingencies 91, 97, 110, 111, 113
control balance desirability, 97, 111
control deficit, 110, 111, 112
control ratio, 110-112, 113
control surplus, 110-111
control theories, 56, 97, 98-105, 108, 112, 163
conventional behavior, 66, 103
correctional perspective, 39
cortisol, 38, 46, 47
Coser, 131, 141
cost-benefit analysis, 7, 16
Covington, 153-154, 155
Cressey, 50, 61

crime and deviance, 79, 95, 96, 104-105, 107, 113
    victimless crimes, 131
crime prevention, 24, 61, 78, 114, 138
    crime prevention through environmental design (CPTED), 7, 18
crime reduction, 22, 59, 125
criminal act, 10, 27, 29, 52, 68, 78, 92, 107, 118
    criminal activity, 4, 16, 18, 59, 60, 73, 125, 140, 165, 166
    criminal actor, 27, 29
    criminal conviction, 37
criminal justice system, 3, 9, 12, 13, 22, 23, 45, 76, 120, 122, 123, 124, 125, 130, 138, 139, 140, 141, 145, 147, 153, 155, 156
    criminal justice policy, 32, 33, 94-95, 96, 154, 228
    criminal justice processing, 34
    criminal law, 2, 24, 133
criminal lifestyle, 52
criminal personality theory, 43
    criminal predispositions, 37
criminal subculture, 63, 71
criminality, 2, 3, 5, 15, 16, 19, 23, 37, 52, 53, 55, 65, 74, 75, 78, 105, 120, 121, 123, 126, 141, 142, 146, 147, 148, 149, 150, 154, 156, 157, 165, 166
criminaloid, 27, 31
criminals by passion, 27, 31
criminological theory, 1, 2-3, 8, 16, 23, 24, 25, 29, 46, 47, 50, 79, 89, 96, 113, 117, 127, 141, 142, 144, 156, 160, 161, 166
    criminologist, 9, 22, 28, 32, 33, 35, 37, 38, 42, 43, 70, 129, 130, 131, 136, 137-140, 160-161, 164, 166
    criminological anthropologists, 29
critical criminology, 129, 130, 137, 138, 141, 142
critical theory, 129, 130, 142
    critical realism, 129, 138
Cromwell, Olson & Avary, 16, 24
Culbertson, Vik & Kooiman, 152, 156
cultural criminology, 129, 137, 138, 141
    cultural criminologist, 138-139
culture conflict, 81, 88, 96, 101
    culture conflict theory, 83

culture shock, 83
Curran & Renzetti, 138, 141
Currie & Klein, 145, 156
Curry & Piquero, 111, 113

Dahrendorf, 131, 141
D'Alessio & Stolzenberg, 14, 24
Daly, Kathleen, 149-150, 152, 156
    Daly & Chesney-Lind, 143, 144,
        149-150, 156
    Daly's Five pathways to felony
        court for women, 149-150
Darwin, 30-31, 33, 46
    Darwinian, 30-31
Davies and Tanner, 122, 127
De Giorgi, 130, 141
De Haan & Voss, 17, 24
death, 24, 32, 33, 41, 58
    death penalty, 14, 19-20, 23, 25, 26,
        124
    death row, 20, 25
decarceration, 115, 123
decision-making, 8, 10, 11, 16, 17, 21,
        25, 37, 77, 85, 86, 138, 156
decriminalization, 115, 123
defensible space, 7, 21, 23
definitions, 4, 6, 81, 88, 90, 92, 93, 95,
        121, 134, 135
delinquency rates, 57, 164
    deliquent boys, 34, 53, 68, 79
    deliquent subculture, 63, 67-68, 71
Demographic measures, 93
demonology, 7, 8
density, 159, 163, 164
dependent variable, 3, 110, 115, 116
deregulation, 63, 64
designing out crime, 21
determinism, 7, 8, 16, 24, 30, 86
deterrence theory, 7, 12, 14, 15, 16
    deterrence, 7, 12-15, 16, 24, 25, 26,
        41, 127
development (psychological theories),
        27, 40, 44-45, 46, 47
developmental stages, 42
deviance-amplification, 120
deviant, 2, 6, 8, 9, 40, 52, 57, 66, 67, 70,
        72, 74, 91-93, 95, 96, 98,
        103-104, 105-106, 110, 111,
        112, 113, 117-120, 125,
        147-148, 156
DeWees & Parker, 151, 156
Dezhbakhsh, Rubin, and Sheperd,
        19, 24

Differential association, 81, 82, 83,
        88-90, 92-93
    differential association theories, 70,
        88, 96
    differential association-social
        learning theory, 82, 85-87
differential opportunity, 63, 70
differential reinforcement, 81, 90,
    92-93
differential social control, 115, 121, 127
differential social organization, 81,
    90, 93
differential social reinforcement
    theory, 90
digital piracy, 96, 109, 113
Dinitz, 101
direct file, 7, 21, 26
discipline, 21, 44, 73, 76, 101, 105,
    106-107, 151, 155
disintegrative shaming, 115, 120, 121,
    159, 163
disintegratively, 166
disjuncture between aspirations and
    expectations, or actual
    achievements, 63, 71
disjuncture between expectation and
    reality, 64, 71
disjuncture between fair outcomes and
    actual outcomes, 64, 72
disorganized, 50, 52, 53, 54, 55, 59,
    60, 71
disturbances, 40
diversion, 115, 123
dominant authority figures, 138
dominant group, 132-133
double failures, 64, 71
dramatization of evil, 115, 117
Drapela, 74, 79
drift, 97, 102, 113
    drift theory, 7, 16
drug and alcohol, 5, 19, 53, 71, 96, 140
drug offenders, 12, 20
due process model of justice, 7, 11-12
Dugdale, Richard, 27, 33, 46
DUI, 120
Durkheim, Emile, 64-65, 79, 80

economic marginalization hypothesis,
    143, 150, 155, 156
economic status, 52, 152
ectomorphs, 27, 34
Edwards, 144
egalitarian family, 143, 147-148, 151

ego, 27, 41-42, 99, 101, 148
Einstadter & Henry, 8, 24, 46, 76, 77,
    79, 122, 123, 127, 145, 156
Elder, 165, 167
Eley, Lictenstein & Moffitt, 36, 46
Elliot and Colleagues, 159, 162
    Elliot, Ageton and Cantor, 162, 166,
        167
    Elliot and Voss, 74, 79
empirical falsification, 1, 3
    empirical validity, 1, 3, 95
endogenous communities, 49, 57
endomorphs, 27, 34
end-to-end integration, 159, 161
environment, 21, 29, 30, 32, 33, 35, 37,
    38, 39, 40, 41, 45, 46, 47, 50,
    52, 60, 71, 82, 83, 84, 87, 88,
    89, 101, 102, 107, 110, 133,
    162, 163
environmental criminologist, 32
    environmental design, 7, 18, 21
    environmental factors, 23, 32, 34,
        37, 44
    environmental stimuli, 43
epileptoid, 27, 31
eros, 27, 41
ethnic group, 53, 75, 106, 135
eugenics, 27, 33
evolutionary, 30-31, 33
excitement, 64, 69
executions, 19-20, 127
Eysenck, 43, 46

Fagan, 20, 24
failure to achieve positively valued
    goals, 64, 71
faith-based, 115, 125-126
Falchikov, 151, 156
falsely accused, 115, 118
Families Against Mandatory
    minimums (FAMM), 20
family, 15, 18, 23, 40, 52, 53, 55, 56, 57,
    62, 68, 72, 78, 82, 84, 86, 89,
    92, 95, 98, 100-101, 106-107,
    109, 113, 119, 124, 144, 145,
    147, 149, 154, 155, 156, 163,
    165
    family values, 53
fatalism, 64, 69
Federal Bureau of Investigations or
    FBI, 4
Federal Guidelines, 20
Feinman, 150, 156

felicity (hedonistic) calulus, 7, 11
Felson, 18, 24, 75, 79
　　Felson and Boba, 21, 24
female passivity, 146
Feminist theory, 130, 143, 144, 146,
　　151, 152, 154, 157
　　feminism, 137, 143, 144-145, 154,
　　　155, 156
　　feminists, 143, 144, 145
　　feminist criminology, 145, 146, 157
　　feminist theoretical thought, 146, 150
Ferraro, 152, 156
Ferrell, Jeff, 129, 138-139, 141
Ferri, Enrico, 27, 30, 32
fetishism of money, 64, 73
Finestone, 57, 61
Flavin, 154, 156
Florida, 20, 56, 124
focal concerns, 64, 68, 69-70
Forde & Kennedy, 19, 24
formal sanction, 15
France, 32
Frankling & Fearn, 145, 156
free will, 7, 10, 16, 22, 24, 29, 31, 37
Freud, Sigmund, 27, 41-43, 44, 46
　　Freudian, 99
Friedrichs, 140, 141
Fuller & Wozniak, 140, 142
fully integrated theoretical integrations,
　　162

Gaetz, 19
Gall, 28
Galliher, 11, 24
Galton, 33
gang, 36, 57, 59, 68, 69, 70, 71, 74, 76,
　　77, 78, 79, 80, 102
Gannon-Rowley, 54
Garner, Eric, 58-59
Garofalo, Rafaele, 27, 30
　　Garofalo, 32-33
　　Garofalo & Clark, 18
Gavazzi, Yarcheck & Chesney-Lind,
　　149, 156
Geis, 19, 24
Gelsthorpe & Morris, 151, 156
gender differences, 79, 105, 106, 121,
　　127, 147, 156
　　gender inequality, 144, 145, 152,
　　　157
　　gendered pathways perspective,
　　　143, 149, 152, 153
　　gender-specific, 153

general deterrence, 7, 12, 14, 25
General Strain Theory (GST), 63,
　　64-65, 71, 73, 74, 75, 76, 77,
　　78, 79, 80, 161
general theory, 1, 2
　　general theory of crime, 24, 62, 95,
　　　104, 113
　　general theory of deviance, 110, 114
genes, 28, 29, 35-36, 37, 47
　　genetics, 35-37, 39, 43, 46, 47
get tough policies, 21
Gibbons, 138, 142
Gibbs, 14, 15, 24
Giuliani, Rudolph, 58
Glaze & Parks, 21, 24
Glick & Fiske, 152
Goffman, 116, 127
Goldman & Ducci, 36, 46
Goode, Erich, 95, 120, 127
Gottfredson and Hirschi, 62, 97,
　　104-109, 112, 113, 114
Grasmick and Bursick, 15, 25, 61
　　Grasmick, Tittle, Bursik and
　　　Arneklev, 108, 113
Greenblat, 151, 156
Greenberg, Michael, 58
Grimes & Turk, 120, 127
Grosmaire, Ann, 124
guardianship, 18-19, 26
guilt complex, 42

habitual criminal, 28, 31
Hadjar Baier, Boehnke & Hagan, 151,
　　156
Hagan, John, 143, 147-148
　　Hagan and colleagues, 147, 148, 151
　　Hagan et al., 148, 151
　　Hagan Simposon & Gills, 147, 156
　　Hagan, Boeknke & Merkens, 151,
　　　156
　　Hagan, Gillis, & Simpson, 147, 156
Hamm, 139, 142
hard determinism, 16
Hawkins , 135, 142 Hawkins &
　　Tiedeman, 120, 127
Hawley, 17, 25
Hay and Evans, 74, 75, 79
　　Hay and Forrest, 107, 113
hedonistic, 7, 11
hegemony, 129, 137
Heimer, 121, 127
　　Heimer and Matsueda, 121, 127
Heidensohn, Frances, 144

Helland and Tabarrok, 15, 25
Henry and Milovanovic, 137, 142
Henry Street Settlement House Board
　　of Directors, 59
heritability, 36
Hickman, Piquero, Lawton, and
　　Greene, 110, 113
Higgins, 107, 113
　　Higgins and Tewksbury, 108, 113
　　Higgins & Lauterback, 111, 113
　　Higgins, Lauterbach & Tewksbury,
　　　111, 113
high crime rates, 56, 60
Hindelang et al., 17, 18, 25
　　Hindelang, Gottfredson, and
　　　Garofalo, 18
Hipp, 54, 56, 61
Hirschi, Travis, 62, 97, 98, 103-104,
　　108, 113, 121, 127, 160, 161,
　　162, 167
Hjalmarsson, 122, 127
Hobbes, Thomas, 9, 98
Hoffman and Miller, 74, 79
Hollon & Beck, 77
homicides, 19, 127
Hooten, 27, 33-34, 46
Hormones, 35, 38, 39
Horowitz & Pottieger, 145, 156
hot spot, 7, 21-22, 24, 25, 26
human agency, 17, 139
human rights, 11, 24, 136
Hunnicutt & Broidy, 151, 156
Hurricane Katrina, 118
hyperactivity, 38, 166

id, 28, 41-42
illegitimate opportunities, 70-71, 120
Illinois, 124
imitation, 81, 85, 89, 90, 92, 93
immigrants, 50-51, 83
　　immigrant culture, 50, 84
　　immigration legislation, 35
improper policy, 35
inappropriate behavior, 120, 146
incarceration, 11, 20, 21, 24, 25, 122,
　　123, 126, 139
independent variable, 3, 115, 116
indeterminate sentencing, 19, 39
Indianapolis, 135
individual (micro) level theories, 1, 2,
　　40, 49, 54
individual behavior, 2, 58, 67, 131
individualism, 64, 73

individual's learning history, 85, 86, 92
infant mortality rates, 53
informal deterrence, 7, 15
informal social sanction, 15
innovation, 64, 66, 71
insane criminal, 28, 31
institution imbalance, 73
institutional balance of power, 64, 73, 78
instrumental control, 147
integrated theory, 1, 2, 43, 45, 162
interaction, 37, 40, 58, 82, 85, 86, 87, 88, 89, 90, 91, 92, 116, 122, 134
interdependency, 115, 120
interest groups, 129, 132
internalized control, 97, 100-101
Internet, 22, 53-54
intimate partner violence (IPV), 143, 151-152
involvement, 68, 70, 79, 97, 103, 107, 125, 127
Irwin, 122, 127
Italian School of Criminology, 30

Jackson III, Curtis (50 Cent), 165
Jacobson, Prescott, & Kendler, 36, 46
Jensen & Rojek, 21, 25
Jingxi, Tay, 109
Job Corps, 76-77
Johns, 140, 142
Johnson, 122, 125, 127
Johnson, Dwayne, 165
juries, 32
Jurong Police, 109
just deserts, 7, 12, 23
juveniles, 15, 21, 52, 53, 55, 57, 68, 69, 71, 72, 76, 95, 115, 117, 118, 120, 122, 145-146, 150, 153, 156, 164
    juvenile court, 21, 52, 53, 120
    Juvenile Law Center, 119
    juvenile offenders, 21, 25
    juvenile violence, 56

Kairos Prison Ministries, 125
Kalidass, M, 109
Kam, Cleveland & Hecht, 75, 79
Kansas City Patrol Experiment, 22
Kant, Immanuel, 9
Katz, Levitt and Shustorovich, 20, 25
Kelling & Coles, 58, 61
    Kelling & Sousa, 58, 61

Kentucky, 13
Kerman, Piper, 143, 149
Killias & Clerici, 152, 156
Kincade, Antoin , 38
King, Martin Luther Jr., 139
Kirchner and Higgins, 108, 113
Kirk & Matsuda, 55, 61
Klein, 144, 156
    Klein & Kress, 145, 156
Kobrin, 57, 61
Kornhauser, 54, 61
Krahe, 75, 79
Kraska, 122, 127
Kray twins, 27, 36
Kretschmer, 34, 46
Krohn, Marvin D, 163-164, 166, 167
Kubrin Stucky & Krohn, 75, 79
    Kubrin and Weitzer, 54, 61
Kurlychek, Brame, & Bushway, 122, 127

La Bodega de la Familia, 154, 157
Labeling theory, 115, 116, 117-121, 122-123, 125, 127, 130, 131, 132, 163
labels, 115, 116, 120, 122
lack of a capable guardian, 18
LaGrange, 19, 25
Lanier & Henry, 24, 130, 142
Lanza-Kaduce, Capece, and Alden, 94, 96
Latimer, Dowden and Muse, 125, 127
Lauritsen, Heimer, & Lynch, 150, 156
Lavater, 28
law enforcement, 4, 14, 18, 21, 50, 58, 118, 122, 132, 133, 134, 135, 138, 141, 145
laws of imitation, 81, 83, 96
laypeople, 32
learning disabilities, 39
learning environments, 64, 70
left realism, 129, 137, 138
legal images, 134
legislation, 12, 20, 24, 35, 134, 135
legitimate means, 65-67, 163
    legitimate opportunities, 65, 70-71, 74, 76, 78, 120
Lemert, Edwin, 115, 119-120, 127
    Leiber & Wacker, 151
        Lemert eight step process, 119
Liberal feminism, 143, 144
life course criminality, 166
    life course perspective, 149, 159, 164-166

life imprisonment, 33
lifestyle theory, 160
    lifestyle/exposure theory, 17
likelihood, 1, 3, 14, 19, 21, 38, 75, 94, 108-109, 110, 122
Lilly, Cullen & Ball, 83, 96, 101
Locke, 9
Lombroso, Ceasar, 27, 30-32, 37, 46
Loney et al., 38, 46
looking-glass self, 115, 116
Lopes et al., 121, 122, 127
low socioeconomic, 50, 78
Lowenkamp, Cullen & Pratt, 56, 61
lower class, 57, 67-70, 71, 74, 76, 78, 80, 102, 132, 148, 150
Lowman, 138, 142
Lyons et al., 36, 46

Macdonald and Chesney-Lind, 146, 156
MacKenzi & Piquero, 28, 35
macro-environment, 82
macro-level, or micro-level theories, 1, 2, 14, 19, 49, 54, 58, 62, 81, 87, 90, 93, 130
Madoff, Bernie, 63, 67
Mallicoat, 145, 156
Mandatory minimum sentencing, 12, 20, 27
    mandatory minimums, 8, 20
Marciniak, 151, 156
Marcum, 21, 25
Maricopa County, 121
marijuana, 79, 86, 123
Marquart, Brewer, Simon and Morse, 153, 157
Marx , 136
    Marxist feminism, 143, 144, 145
    Marxist theory, 130, 131, 136
masculinity, 68, 69, 121, 143, 148, 150
    masculinity hypothesis, 143, 147
mass incarceration, 8, 21, 24
Massachusetts, 20, 149
Matsueda , 121, 127
    Matsueda & Heimer, 54, 121, 127
Matthew, 138, 142
Matza, 16, 102, 113
Maume & Lee, 75
Maxfield & Babbie, 4, 6
Mazerolle, Burton, Cullen, Evans, & Payne, 74, 79
    Mazerolle, Roehl & Kadelleck, 58, 61

McBride, Conor, 124-125

McCart, Priester, Davies, & Azen, 77

McCarthy, 17, 25

McClellan, Farabee and Crouch, 152, 157

McHugh & Frieze, 152, 157

McKay, Henry, 52, 53

Mead, George Herbert, 116, 127

meanings, 52, 115, 116, 138

mechanical society, 64

Megan's Law, 118

Meier & Miethe, 18, 25

mental disorder, 53
    mental health problems, 28, 101
    mental illness, 39, 149, 150, 152, 154
    mentally ill, 31, 35, 39

Merton, Robert, 63, 65-67, 70, 71, 73, 76, 78, 79

meso-level, 81, 87, 93

mesomorphs, 28, 34, 85

Messerschmidt, James, 143, 148, 151, 157

Messner & Rosenfeld, 63, 73-74, 75, 78, 79, 80
    Messner & Tardiff, 17, 25
    Messner, Baumer & Rosenfeld, 55, 57, 62

micro and meso levels, 87

micro-environment, 82

Mid-City Project, 76-77

middle-class, 67-68, 71, 74, 75, 131, 132
    middle-class expectations, 64, 67

Midwest, 56

Miles & Carey, 36, 47

Miller, Walter, 63, 68-70, 76, 80

minorities, 58-59, 70, 166

minority communities, 21

minority groups, 54, 75, 106, 133, 141

Mitnick, Kevin, 165

Mobilization of Youth, 49, 59, 61, 76-77

Mocan and Gittngs, 19, 25

Moffit, Terri, 36, 37, 47, 164, 166, 167
    Moffitt & Silva, 38, 47

molecular genetics, 35

Monachesi, 10, 25

monoamine oxidase (MOA), 37

Moore, Scarpa & Raine, 38, 47

Morenoff, Sampson, & Raudenbush, 55, 62

Morris & Higgins, 94, 96

motivated offender, 8, 18

multiple scope levels, 87

Mustaine & Tewksbury, 18, 19, 25

Naffine, 150, 157

Nagin & Pogarsky, 14, 15, 25

Narcotics Anonymous (NA), 76

National Crime Victimization Survey, 1, 5, 156

National Incident Based Reporting System, 1, 4

Nebraska, 56

Negative reinforcement, 81, 85

neighborhood, 19, 22, 25, 53-60, 61, 62, 68, 71, 76, 83, 84, 100, 119, 146, 163

Neighborhood Watch, 52, 59, 61

neoclassical school, 7, 8, 16-19

neurological examinations, 39

neurotransmitters, 28, 37, 38

neutralization, 82, 97, 102, 114

New Mexico, 20

New Orleans, 118

New York City, 58-59, 61, 76, 154
    New York City Police Department, 58
    New York State Prison Association, 33

New Zealand, 124

Newton, Issac, 9

Nobles & Fox, 111, 113

noncapitalist, 145

non-conformity, 100

non-corporal discipline, 105

noncriminals, 30, 44, 86, 95

nondelinquent, 34

non-economic institutions, 73

nonpatriarchal, 145

nonpunitive, 76

North Carolina, 94

nutritional program, 39

Nye, 97, 99, 100-101, 113

Oakland, 124

objective and perceptual measures of deterrence, 8, 14

objective strain, 64, 72

occasional criminal, 28, 31

offending, 5, 18, 39, 74, 75, 80, 82-83, 86, 87, 89, 90, 91, 93, 105, 107, 112, 119, 146, 150, 152, 156, 157, 165

Old World, 53

Olsen, 64, 80

On the Origin of Species, 30, 68

one-sex peer unit, 64, 69

online, 21, 22, 25, 53, 58

operant conditioning, 81, 84, 90, 91

opportunity hypothesis, 143, 147, 150

Orange Is the New Black, 149

Orcutt, 118, 127
    Orcutt & Schwabe, 94, 96

Oregon, 124

organic society, 64

opportunity hypothesis, 143, 147, 150

Osgood and Chambers, 56, 62

Outward Bound, 143, 153

overcrowding, 20, 21, 123

Packer, 12, 25

Pager, 122, 127
    Pager & Quillian, 122, 127

parental management, 97, 105, 106, 107, 108

Park, Robert E, 50

parsimonious, 1, 3

paternalism, 143, 145, 156

Paternoster and Bachman, 127, 155
    Paternoster and Pogarsky, 17, 25
    Paternoster, Salzman, Waldo and Chiricos, 15, 25

pathology, 39, 127

patriarchal family, 143, 147, 148, 151
    patriarchal society, 144, 145

Pavlov, 81, 84, 85

peacemaking criminology, 129, 137, 139, 140, 141, 142

pediatrics, 35

peer associations, 92, 100, 146, 240

peer norming, 95

Pennsylvania Supreme Court, 118

Pepinsky, Harold, 139
    Pepinsky & Quinney, 129, 139

personal control, 97, 99-100

personality theory, 27, 43-44
    personality dimensions, 43
    personality traits, 43, 85

Peters, Thomas & Zamberian, 21, 25

Philadelphia, 119

phrenology, 28

physical appearance, 29, 35

physical guardianship, 18

pink-collar ghetto, 151

Piquero and Bouffard, 108, 113
    Piquero and Hickman, 110, 113, 114

Piquero and Sealock, 75, 80
Piquero, MacDonald, and Parker, 167
policy implications, 1, 3, 5, 7, 9, 19, 27, 28, 39, 40, 44-45, 49, 50, 57-58, 63, 65, 76, 81, 94-95, 97, 98, 112, 115, 116, 129, 139, 143, 146, 153
  policymakers, 45
Pollak, 145, 157
Ponzi scheme, 67
Portland, 124
positive reinforcement, 81, 85
positivism, 28, 29
postmodern, 129, 137, 142
power, 2, 8, 9, 10, 11, 12, 22, 52, 69, 73, 78, 110, 127, 129, 131, 132, 133, 134, 135, 136, 137, 140, 141, 144, 145, 147, 148, 152, 162
power control theory, 143, 147, 148, 155, 156
Pratt & Gau, 54, 62
  Pratt and Cullen, 56, 62, 107, 114
  Pratt et al., 14, 15, 19, 25, 36, 136
  Pratt, Cullen, Sellers, Winfree, Madensen, Daigle, Fearn, and Gau, 93, 96
predisposition, 28, 29, 37, 40
President Regan, 21
prevention program, 78
primary and secondary reference groups, 93
primary deviance, 115, 119, 121
Prison Fellowship Ministries, 125
prisons, 11, 12, 27, 28, 29, 35, 36, 37, 67, 123, 124, 125, 126, 127, 138, 140, 153
  prisoners, 33, 34, 125, 157
Probabilistic concept of causality, 1, 3
process of concern, 82
process, 3, 10, 12, 17, 21, 28, 33, 35, 39, 40, 42, 43, 44, 51, 68, 70, 76, 80, 81, 82, 83, 84, 85, 86, 87-90, 91, 93-94, 98, 100, 110, 116, 117, 119, 120, 125, 132, 133, 134, 135, 145, 163
Project on Human Development, 55
projection, 42
proletariat, 136
prosocial behavior, 42, 92, 133
prostitutes, 33, 58
psuedo-criminal, 31

psychiatry, 35
psychoanalysis, 44-45
psychoanalytic theory, 41, 42, 43, 44, 131
psychological consequences, 137
psychological dispositions, 23
  psychological theories, 3, 27, 28, 39, 40, 41, 44
psychology, 2, 27, 30, 35, 38, 39, 85, 86
  psychologists, 39-40, 43, 45
psychosis, 39
Pulls, 97, 101-102
punishments, 2, 3, 9, 10, 11, 12, 14, 15, 23, 91, 92, 139, 148
pure deviant, 115, 118
pushes, 97, 101-102

Quakers, 139, 142
Quinney, Richard, 129, 134-135, 139, 142
  Quinney & Wildman, 139, 142

racial, 26, 53, 54, 61, 70, 75, 106, 113, 135, 166
  racial heterogeneity, 49, 56, 81
  racial profiling, 58, 129, 135
  racial threat, 135
Radelet & Akers, 14, 25
radical feminist, 143, 144, 151
radical theory, 129, 130, 136, 139
rape, 4, 110, 118, 130, 142, 152, 156, 157
Raphael and Stroll, 21, 25
rational beings, 10, 97, 98, 112, 343
  rationality, 10, 16, 30, 104
Rational Choice Theory, 7, 8, 16-17, 21, 139
reaction formation, 28, 42, 64, 68
rebellion, 64, 66
recidivism, 10, 21, 77, 100, 120, 123, 125-126, 128, 153, 156, 157
Reckdenwald & Parker, 151, 157
Reckless, 97, 99, 101-102, 114
rehabilitation, 95, 125, 139
reign of terror, 139
reinforcement, 45, 81, 84-85, 90-91, 92, 101
Reisig, 59, 62
  Reisig, Holtfreter, & Morash, 149, 157
Reiss, 61, 99-100
  Reiss, Nye, Reckless, Sykes and Matza, 99

Reiss's Theory of Personal and Social Control, 97, 99-100
relational control, 148
removal of positively valued stimuli, 64, 72
reparation, 33, 115, 123, 124
replacement discourse, 129, 140
residential mobility, 49, 55, 56-57, 61
resources, 50, 52, 55, 60, 129, 131, 132, 136, 140-141, 153
restitution, 115, 123
restorative justice, 115, 123-125, 126, 127, 128, 129, 140
retreatism, 64, 66, 71
retreatist subculture, 64, 71
retributive, 19, 23, 141
Rhee & Waldman, 36, 47
rhythm, 17
Richmond Youth Survey, 108
Risk-Need-Responsivity model, 77
ritualism, 64, 66
robbery, 4, 20, 24, 34, 36
Robinson, 54, 62
Rodriguez, 125, 128
Roh and Choo, 60
role models, 59, 69, 71, 81, 85, 103
Roncek & Maier, 19, 25
  Roneck & Bell, 19, 25
Rousseau, 9
Routine Activities Theory, 2, 7, 8, 16, 17-19, 21, 23, 24, 25, 55, 56, 139, 160
Rowe, 36, 47

Sampson, Robert J, 56, 62, 80, 81, 91
  Sampson & Groves, 55, 57, 62, 90, 92
  Sampson & Laub, 122, 128, 164, 165, 166, 167
  Sampson, Raudenbush, and Earls, 55-56, 62
Schaefer, Vito, Marcum, Higgins & Ricketts, 94, 96
Scheider, 14, 26
Scheindlin, Shira, 58
Schlossman & Sedlak, 57, 62
Schmalleger, 2, 4, 5, 6, 16
Schoepfer & Piquero, 75, 80
Schwartz & Friedrichs, 137, 142
  Schwartz, Steffensmeier, Zhong & Ackerman, 150, 157
Schwendinger & Schwendinger, 130, 142

scientific method, 29, 30, 32, 33, 35, 45
  scientific method of criminology, 29, 30
scope, 1, 3, 82, 86-87, 89
secondary conflict, 83-84
secondary deviance, 115, 119, 121, 123
secret deviant, 115, 118
self as a social construct, 115, 116
self-report surveys, 1, 5, 104, 164
self-control, 45, 62, 95, 97, 101, 105-109, 111, 112, 113, 161
  self-control theory, 35, 107, 108, 109, 113, 161
self-esteem, 74, 85
Sellin, 14, 26, 83, 96
sentencing guidelines, 2, 8, 20
serial monogamy, 64, 69
serotonin, 38, 47
Settersten, Furstenberg & Rumbaut, 122, 127
severity, 8, 10, 14, 120
sexism, 137, 157
sexual behavior, 42
shaming, 115, 120, 123, 159, 163, 166
  reintegrative shaming, 115, 120, 123-124, 126, 128
Shaw, Clifford, 52-53
Sheldon, 34-35
  Sheldon and Glueck, 34
Shepherd, 19, 26
Sherman et al., 22, 26
Short, 161, 167
short-term trajectory, 165
Siegel & Williams, 150, 157
Simon, Rita, 147
  Simons, Chen, Stewart & Brody, 75, 80
Simonson & Subich, 151, 157
Simpson, 144, 157
Singapore, 109
Sisters in Crime, 146, 155
situational choice theory, 8, 16
situational learning theories, 62
Sixth Amendment, 13
Skinner, 81, 84-85
Smart, 144, 157
smartness, 64, 69
Smith & Akers, 14, 26
  Smith and Paternoster, 120, 128
Smith College, 149
Social and non-social reinforcers, 92
Social bonding theory, 104, 108, 120

social bonds 103-104, 108, 161, 162, 165, 166
social capital, 49, 55, 57, 61, 62, 156
social contract, 8, 9
social control theory, 55, 163
social disorganization, 54-55, 57, 61, 62, 70, 83, 93, 99, 103-104, 120, 151, 153, 161
  social disorganization theory, 2, 49, 50, 54-55, 56, 58, 59, 60, 61, 62, 138, 161
social ecology, 25, 49, 50, 62
social guardianship, 18, 26
social institutions, 52, 79, 99, 100, 164, 165
social justice, 130, 139
social learning theory, 2, 49, 81, 82-94, 95, 96, 161, 162, 163, 165
  social learning mechanisms, 90
  social learning variables, 93
social network theory, 82
social process theories, 86
social visibility, 115, 119
socialist feminists, 143, 145, 156, 157
socialization, 15, 28, 36, 40, 41, 42, 62, 82, 97, 98, 106, 146, 162
socially acceptable goals, 49, 50, 55
socioeconomic status (SES), 71, 80, 114
soft determinism, 8, 16
somatatyping, 34
Soon, Lee Eng, 109
South Carolina, 56
Spano & Nagy, 19, 26
special interests, 132-133
specific deterrence, 8, 12, 15, 26
Staff Training Aimed at Reducing Rearrest (STARR), 77
Staten Island Ferry, 58
status frustration, 64, 68
Steffensmeier , 150, 157
  Steffensmeier and Allen, 154, 157
  Steffensmeier, Kramer & Streifel, 145, 157
Steiner & Wright, 21, 26
sterilization, 35
stigmata, 31
Stinchcombe, 3
stop and frisk, 58
strain, 64, 65, 67, 70, 71-72, 73, 74, 75, 76, 78, 79, 80, 83, 162, 166
strain theory, 63, 64-65, 71, 73, 74, 75, 76, 77, 78, 79, 80, 120, 161
structural variables, 93

structured action, 143, 148, 157
subcultural theory of deviance, 102
subjective strain, 64, 72
Sugarman and Frankel, 151, 157
Suicide: A Study in Sociology, 64
suitable target, 8, 18
Sullivan, Mino Nelson & Pope, 154, 157
superego, 28, 41, 42, 101
surveillance, 21
Sutherland, Edwin, 70, 81, 82, 83, 87-90, 96
Sutherland's nine propositions, 88-89
Sweeton, 122, 128
Swim & Cohen, 152, 157
Sykes and Matza, 97, 102, 114
symbolic interactionism, 83, 115, 116, 131, 138
  symbolic interactionist, 81
  symbolic interactionist perspective, 83

tag, 115, 117
Takagi, 130, 142
Tallahassee Police Department, 124
Tannenbaum, Frank, 115, 117, 128
target hardening, 7, 8, 21, 22, 23
Target suitability, 18
tautology, 1, 3
  tautological, 42
Tech Boyz, 81, 94
tempo, 17-18
testability, 1, 3, 42
testosterone, 38, 46, 146
Tewksbury & Mustaine, 19, 26
thanatos, 28, 41
The Outsiders, 117, 126
The Professional Thief, 70
theoretical competition, 159, 160-161, 166
theoretical integrations, 147, 159, 160, 161-162, 167
therapy, 32, 44, 77, 140
thieves, 33, 58, 70
Thornberry, Moore and Christenson, 74, 80
thoughtfully reflective decision making (TRDM), 8, 17
three strikes laws, 8, 12, 15, 20, 25
  tough on crime, 19, 138
tightening security, 21, 22
timing, 17-18, 91, 164
tipping point, 159, 163, 166

Tittle, 97, 108, 110-112, 113, 114, 121, 128

Tonry, 14, 25, 26, 61, 62

Toronto, 151, 156

toughness, 64, 69

tragectory, 159, 164-165, 166, 167

traits, 28, 35, 43, 46, 85, 124

traumatic experiences, 40, 154

treatment (psychological theories), 2, 3, 9, 10, 21, 26, 39, 40, 45, 120, 121, 123, 139, 144, 145, 153, 153, 157, 161

trouble, 64, 68-69, 112, 124
troublemaker, 122, 126

Tseloni, 18, 26

Tullis, 125, 128

Turk, 129, 133-134, 142

twin studies, 28, 35, 37, 47

Tyler et al., 125, 128

typology, 31, 34

Uggen, 122, 128
Uggen, Vuolo, Ruhland, Whitham & Lageson, 122, 128

Uniform Crime Report (UCR), 1, 4

United States Congress, 132

United States District Court, 58

universalism, 64, 73

University of Chicago or "Chicago School", 50-51, 83-84, 138

USA Today, 94

usefulness, 1, 3, 121, 153

utilitarianism, 8, 11

van Goozen, 38, 47

Van Ness & Strong, 124, 125, 128

Van Voorhis, Salsibury, Wright & Bauman, 150, 157

Veysey & Messner, 55, 56, 62

vicarious strain, 64, 72, 74, 75, 79, 80

victimization, 5, 17, 18, 19, 21, 22, 23, 25, 26, 61, 62, 74, 75, 79, 80, 152, 154, 156, 157
criminal victimization, 25, 55, 75, 137
rape victimization, 130
sexual victimization, 19

Vietnam War, 130

violence against women, 130, 131, 152, 156

violence, 34, 37, 38, 56-57, 61, 62, 69, 71, 79, 123, 125, 130, 139, 142, 147, 151, 152, 156, 157

violent offenders, 20, 47, 123

Virkkunen, 38

Vold, 129, 133, 134, 142
Vold & Bernard, 8, 26, 33, 47, 133
Vold, Bernard & Snipes, 9, 26
Vold, Turk, Quinny and Blalock, 133

Voltaire, 9

volunteers, 57

Walby, 152, 157

Walters and White, 44, 47

War on Crime, 12, 21

War on Drugs, 12, 21, 140, 142

Watergate scandal, 131

Webster, Doob & Zimring, 19, 26
Webster-Stratton, Reid & Hammond, 76, 80

Weisburd et al., 22, 26
Weisburd, Waring & Chayet, 14, 26

Weiss, 140, 142

West Africa, 149

Whaley, Smith, and Hayes-Smith, 94, 96

Williams, 161
Williams & McShane, 29, 31, 47, 83, 86, 96, 118, 128
Williams and Hawkins, 15, 26

Rev Williams, Theron, 135

Wilson and Hermstein, 43, 47, 81, 85-86

Wilson and Kelling, 57, 58, 62

Women's Liberation Movement, 18, 144, 147
Women's Liberation, 130, 145, 150

Wood and Dunaway, 110, 114

Wooldredge, 54, 62

World War II, 18

Wright & Benson, 55, 62

Yodanis, 152

Young, Jock, 137

Young criminals, 43
youth criminality, 75

Zahn, Day, Mihalic, and Tichavsky, 153, 157

Zavala and Spohn, 75, 80

Zhang, 21, 26

Zimring, 12, 26
Zimring and Hawkins, 15, 26

zone of transition, 49, 51, 53